Praise for *Coaching Salespeople into Sales Champions*

"Winning in sales is no different than winning in life. As someone who has done a lot of personal and professional coaching over the years, I see tremendous value for anyone who reads this book. If the reader will embrace Keith's philosophy around coaching, they can certainly expect to win in all areas of their life, while making a profound and measurable impact on their salespeople's performance and attitude."

Dr. Denis Waitley
Best-Selling Author of *The Seeds of
Greatness* and *The Psychology of Winning*

"There is no other single activity to boost sales that works better than sales coaching and this book is the best ever written on how to do it well."

Brian Tracy, Author of *Getting Rich Your Own Way*

"Fluffless! Rosen continues to give practical, A to Z how-to advice. After you read it, simply do it!"

Anthony Parinello, Author of *Selling to VITO*

"Keith has done a tremendous job outlining the importance of coaching vs. managing. Implementing Keith's playbook will drive the development of high performance salespeople and superior results."

Kelly Carioti, Vice President of PepsiCo,
Specialty and Self-Service Retail

There are very few good books published for sales managers and most of them are filled with biased ideology and abstract concepts. Keith Rosen's book is refreshingly practical. It contains concrete steps on what to coach, how to coach and how to bring out people's hidden talents without resentment, or frustration. This is the clearly the best book on sales coaching I've seen in a long time."

Gerhard Gschwandtner, Founder and
Publisher of *Selling Power*

"This is a book that will truly take entire sales organizations to the next level. Keith is spot on, and his approach to accountability in the coaching process is what so many sales people and sales managers are missing."

Tom Ziglar, CEO of Ziglar, Inc.

To lead is to serve and to truly serve is to coach. In a world of hyper competition and talent shortages, pithy leadership quotes won't be enough. In Keith Rosen's brilliant book you'll not only learn how to create a winning culture and a competitive advantage for your team through coaching but also how to create and leave a legacy that you'll be proud of. These lessons, if applied, have the power to transform your team, your management career and your life.

Vince Thompson, Author of *Ignited*

When it comes to building a top sales organization, Keith has got the market cornered on tactical leadership strategies for today's workforce. *Coaching Salespeople into Sales Champions* is a winning playbook for managers who need to strengthen and invigorate their sales team through executive sales coaching.

**David Hirsch, Director of Business to Business Vertical Markets Group, Google**

"We can give salespeople all of the training in the world, we can inspire them and motivate them, we can even provide them with the latest and greatest technology . . . . but in today's highly competitive marketplace, we can measurably accelerate their success through coaching and this is THE TACTICAL PLAY BOOK to help get it done!"

**Michael Norton, Chairman of the Board and Founder, CanDoGo™**

"Keith offers insightful BUT practical coaching. It is easy to get so blinded by the drive for results that you don't even realize your actions are working against you. *Coaching Salespeople into Sales Champions* will help you identify what truly supports your sales team and provides a guide to putting it into action every day."

**Margo Manning, Senior Vice President of Sales and Training, Dave and Buster's, Inc.**

"This book will inspire you to take a fresh new look at what you have become familiar with doing every day, as you lead and interact with your sales team. Each chapter is full of approaches that have been proven to work, tools to develop better skills, and application of concepts that are illustrated through real life scenarios. Time invested with this material will improve your coaching and interpersonal skills, while unlocking your sales team's hidden potential. Coaching Sales People into Sales Champions is a must-read for any sales manager."

**Robb King II, Vice President of Operations, Paul Davis Restoration, Inc.**

"Keith Rosen has crafted an intuitive coach's handbook for sales executives who are looking to maximize their force's talents to generate more sales in an increasingly competitive marketplace."

**David Thompson, CEO & Co-founder of Genius.com**

"*Coaching Salespeople into Sales Champions* is highly recommended reading for managers and executives who are looking to improve their sales organization and avoid the myriad of pitfalls that can hurt sales performance. Keith effectively addresses the burning issue regarding successful leadership and coaching sales teams, which we all know is a huge challenge in every company."

**Razi Imam, CEO of Landslide Technologies Inc.**

Keith's high energy seminars gave my sales team the skills and confidence to take their process to the next level. In his latest book "Coaching Sales People into Champions," Keith once again addresses "real world" skills for both sales managers and sales people. Simply put: if you want your salespeople to have the same laser focused intensity that my sales team now has, I suggest you not only read this book, but study it and implement it!!

**Michael B. Kirven, CEO of Bluewolf**

# Coaching Salespeople into Sales Champions

A Tactical Playbook for Managers
and Executives

## KEITH ROSEN, MCC

**WILEY**

John Wiley & Sons, Inc.

Published by John Wiley & Sons, Inc., Hoboken, New Jersey.
Published simultaneously in Canada.

For general information on our other products and services or for technical support, please contact our Customer Care Department within the United States at (800) 762-2974, outside the United States at (317) 572-3993 or fax (317) 572-4002.

Wiley also publishes its books in a variety of electronic formats. Some content that appears in print may not be available in electronic formats. For more information about Wiley products, visit our Web site at www.wiley.com.

*Library of Congress Cataloging-in-Publication Data:*

Rosen, Keith.

   Coaching salespeople into sales champions: a tactical playbook
for managers and executives/Keith Rosen.

     p.   cm.

   ISBN 978-0-470-14251-6 (cloth)

   1. Sales force management.   I. Title.

   HF5439.5.R67   2008

   658.3'044—dc22

                                              2007035349

Printed in the United States of America.

10  9  8

To my wife, Lori, and my three children,
Jessica, Jett, and Nicole,
who continually remind me that at any age,
"dreams really can come true."
You keep my eyes focused on my priorities
and the daily miracles in life that really matter.
You are the center of my universe
and will always be my greatest source of inspiration.
I am forever grateful to have you in my life.

# CONTENTS

## CHAPTER EIGHT

## CHAPTER NINE

# About the Author

## KEITH ROSEN, MCC—THE EXECUTIVE SALES COACH

Keith Rosen is the President of Profit Builders and the executive sales coach that top managers, sales professionals, and executives in many of the world's leading companies call first. As a prominent, engaging speaker, Master Coach, and well-known author of many books and articles, Keith is one of the foremost authorities on assisting people to achieve positive, measurable changes in their attitudes, in their behaviors, and in their results.

For his work as a pioneer and a leader in the coaching profession, both *Inc.* and *Fast Company* magazines named Keith one of the five most respected and influential executive coaches in the country. *Software Sales Journal* named Keith's coaching firm, Profit Builders, one of the Top Nine Best Training Firms.

Keith is also the author of *Time Management for Sales Professionals, The Complete Idiot's Guide to Cold Calling,* as well as *The Complete Idiot's Guide to Closing the Sale.*

Keith's articles can be found in *Selling Power Magazine* and has appeared in feature stories in the *New York Times, Inc.* magazine, *The Washington Times, Sales and Marketing Management,* the *Wall Street Journal,* TheStreet.com, and Entrepreneur radio. Keith is also a frequent contributor on Selling Power Live, CBSNews.com, and has been appointed as the Expert Sales Advisor for AllBusiness.com.

Keith lives in New York with his wife and three children.

If you're ready for better results quickly, contact Keith about personalized, one-to-one or team coaching and training at 1-888-262-2450 or e-mail info@profitbuilders.com. Visit Keith Rosen online at www.ProfitBuilders.com for Podcasts and videos and be sure to sign up for his free newsletter *The Winner's Path*.

# ACKNOWLEDGMENTS

To my mom for encouraging me to follow my passion and write.
To my dad, for being my first coach and lifelong advocate.

And to my wife, my lifelong partner in this journey, who inherited their roles with grace. Thank you for your unconditional support.

# Introduction

## THE ULTIMATE TACTICAL SYSTEM FOR MAXIMIZING PERFORMANCE

I was standing on the balcony of a high-rise suite at the Waldorf Astoria on 49th and Park Avenue, enjoying the breathtaking, palatial view of Manhattan. Gerhard Gschwandtner, the publisher of *Selling Power* magazine, and I had just completed an impromptu video shoot of me coaching three people I had never met before. As the cameras were rolling, they were filming the first time I had ever met these participants face to face.

A sales manager and two of his salespeople were the first to respond to this opportunity to be coached live for this special segment. Immediately following the taping, Greg, the sales manager, approached me with some follow-up questions that surfaced after his coaching experience. He was an enthusiastic, compassionate, and admirable manager who was truly committed to leading his team to greater success. Yet, like most managers, he was never formally trained to be a sales manager. After observing my successful coaching session with his two salespeople, his eyes were wide with excitement. The problems that his salespeople had been struggling with for months which he desperately tried to handle were resolved in a 15-minute coaching session. Greg desperately wanted to learn my secret and asked for more remedies for his most pressing challenges—all of which are addressed in great detail in this book.

- How can I get my salespeople to follow the system so they can start achieving their monthly sales goals on a consistent basis?

- How do I turn around an underperformer or make the decision to let someone go?
- How do I attract and retain top talent, especially new hires?
- How do I get and keep salespeople motivated without using consequences or threats?
- How do I continually leverage their strengths to maximize their productivity?
- How do I handle difficult or toxic salespeople?
- How do I get them to self-generate solutions to their problems so they don't have to be so dependent on me as the primary problem solver?
- How do I create buy in from my staff on what they need to do?
- How do I free up more time to focus on the activities that desperately need my attention?

Do these obstacles sound familiar? The fact is, regardless of experience, most leadership efforts are doomed from the start. Managers lose talented salespeople and maintain an atmosphere of mediocrity not because of a lack of effort but because they lack a coaching system they are comfortable with and can trust to leverage the talents of their salespeople in order to generate consistent, worthwhile results.

## ANNIHILATING THE ALBATROSS OF LEADERSHIP

Great managers realize that one of their key roles is to maximize the productivity of their team and ensure they are operating at peak performance. The consequences of not having your sales team live up to their potential are severe: a decrease in sales, lower morale, higher turnover, and client attrition. Additionally, there's the stress every manager feels from the added workload each time there's a vacancy in a position, sales that need to be made, and territories that have to be covered.

Now, compound this challenge with the additional responsibility managers often have. Aside from being responsible for the production and development of their sales team, some managers are often responsible for hitting their own sales numbers and production goals.

With long work hours, deadlines, and personal responsibilities, something gets sacrificed. As such, managers find that developing, coaching, and retaining their staff takes a back seat to the problems and challenges that arise daily. Even with their best intentions, managers don't often have the time and resources needed to effectively coach their staff or a strategy to identify and develop the essential skills and core characteristics needed to become a masterful coach. As a result, morale and productivity suffer.

Through the eyes of a salesperson, this lack of attention and support translates to a feeling of isolation. Quite often salespeople believe that management simply doesn't care, won't take the time to work with them, or simply isn't available. This environment becomes the perfect breeding ground for high attrition and deteriorating performance.

## HOW DO YOU *DO* THAT?

### Transforming Management Principles into Tactical Solutions

To reveal management's fundamental problem that proliferates dismal results, inefficiency, and failure, simply look at the questions posed by Greg, the sales manager I coached. Notice these questions were not *why*-based or philosophical questions but *how*-based or tactical questions.

Greg had the theory down but struggled to convert these leadership principles into actionable, measurable steps and a process that he can duplicate consistently. *Coaching Salespeople into Sales Champions* cracks the code and solves each of Greg's pressing issues that plague most managers. This book makes it possible for any manager, business owner, or executive to develop the missing discipline of leadership: *coaching*.

Most leadership programs train in ideology rather than in developing a core competency or skill. Nothing more gets accomplished other than identifying another great concept in leadership, an overanalyzed theory, or an attribute the greatest leaders possess. Although they are sound principles, they're devoid of a specific, measurable process and a practical application that generates the results you seek. With a team of salespeople to manage, objectives to reach, and expectations to meet, you need measurable results fast!

Increased global competition, a rapidly changing marketplace, and less face time with customers and employees are forcing companies to reevaluate their selling and leadership strategies.

With more business conducted across various communication platforms and more sales teams operating in a virtual environment, these managers question how proficient they can be at managing their team at a distance—especially since they have never been shown how to do so effectively. Managers do not always have the luxury of calling a face-to-face meeting and instead find themselves supporting, coaching, and managing their people over the telephone. Developing and strengthening your telephone coaching skills becomes essential to leveraging your competitive edge or you're bound to get left behind.

Top leaders know that in order for their people to live their fullest potential every day, they need someone in their corner supporting them throughout the process. As such, a growing need for a proven, long-term solution that can be rapidly deployed to continually develop and retain top talent while maximizing new business opportunities has sparked the evolution of this new kind of manager: *the executive sales coach.*

## GETTING TO GREAT AND PLAYING A BIGGER GAME

### RESULTS YOU CAN EXPECT

*Coaching Salespeople into Sales Champions* is the essential playbook that executives, managers, and business owners need to become an executive sales coach. This book will show you with great clarity how to get your salespeople to bring in more sales, how to quickly turn around or terminate an underperformer, and how to integrate a proven, step-by-step internal coaching model to most effectively maximize your team's natural talents and strengths. Now you can break out of survival mode and focus on helping the company thrive.

If your marketplace has changed, then you need to change with it. Einstein said it best. "The level of thinking that got us here is no longer enough." *Coaching Salespeople into Sales Champions* takes into account the many pressures facing management today. It offers a framework for thinking and behaving in new ways that will harness the true power managers possess and show you how to use that power to achieve your objectives. The incorporation of the core principles and strategies of the executive sales coach into your leadership style will cause a shift in the way you manage and how your people think, act, and produce results.

Over two years in the making, this book is my response to all the problems I've coached managers and business owners through during my years as an executive sales coach. I've listened to your requests to find a proven, permanent resolution to the timeless struggles managers have with their salespeople that cause anxiety and frustration.

Rather than fill this book with fabricated case studies and hypothetical scenarios that may not be applicable or relevant in the real world, every story you read is based on actual events, genuine scenarios, and *real* people you can relate to who I have actually coached. *Coaching Salespeople into Sales Champions* encapsulates my 20 years of practical, hands-on, in the trenches coaching experience that has made me the coach I am today. This book dispels the common managerial myths and exposes the self-sabotaging behavior managers unknowingly engage in that prevents positive change.

You'll discover how to facilitate a coaching conversation that fits your management style—the same system I have used to coach thousands of salespeople, business owners, and managers. You'll also find out what to say in any situation as well as the language and dialogue that the world's greatest coaches use. I've also included dozens of actual case studies spanning over 15 different industries and professions, templates, scripts, masterful coaching questions and an easy-to-follow coaching process regarding how to apply these techniques.

*Coaching Salespeople into Sales Champions* is the aspirin for all your management headaches. This book will be a resource that you can reference daily. You'll soon have a book that's loaded with Post-it Notes and a cover that refuses to stay shut. After you implement the strategies outlined in this book, please don't hesitate to share your successes with me. I'd love to hear about them, so feel free to contact me via my web site at www.ProfitBuilders.com where you will also find additional support materials. So, have a highlighter and a notepad handy and get ready to begin your journey into coaching that is sure to protect and maximize the value of your company's greatest asset: people. Coach your salespeople to become the sales champions they can and want to be.

# The Death of Management

## BECOMING AN EXECUTIVE SALES COACH

"What is that guy doing?" It was just an odd maneuver. Something out of the ordinary from what would have been a typical everyday experience at the drive-through of a Burger King. I was heading home from a day at the beach, unaware that I'd be having a breakthrough that would lead to the development of the concepts and strategies in this book.

I watched as the customer in front of me drove from the ordering to the pickup window of the drive-through, but it was closed. "How odd," I thought. Instead of the usual routine, the cashier came outside to deliver the food, headset intact and bags of food in hand. The customer then drove off.

As I pulled up, I wondered if I too would have the same experience. Then, out of the corner of my eye, I noticed a digital timer mounted on the wall above the cashier's head. At that moment, the manager at the drive-through window waved me forward, without my food. "We will bring it out to you. Just pull up, please," he requested.

The manager sent a young man out to my car who handed me my food. I had to ask: "I'm curious, why did we have to pull up, especially when there was no one behind me?"

"The timer," he replied. "That's how the manager is rated in performance. We're supposed to serve each customer within a certain period of time. By moving everyone ahead like this, he can manipulate the results of the timer."

It is a scientific fact that human beings have not tapped into their fullest potential. People drive growth and innovation. This applies to our business, our company, our managers, and, subsequently, our salespeople. Taking on the burden of management and the responsibility for increasing the value of each person on your team is a noble undertaking. This unique class of people is referred to as our manager, our brave and fearless leader, our CEO, our president, or our senior executive VP. It is unfortunate, in many cases, this role has been taken on by people who are untrained for it.

This book evens the playing field by giving managers the practical hands-on tools that sales coaches can use every day when they're in the trenches.

Management, coaching, empowerment, accountability, motivation, leadership. These noble words have become so diluted in meaning and so irrelevant in business that many managers mistakenly believe that they actually know how to manage and coach their salespeople. They even think they do a good job.

In this first chapter, I will introduce you to the missing discipline of sales coaching in leadership. A new breed of managers is taking the helm, the executive sales coach, that is changing traditional management strategies. I will dispel the myths and misconceptions of traditional management and explain why it simply does not work. I will also introduce you to a new, more powerful approach to developing your salespeople into sales champions. Finally, I will describe the characteristics of the world's greatest sales coaches and the obstacles that must be conquered in order to become one.

## BUT I'M ALREADY COACHING . . .

At least once or twice a week, I talk with managers about their leadership styles. At some point during the conversation, a manager will mention that he coaches his team. I ask, "Really, that's great to hear that you're using the coaching model. Where were you trained as a coach?"

The response I hear most often is "Oh, I've never been formally trained."

I then ask, "Well, have you worked with a coach yourself? Have you ever been coached?"

To my surprise, the answer is usually "No."

Most managers don't understand that they can't just change their title from manager to sales coach without changing their skill set. They don't understand the difference between being a manager and being a coach.

Let me explain. Calling yourself a coach without the proper training is the same as me waking up tomorrow morning and saying, "Today, I'm going to be a doctor (or a lawyer or a CPA or a professional athlete)." I can say it, but I can't be it.

A sales coach must be proficient at coaching and that requires ongoing study and training. This book will guide you through the process of developing and mastering your coaching skills.

## MAKING THE SHIFT FROM SALES MANAGER TO EXECUTIVE SALES COACH

Management is dead. This is a pretty bold statement to make, I know. Yet, the thousands of managers I've worked with throughout my career are testaments to the truth of this statement.

I ask managers, "What exactly is it you manage?" Although they say they manage people, the truth is that managers today spend most of their time managing processes, projects, data, problems, and information. If you do not have a defined process that moves your people forward so they can achieve greater results, then what is it you are managing? You're managing the status quo. You're managing a ledger entry in your company's P&L statement. You're managing sales reports and activity. Ultimately, under this antiquated model, when it comes down to your people, you are managing the mediocre and the underachievers.

The ultimate problem with management inefficiency and failure is that the leadership principles taught today are just that, principles, devoid of specific measurable actions. Most leadership training programs concentrate on ideology rather than on developing a core competency or skill. Nothing more gets accomplished other than identifying another great concept in leadership or an attribute the greatest leaders possess. Status quo is managed, and life goes on.

The Executive Sales Coaching model discussed in this book fills the void between management philosophies and execution. Coaching translates theory into tactical, measurable actions.

I remember a story about a young boy who found a butterfly cocoon. Each day, the boy went to visit the cocoon, until one day a small opening appeared. The boy watched the butterfly for several hours as it struggled to force its body through the little hole.

Suddenly the butterfly stopped trying to make its way out of the cocoon. It didn't seem to be making any progress. The butterfly was no longer moving. With good intentions, the boy felt that he needed to help the butterfly. He took a pair of scissors and very slowly with surgical precision, snipped the remaining bit of cocoon being careful not to hurt the butterfly. The butterfly then easily emerged.

Except something was strange. The butterfly's body was swollen, and its wings were all shriveled and deformed. Nevertheless, the boy continued to watch the butterfly, expecting that, at any moment, the wings would expand to support the body, which would contract in time. Unfortunately, neither happened. In fact, the butterfly spent the rest of its life crawling around with a swollen body and deformed wings. It was never able to fly.

What the boy in his kindness and impatience did not understand was the natural evolution of life. The restrictive cocoon and the struggle through the small opening of the cocoon is nature's way of forcing fluid from the butterfly's body into its wings, so that it would be ready for flight after it emerged from the cocoon.

Sometimes struggles are exactly what we need in our lives. If we went through life without any obstacles, both our minds and bodies would atrophy. There would be no opportunities for us to learn and grow from each experience. We would never be able to spread our wings and fly on our own. The premise of coaching is to develop a safe place to co-create new possibilities with people so they can reinvent themselves and who they are at their very core. Coaching provides the opportunity for people to generate solutions and solve problems on their own, while bringing out their very best.

I'm reminded of a conversation between two people who met at a networking event. When talking about what each did for a living, one person said, "I love my job. I'm the director of a camp for young children." The other person replied by saying, "That sounds like fun! I work with children, too." When asked what type of work he did, the person responded, "I manage a team of salespeople."

The point is, let your employees solve their own problems or you will wind up managing a team of salespeople that is fully dependent on you.

## THE MISSING DISCIPLINE OF SALES COACHING

### WHAT IS COACHING?

The coaching model is based on the belief that the question is the answer. The coach is responsible for people finding the answers themselves and developing their own problem-solving skills.

Coaching uses a process of inquiry so that people can access their own energy or inner strength to reach their own level of awareness. Tapping into a person's previously unused strengths and talents advances personal growth and learning, which challenges people to discover their personal best.

Coaching builds accountability by providing a safe forum for people to honor the commitments they have made. These commitments advance personal and organizational growth.

Coaching is collaborative as well as interactive. Coaching is like a dance rather than a premeditated or prescripted process. The shared experiences, insights, and solutions generated during meetings move the person forward, which also allows the coach to grow even more.

Coaching is about having clients grow on their own. Coaching helps people become more observant so they can better respond to the events, problems, or situations that arise.

Coaching isn't about giving information. It is about responding to the needs of other people. People will resist if information is forced on them.

Coaching consists of motivating people to reach their highest levels by offering them opportunities and possibilities, not obligations. Coaching is the art of creating new possibilities that didn't exist before.

## DEFINING THE ROLE OF A SALES COACH

The following is an overview of a coach's role and core responsibilities.

**Overview of a Coach's Role**
1. Focuses on strengths, not weaknesses.
2. Facilitates, which is defined as "Making things easier."
3. Brings out the best in people by supporting, assisting and maximizing people's strengths.
4. Requests change and growth, as well as informs and guides.
5. Has the *right* questions, not necessarily *all* the answers.
6. Empowers people to be accountable for their success and failures.

**A Coach's Responsibilities during a Coaching Session**
- Helps people uncover their true passions and orient their lives around them.
- Assists in discovering and leveraging people's natural strengths, skills, and gifts to bring out their best.
- Works with people to create what they really want out of life, personally and professionally.
- Co-creates new possibilities that didn't exist before as well as an action plan and a path to help people achieve their goals.

- Provides guidance, support, insight, structure, account-ability, encouragement, and tools people can use today.
- Provides a constructive, safe environment and becomes an unconditional partner during people's personal evolutions.
- Challenges people's thinking, attitudes, and assumptions about things in order to increase their awareness of the truth, enrich the quality of their lives, and boost their effectiveness as salespeople.
- Builds the momentum people need to reach their goals or generate the results they want in half the time it would take for them to do it on their own.

## A COACH VERSUS A MENTOR

Many people use the words *coach* and *mentor* synonymously. The fact is there's a clear distinction between the two.

**Coach**    An expert on people and personal development. Typically a skilled specialist regarding a certain topic, competency, or industry. A coach's role is to provide structure, foundation, and support so people can begin to self-generate the results they want on their own. Learning and growth are achieved by both parties involved. In coaching, the relationship is objective, and the focus is not only on *what* the person needs to do to become more successful but also *who* the person is and how he thinks. A coach works on the whole person and is multidimensional, rather than focusing only on what the person is already doing. The coaching relationship is built on choice rather than necessity.

**Mentor**    An expert in a field, industry, or at a company who typically acts as an internal advisor. Usually this is done on a professional level to advance the mentored person's career. Often mentors have their own approach already in mind and use the system that has worked for them in the past, without taking into consideration the style, values, integrity, or strengths of the people they mentor. Mentors may also have something to gain professionally and, as such, have their own personal agenda. Often, mentors are not trained, and their guidance is based more on their experience rather than the skills or proficiencies needed to mentor.

Often, the mentoring relationship is need-driven rather than driven by choice.

## NINE BARRIERS TO COACHING A SALES TEAM

For any executive sales coaching initiative to be effective and long-lasting, there are important obstacles that a manager or internal sales coach needs to address.

### BARRIER ONE: NO COACH THE COACH PROGRAM

One of my clients recently called me with questions about building an internal coaching program. It seems the person who was spearheading the initiative was having a difficult time putting the processes and procedures together as well as getting the managers to embrace the new philosophy and approach. Since the company felt they could build the internal coaching program on their own, they didn't hire an outside expert or consultant. The person in charge of the initiative wasn't even a coach but someone in HR. Without a coach training program to develop coaching skills and competencies, you can change your managers' titles, but not their essence, their thinking, or their skills.

### BARRIER TWO: COACHING IS A CHOICE—NOT AN OBLIGATION

The coaching relationship is a choice, not an obligation. The relationship between the coach and the people who are coached is a designed alliance, a collaborative partnership, and more. As such, remedial or sanctioned coaching is often met with resistance rather than with open arms. How is coaching being offered to your team or to your employees? A perk, an incentive, an option, an obligation, or a remedial response to underperformance? Are you offering it to your entire team, to a select few, or to just one person?

### BARRIER THREE: SURRENDER YOUR AGENDA WHEN COACHING

What if your boss walked up to you today and said, "Your career, your bonus, your position in this company, and your salary will depend on how well your team performs. That said, I want you to start coaching all the people on your team, one on one. Hold them accountable and be unconditionally supportive, while surrendering your agenda and maintaining objectivity." Could you do it?

My clients consist of a myriad of companies and professions, all shapes and sizes, selling products and services in practically every industry and profession. Yet, the one truth I share with them is this: "When you work with me as your coach, this will be the only relationship you have where it will always be 100 percent about you."

If you're an internal coach, this may be a stretch to fully surrender any agenda or attachment to your sales team's performance, especially since their performance directly reflects on you. In such cases, there's an inherent challenge for you, as the business owner or manager, to separate your agenda from theirs and have no personal expectation from the relationship other than your unconditional commitment to their continued growth and success. It's going to take some adjustment on your part to develop an unconditional and authentic relationship with your salespeople. We tackle this in much greater detail in Chapter 2.

## BARRIER FOUR: YOU'RE COACHING PEOPLE, NOT CHANGING PEOPLE

There's a big difference between coaching people and changing people. However, for executives or front line managers who are commissioned to hit some aggressive sales numbers, coaching is the last thing they want to talk about. The real distinction is that coaching is a process of discovery. A coach cannot push for results or attempt to change people overnight. The traditional scenario to facilitate change is typically a stressed-out manager who lays the same stress on his salespeople that his boss dumped on him. "Work harder; get focused; our jobs can be on the line; just bring in some more business." This hollow approach seldom drives change.

## BARRIER FIVE: CONNECTION—IT HAS TO BE THE REAL THING

In coaching it's critical for unrestricted, honest communication in the coaching relationship. It's extremely challenging to connect with your salespeople at a deeper level, the type of connection necessary between the coach and the person being coached. Many employees are afraid that if they disclose too much, it will be held against them in the future. So they limit their vulnerability level to what is absolutely needed to perform their job function. This restricts safe and open communication, limiting the chance to connect with your people in a way that allows coaches to get to the real issues and barriers;—barriers that are preventing improved performance.

### BARRIER SIX: CONFIDENTIALITY AND NO JUDGMENT? SURE, BOSS!

Lets get right to what you're thinking. Your role as supervisor or boss presents some inherent problems with coaching that need to be addressed head on.

Given the parameters, guidelines, and principles necessary to be a masterful coach, trust is critical to make the connection. After all, if your employees can't trust you as their manager, forget even trying to coach them. Coaching requires an elevated level of trust that transcends the superficial trust between employees and management.

And what if some of your salespeople already have a problem with you as their boss and now you're going to try and coach them? How does that get handled? Do you think any of your employees are going to just come out and say that? Think again.

As a result, this relationship could quickly turn into more of a mentoring rather than a coaching relationship. This is a major reason why companies bring in an expert coach from the outside who doesn't have any direct ties to the company as a manager would.

### BARRIER SEVEN: ANYONE CAN MANAGE, NOT EVERYONE CAN COACH

"I'm really not cut out to be a coach." The hard fact is there are managers who want to be coaches, managers who need to be coaches, and managers who shouldn't be coaches, and probably shouldn't be managers, either.

Companies that force all managers into a coaching role make a costly assumption that all of their managers would actually make great coaches, just like every college athlete should automatically make the pros. The rules work the same. Desire, attitude, ability, and skill will always be the formula for becoming a successful coach, or athlete. Then there is the mistake of pushing managers to do something they don't want to do. Managers can easily sabotage their own coaching efforts, and in the end, corporate may learn the wrong lesson: "I guess our internal coaching program didn't work."

## BARRIER EIGHT: FULL ACCOUNTABILITY

If you want to become powerful, hire a powerful coach. It's a simple, yet highly effective strategy. If you want your salespeople to be powerful, you need to be a good role model for them. As you evolve, so does your team. Consider this truth: Your team is a reflection of you. If you're not prepared to be 100 percent accountable for the success and failure of your team, if you skirt accountability in any way, if you lack professionalism or proficiencies in certain areas, your team will reflect these weaknesses. If you choose to evolve, so will your salespeople. If you want a world-class sales team, you have to become a world-class executive sales coach.

## BARRIER NINE: COMPETITIVE MANAGERS

The most effective leaders develop other leaders. They encourage their people to perform as well as they do—even better. That is the sign of a true master and the real testament of a great manager. But what if the manager perceives his coworkers and subordinates as a threat? What if the manager is driven strictly by ego, the need to prove himself and his worth? What if this manager thinks he has survived only by keeping a competitive distance from his peers and salespeople? I've known managers who don't share their tools and best practices with their salespeople for fear their salespeople will outdo them. These are likely to be inferior managers who will seek to selfishly leverage the coaching relationship in a way to better themselves and their position rather than for the betterment of their sales team.

Now that we've listed the barriers that can get in the way of implementing an effective internal coaching program, do not be disheartened. With greater awareness comes choice. The good news is you possess the power to make a difference. The majority of these internal obstacles can be overcome using the strategies outlined in this book. The remainder of this chapter outlines some very specific steps you can take as you begin your journey as a coach.

## CONSULTANT, TRAINER, OR COACH?

When potential clients call my office, I begin the process by conducting a preliminary needs assessment to ensure there is a strong fit between us as well as a clear understanding of their objectives. I assess what they are expecting from a coach, have them share their background and goals with me, uncover the additional areas we would be working on together, and qualify them to ensure they are a client that I would like to work with. Inevitably, I would hear myself saying, "It sounds like you need more than just a coach to reach your goals. I'm also hearing that you are looking for someone who can give you the best solutions and answers to certain issues with the intention of minimizing the steep and often costly learning curve. That's why you really need a coach who is also a trainer and a consultant."

It is at this point in our conversation when I would share with them the distinction between these three types of professionals and the role each would play in achieving the client's goals. Here is a scenario that will help distinguish between the three, determine the value proposition or deliverable each brings into the relationship, and the approach that can be expected from each.

Let's say you're looking to expand your selling and prospecting efforts and want your sales team to call on some different types of companies in your market. Since you are not sure which ones make most sense nor do you have a strategy to execute, you call on a consultant, a trainer, and a coach for help. Based on this scenario, here's what each would be able to offer. Keep in mind, I'm only drawing a distinction between these three professionals based on their core deliverables and not what each person may be able to offer based on their specific level of experience and expertise.

## THE CONSULTANT

The consultant may provide you with some market research and aggregate certain data based on your target market. The consultant may report either verbally or in a written report about market conditions, market trends, samples of research they've conducted, a concise solution, and possibly an overview of an action plan needed to execute the solution. The consultant may also suggest hiring other experts by outsourcing, hiring full-time, or employing the services of other professionals such as legal, tax, accounting, human resources, IT, recruiting, trainers, coaches, and so on.

## THE TRAINER

Once the consultant finishes, enter the trainer. Now, based on the overall solution the consultant laid out, there may be a component that calls for some professional training and further development of your employees' skill set. As such, the trainer's role may be to develop and deliver the actual training needed to achieve the overall objectives. The trainer may perform some further due diligence by interviewing participants, salespeople, and managers, possibly even some clients, to get a better assessment of the issues and what areas require further training and further skill development. The trainer would then develop the training module and deliver the training. Depending on the trainer's style and approach, the trainer may incorporate a variety of additional approaches such as:

- Action steps, assessments, or exercises to be completed prior to the training event
- Role playing
- Skill practice scenarios
- One-to-one training
- Roundtable discussions.
- Interactive forums: question and answer, panel discussion
- Development of collateral materials, scripts, templates, and so on
- Co-creation and collaboration on certain exercises and objectives to be completed by the end of the training event

## THE COACH

When the training event is over, what safeguards do you have in place to ensure that the concepts and ideology learned during the training are understood, effective, and long lasting? How are the participants held accountable for applying what was learned? What process is in place for discovering the areas participants are still struggling with in order to develop a better solution? And, finally, what discipline will be used to ensure your people have developed and can maintain the mindset of a champion? I have found that continued accountability and support is essential to ensure the success of any type of long-term coaching and training initiative within an organization.

Since learning does not stop when delivery of the training is over, the sales coaching program is intended to be one component of a comprehensive set of methods for continuous improvement of the performance of the sales team. The trainer's responsibility is to teach you the fundamentals and how to play the game; it is the coach who then further sharpens your game and makes you a champion. Trainers teach you how to play the game; coaches teach you how to perfect your game, while building in the added accountability to ensure you actually play and achieve your high score in every game.

Through ongoing individual and team sales coaching sessions delivered via the telephone or in person, the coach will work with the sales team on the essential techniques, skills, and competencies that will result in accelerated levels of individual and team performance, productivity, and profitability. Scheduled weekly phone meetings will accelerate progress.

By understanding the differences between the consultant, trainer, and coach, you can accurately identify which professional is needed to develop the missing competencies and skills of your sales team. Sometimes it's going to be a training issue, other times a consulting issue, and in many cases it will be more of a coaching issue. Moreover, there will be times when the solution requires a combination of these approaches. A better understanding of these three distinct disciplines will help you accurately determine which approach would be most effective for your situation.

## MANAGERS DON'T HAVE TIME TO MANAGE

The Arizona sun just started to shine over the mountains and come through my hotel window as I finished organizing my notes for the seminar I was delivering in a couple of hours. I was keenly aware that this new day would bring a new experience. I was going to test out a new methodology in front of an audience for the first time. I was certain my ideas would trigger a reaction and infuse new life into this program while championing longer-lasting results.

The title of the program was "Coach Your Sales Team to the Top." Essentially, I was going to leave it up to the audience of approximately 60 front line managers to design the content of the program on the spot. The concept? Facilitating what I call Participant Driven Seminars not only fuels greater audience participation and collaboration but also helps identify the stronger, natural leaders of the group.

This format enables participants to tap into and experience firsthand the significance of empowerment, the power of coaching, and the real value of investigating and identifying problems. They would be developing their own solutions and creating an executable action plan everyone could follow.

When we came to the topic of execution and follow-through, I started to hear most of the grumbling, complaining, and resistance.

I typically get this reaction during a seminar when I discuss time management and strategic execution. However, the decibel level of this grumbling was much higher than average. You see, this particular company was Vetter Staffing, Inc., an executive recruiting firm, one of the largest in the country. And like many companies today, this company's management team was responsible for their own level of personal production.

I opened up the seminar with some questions. I posed the first question to the management team. "Can someone share with me how you wound up in the position you're currently in?"

As I listened to their responses, I realized that most managers in the audience were top producers themselves before becoming managers and, subsequently, were promoted into management.

I then asked, "When you were promoted into this new management position, were there any changes in your workload and in your responsibility? How did your job description change in this new position?"

"Nothing's changed, other than the 10 salespeople who started reporting directly to me about a month ago." one manager shared.

Wanting to confirm consensus, I asked one more question. "So, every manager in this room is still responsible for a certain level of personal production and your own monthly sales quota."

I took the head nodding and silence as agreement. I found out that even though their own individual monthly sales quotas had been reduced by 10 to 20 percent, they were still responsible for everyone else's sales and daily sales activity. Therefore, the reduction in their sales goals and that time that was typically used to drive sales would now be replaced with the added responsibility of hiring, training, developing, retaining, and managing an entire team,—a full-time job in itself. Talk about unrealistic expectations.

This common situation is the first major clue as to why a sales team may not be meeting its goals. Something has got to give. Unless managers are putting in 20-hour workdays, they will not have the time to carry out their role to the best of their ability. Tasks, good intentions, and core managerial responsibilities fall through cracks that get wider and wider. Additional demands are placed on these managers, who have fewer resources available to them which are necessary to perform their role successfully.

Here's an interesting fact to consider. This particular company has experienced 85 percent attrition among their sales team over the last two years. Before they hired me as their coach, the company's strategy to staunch this bleeding wound sanctioned by the senior leadership team was "Work harder and smarter."

You are not reading this book to become a traditional manager but to become a powerful, influential manager and executive sales coach. Managing is a lot like parenting in the sense that practically anyone can be a manager but not everyone will be good at it. And becoming a great manager means becoming a great coach. This requires not only your commitment to your own development but also to your investment in the continued development of your team. For Vetter Staffing, bringing in someone like me to work with their managers was certainly one positive step toward giving them the additional tools they need to not only survive but to flourish. The deeper issue that I uncovered during my one-day program was more of a cultural phenomenon that would ultimately have to be addressed with the senior leadership team, where the source of the problem originated.

Although these managers at Vetter Staffing did not have the power to change their role or job description, each had the power to change how they currently managed their teams. They learned at the seminar that a little honesty, introspection, and self-analysis goes a long way, especially as it relates to evaluating the integrity of their commitment as well as the process they are currently using to get their salespeople to perform at their very best.

## UNDERSTANDING THE COMMITMENT TO COACH YOUR SALES TEAM

In the forward-thinking, pioneering companies that have embraced some form of a coaching model, coaching is offered as a perk to employees. These companies offer coaching to those employees that they want to invest in, support, and assist in their growth or succession plan. Not a bad way to position coaching, but there's more to the story:

- For a salesperson in your company, how many hours does it take to achieve success?
- How much time does it take to become a sales champion?
- How long will it take you to foster a healthy relationship with a salesperson?
- What is an acceptable period of time for a salesperson to foster a healthy relationship with a prospect or customer?

You might be surprised to find out that these questions are not meant to be rhetorical but to drive a lesson home. If you're not coaching on a daily or weekly basis, you're lying to yourself and your employees. You cannot define your internal coaching program by the monthly or quarterly meetings you hold or the performance evaluations you do each year.

Many self-proclaimed coaches or managers share the following illusion they believe to be true: "Sure, we have an internal coaching program. I mean, I'm not meeting with each person on my team every week on an individual basis, but we do hold sales meetings every Monday to go over their numbers and their progress. And we do two formal performance evaluations each year for every salesperson. With the demands I already have pulling on me, there's no way I'd be able to meet with them one to one consistently on a weekly basis."

Oh, the lies we tell ourselves. Let me shatter this costly illusion right now. This does not, in any way, resemble a sales coaching program. The bottom line is this: If you or an outside sales coach you have hired are not meeting with your salespeople individually on a consistent basis, either weekly or biweekly, then you are not coaching them.

If you want to grow your team and your business, ongoing sales coaching is an essential nonnegotiable activity every manager needs to be involved in. The most valuable investment any manager can make would be in the weekly coaching of each member on her team, especially a new hire. If you are unable to do so due to your workload or the size of your team, then biweekly sales coaching would be an alternative solution. And if this still isn't an option for you, consider outsourcing the sales coaching to a professionally trained, certified executive sales coach.

A client of mine shared her concern about Ike, a salesperson who recently decided to quit. During Ike's year-end review, management uncovered some key issues that had compromised Ike's performance throughout the year, issues that could have easily been addressed and eliminated with additional training and coaching. Unfortunately, because this problem wasn't addressed until Ike's year-end review, what was initially a small concern quickly escalated into a large-scale catastrophe that turned into a lose-lose situation. My client lost a good employee, and Ike lost a good job.

Unless you are continually checking in and meeting with your staff throughout the year, the year-end review or performance evaluation is often the first time that both the employee and employer get to share their successes as well as their challenges.

Weekly coaching sessions enable you to identify and eliminate problems that can compound over the year and cost the company money, new business, and countless hours in attempting to salvage an employee. And if you're losing salespeople as a result of coaching negligence, it will cost your company even more time and money to hire and train new salespeople.

---

### ❧ FROM THE SIDELINES ❧

There is nothing more important managers can do that will have a direct and measurable impact on the bottom line than investing time each day coaching their salespeople.

---

## GET A COACH FOR THE COACH

Top executives and managers should be disciplined enough to hold themselves accountable to execute the strategy and take the actions needed to build a thriving team. That said, challenges exist that impede the efforts of even the world's most well-intentioned managers.

First, let me point out that the word *should* is a dirty word. I try my best never to use it, as a *should* is typically somebody else's agenda rather than what is in the best interest of that person. *Shoulding* on yourself or someone else would sound like, "I *should* be farther along in my career." "If they've been in the business as long as they say they have, then they *should* already know how to perform that task." "At this point, I *should* be able to manage my workload better." "Results *should* be showing up faster than they are."

If you're on top, there's often no one up there with you to support you and ensure that you're being accountable to your business, your employees, and yourself. Being accountable doesn't always mean that you're getting everything done. It also means taking ownership of the situations around you, which also includes all the *shoulding* you're doing on yourself and on others.

Top executives face problems and issues on a daily basis, so there is always a great reason why they cannot do something they need to do. Just as your salespeople have certain blind spots when it comes to looking at themselves or identifying the source of a problem, managers also have blind spots. Blind spots are well named because they are hard to see; many have been around for a long time. When something goes on for a while, whether it's a limiting belief, a faulty approach or tactic, or a behavior we're tolerating from others, we become numb or blind to them. Sometimes, we all need someone to point out the truth to us. Only with the help of a coach can you identify your blind spots.

Here's why. You cannot grow with what you already know. Breakthroughs require tapping into new wisdom, additional information, and getting out of your own head. Otherwise, you'll find yourself recycling the same level of knowledge and insight you already possess.

For example, it's easy for a manager to get fired up in a seminar and decide that on Monday he's going to start a training program for his people or take on some other initiative. The problem is that Monday morning the phone starts ringing, and the manager gets involved in his daily routine.

Top executives need more than just a solid strategy, systems, and procedures to accomplish their goals. The number one reason for business failure has less to do with the people, strategy, product, process, service, or profitability and everything to do with consistent execution on every level. Yes, execution is a manager's responsibility, but who will ensure that the manager is executing on a consistent basis?

An increasing number of managers are turning to coaches because they offer expertise, third-party perspective, targeted advice, and a safe sounding board. Managers can talk to a coach about their challenges without worrying about being judged or criticized.

One benefit of having your own executive sales coach is knowing there is someone who will be frank with you should you attempt to use avoidance behavior, diversionary tactics, or excuses. Your coach will work with you to develop a strategy and timetable to accomplish your core objectives and then create the structure to hold you accountable. Since you are the one setting the goals, creating the timetable, and paying for the coach's expertise and time, there is plenty of incentive to follow through on your commitments.

# FIVE CORE CHARACTERISTICS OF THE WORLD'S GREATEST SALES COACHES

Regardless of your position or your profession, I've noticed commonalities among the greatest coaches I know and have trained.

1. *You can't take someone where you haven't been yourself.* Sure, you may be in sales but has your coach ever held a sales position before, let alone been a top producer in her industry and company? If you're a business owner, manager, or executive, has your coach experienced the same challenges and successes and learned the valuable time-saving lessons that will help you build a high-performance team or grow your business? Having an experienced coach in your corner who also happens to be a successful business owner and salesperson gives you the additional edge that's sure to cut down the time-consuming and often costly learning curve it takes for you to learn and achieve what's most important to you.

2. *A top coach is a model of what is possible to achieve.* The most effective way to teach others—our employees, clients, even family members—is to exemplify that which we want to teach. From the time you walk into the office, your appearance and disposition, as well as how you handle problems, talk to clients, complete tasks and projects, your work ethic, and how you demonstrate your commitment to your people as their manager, sends a message to your staff that says, "This is how it is done." The "Do as I say not as I do" approach to managing is no longer effective. Managers need to think beyond their spoken word and evaluate their behavior to fully identify the overall message they are really sending to their staff.

   A hard truth to embrace but one that rewards every manager who does is this: Businesses take on the complexion of their owners and management, both their strengths and weaknesses. You can't expect your team to go the extra mile, feel great about their work, be highly organized, and be fully accountable for their performance if their leader is not.

The greatest leaders know that in order to have an impact on others, they need to change themselves first. If you want to accelerate team performance in ways other than through training and coaching, upgrade the message you send in your communication, which also encompasses your actions as well as your behavior. You owe it to yourself as well as to your team. You are their manager and have a responsibility that transcends monthly numbers or year-end sales targets. You create the atmosphere and culture among your team. You develop the parameters that determine exactly how effective your sales team can be each day. Are you setting them up to thrive or simply survive? When you have the power to make a difference in just one person's life, you are a leader.

3. *Sometimes they really need the answer!* So, give it to them rather than throwing another question at them, which does nothing more than frustrate the person you are coaching. The sad truth is, most coaches can't give the answer. Why? Go back to the first quality. You can't get the answers from a coach who hasn't been where you want to be.

   Interestingly, most people need more than just a coach to reach their goals. They also need someone who can give them the best solutions, sometimes the answers, and reduce their learning curve (via training, advising, and consulting). Only an experienced coach who possesses great business acumen and experience in the real world can do this.

4. *Coach from your heart, not from your head.* When I first started coaching I had a master list of questions I used to ensure I was in fact asking the right questions. (I'll share these questions with you in the Appendix.) After coaching dozens of people over the course of my first several months as a new coach, I realized that the greatest coaches coach from their hearts, not their heads. That is, rather than focus on the "Five Steps to Coach Anyone" or some cookie cutter model that can be bought off the shelf, the truly masterful coaches go many layers deeper in themselves to become the most effective coaches they can be.

There is certainly a place for templates and a step-by-step model when coaching as I've outlined throughout this book. However, once you have evolved into a coach, it defines who you are, not just what you do. It becomes part of you. Rather than simply "doing" coaching, you are now coaching from your heart as a natural expression of yourself.

The most effective way to uncover and connect with someone else's heart, spirit, drive, and passion is to first tap into your own. The more you, as a coach, trust and use your gut feelings, your intuition, your instincts, the more of an impact you will have on the people you coach.

5. *Develop your personal style of coaching.* When people ask me what my style of coaching is, I say, "Direct yet light, exploratory, action-oriented, comprehensive, easily adaptable, conversational, enjoyable, tactical, and results-oriented. I'm your safe sounding board, your advisor, accountability partner, cheerleader, personal trainer, and consultant."

Building off the attribute we discussed under number 4, developing your own coaching style is something that doesn't happen immediately but as an organic process as you coach more and more people. The most effective coaches have learned to trust their heart and, in turn, trust their personality. Their style of coaching complements who they are naturally. These are the coaches who reign supreme, for they know that the very thing that their salespeople or clients find attractive in them is *who* they are, not simply *what* they do. Give yourself permission to be the authentic you and let your gifts radiate throughout the coaching you deliver.

It is perfectly normal and natural to have resistance to making the transformational shift from sales manager to sales coach. Considering what is required of you, it is a tall order. Much more is expected from the sales coach than the sales manager. However, imagine what would be possible for you and for your sales team once you make this transformation. For those managers who are willing to do so, the rewards are abundant.

CHAPTER

# The Coach's Mindset

## Six Universal Principles of Masterful Coaching

In Chapter One I introduced a new model and philosophy for managing your sales team. I wish I could say that simply changing your strategy and management style will yield the results you are looking for, but I can't.

It takes more than upgrading what you do to become a masterful sales coach. You also need to change how you think and behave on a consistent level. Think about the managers throughout your career who you respect and admire. I'm sure it's more than just their business and sales acumen that impressed you. When you think of those people, how do you describe them? Chances are, it would sound like this: "She is great!" "She is very attentive and cares about her people." "She really takes the time to ensure each of her salespeople get the support and attention they need to succeed here." "She will definitely challenge you and hold you accountable but does it in an empowering and positive way." "I think she has my best interests in mind."

These feelings or beliefs that you hold for your favorite managers have less to do with their tactical approach and more about how they act and communicate with you. And how you present yourself and communicate with your salespeople are a direct result of your attitude and mindset and how you approach management and coaching. Besides, if technical ability or knowledge were the deciding factors of leadership success, then we would hear people describe their manager this way: "Wow, she is very well trained."

Now that you have a foundation for this new model of executive sales coaching, I'm going to share with you the first step in becoming a masterful coach: Start to think like one. I will introduce the six universal principles of masterful coaching, using an experience I had coaching a manager. This story will exemplify the winning attitude and philosophies of a masterful coach as well as the self-imposed barriers and faulty thinking that create many of the problems managers desperately hope to avoid.

## MANAGEMENT'S ETERNAL CONUNDRUM

Michele and I have been working together for about six months now. She's the owner and operator of DesignWorks, a marketing and Internet strategy firm located in Pennsylvania. At the time Michele and I began the coaching process, she had 10 salespeople on her team. All of her salespeople were responsible for managing the entire sales cycle: from mining to uncovering qualified prospects via cold calling, referrals and networking, scheduling the initial meeting, and through to the close.

Michele is the kind of person any coach would enjoy working with. She's incredibly savvy, smart, insightful, truly authentic, a great business owner, and open to personal growth and change.

Michele was even a great manager (even though she probably didn't think so at this point), which was what connected us in the first place. At a company event, Michele and I started talking about some of the issues she was facing that were decelerating her company's growth. We discussed coaching as a solution for both her and her sales team. After listening to what coaching could offer, we began working together.

During our initial coaching session, it was obvious that Michele was passionate about her company and her employees. However, with every strength that each business owner possesses, a weakness is sure to follow.

Michele's weakness was that she cared a little too much about her staff. "Too much? How can you care too much?" Here's one telltale sign that overly sympathetic or sensitive managers could be doing more harm than good. Is the nurturing, thoughtfulness, and the attention you are giving to your people blinding you or preventing you from holding them accountable for their performance or from doing the job you expect? If so, then consider that you may be too concerned about protecting them or yourself from controversy, which could be a natural side effect of holding them to a higher level of accountability. (In Chapter 12, we discuss how to turn around an underperformer and hold your people accountable without being the bad guy.)

There was one salesperson in particular that Michele needed to make a decision on regarding her employment. She truly wanted Jennifer, one of her newest salespeople to succeed, but Jennifer was not meeting her goals. Here's where the eternal conundrum surfaces. Should Michele continue to work with Jennifer to try to turn her performance around or should she replace her with someone new?

So, what would *you* do? You will be able to do what Michele did, which got her safely and successfully to the other side of this common problem with minimal risk, fear, worry, and loss of sleep. To get to the solution that would help Michele and her employee, we needed to spend time on her management mindset. She needed to develop a process for approaching this challenge, one that was bound to happen again in her current role as sales manager.

## HITTING ROCK BOTTOM

Here's how the dialogue between Michele and me played out during our initial coaching session. Consider reading this story from two different angles. One is that of a manager who has probably experienced a similar situation before. Secondly, read this as the coach you are becoming so that you can start emulating the approach and mindset needed to coach your own people into sales champions.

"Michele, it sounds as if you're focusing more on a potential and rather grim future rather than on what you can do today to change this situation."

"It sure sounds that way, Keith. And I'm an optimist! I've always been focused and diligent with my work and my goals. And I really do try to go above and beyond what many managers do when it comes to providing their people with the support they need to succeed as a salesperson in my company. I know it's my job to spend the time with my salespeople, listening to them on the phone when they're either talking to a customer or when they're cold calling, even going in the field and running appointments with them. I believe I need to continue to coach and train them so they continue to develop. That's one of the main reasons why I hired you: I feel stuck."

"I can certainly understand your concern," I acknowledged. "Remind me, how long has Jennifer been with you?"

"About 16 months."

"And how long has her performance been in question?" I could tell this question was a bit painful for Michele to answer.

After several seconds of silence, Michele responded reluctantly, "About 12 months."

"So, you've been banking on the possibility that Jennifer may miraculously wake up one morning, turn things around, and start living up to her potential. And that would equate to her bringing in the increased number of sales you want."

"I know she can do it. I just need to push her harder or find out what's really going to drive and motivate her again. She proved that she is capable of selling within the first couple of months working here, turning in a few big sales right out of the gate. But now, she seems to spend her time making excuses as to why she can't sell more rather than making the changes she needs in order to do so. Then she makes comments like, "Well, I did take this job because of the flexibility it provides," and "Like I told you when I started here, I do have a personal life and a family that command a large portion of my time and attention." I just need her to start bringing in more sales now. I must experience at least 15 percent growth in my territory each year for me to hit my goals."

## YOU CAN'T COACH WHAT YOU FEAR

As I listened to Michele's concerns, I identified something I needed to clarify with her regarding what she could expect from my coaching. "Before we continue, it's important you know that I will not be able to coach you around your concern. You're stuck in the area of potential and *what-ifs*. What-ifs are points of time in the future which haven't happened yet. I can't coach you on something that hasn't happened yet. However, I can coach you on what you are currently experiencing today, in both action and in feeling, along with what may have happened in the past.

By focusing on the emotion that is preventing you from action, we can work toward a solution for the future. Once we identify why you have been afraid to address this earlier, then we can work toward making a decision regarding what to do about Jennifer. I sense there's some degree of fear, which is driving some of your decisions."

"Fear?" Michele responded. "I don't think it's fear." Given her reaction, I knew there was some truth to my observation. I proceeded to clarify my position and attacked this from a different perspective, one that she might be more open to hearing.

"Okay. What would you call it? How would you label what you're experiencing now?"

Michele thought for a moment. "Well, it's definitely a bit stressful to think I went through this hiring and training process and now I may have to go through it again due to an error in my judgment. I'm a little worried about not being able to replace her in a territory that really needs a strong presence from my company and how this pitfall will ultimately reflect in my numbers for the year."

To make sure I heard the message she intended, I paraphrased what she said. "If I'm hearing you correctly, it sounds as if you're worried about how this current situation might affect the results you're looking to achieve and when, if at all, you might be able to achieve them. And this is causing you a lot of stress. Is that accurate?"

"Yes," Michele confirmed.

"Michele, what do you think may be behind the stress and worry? What do you think those feelings are based on—the source of those feelings?" I inquired.

"Well, I have growth numbers to meet this year with this team. Our competition is knocking on our back door. So if I don't do something soon, they'll start taking away not only future potential business but also current clients and business that we've worked so hard to earn. Keith, the bottom line is, I have goals that need to be met, period, and in my eyes they are nonnegotiable."

## THE STRONG, FEARFUL LEADER

Let's step out of the conversation for a moment and reflect on what is happening. What are you hearing? Where is Michele getting stuck? What is the opportunity for Michele here? In what areas can coaching help Michele and her team?

For one, Michele is being driven by fear. It is her fuel of choice that keeps her motivated and in action. Unfortunately, the by-product of this is a culture that is based in fear and consequences.

Although we may want to better our lives and accelerate our productivity, many of our decisions are governed by fear. We want more, but avoid taking risks, so we continually produce similar results over and over. We fear change, because we may lose some degree of control over the outcome. We fear expressing how we feel or what matters most to us, in fear that it would make us vulnerable. We fear leaving what's predictable and comfortable, although it may not be best for us. We fear not having and not getting, having what we want and losing it, even getting what we want and no longer wanting it!

Ironically, most of our fears are not based on logic or reality. They are simply not real. Granted, the feeling of fear is very real, and I'm certainly not disputing that. Fear is just another feeling, like happy, angry, frustrated, excited, or sad. These feelings often trigger a physiological reaction. Like these other feelings, our body's reaction to the feeling of fear manifests in a variety of ways: an elevated pulse or heartbeat; temporary paralysis; a knot in our stomach, neck, or back; even perspiration.

There are actually two parts that make up the experience of fear. However, we often collapse these two parts together. If one component of fear is the feeling of fear, the other part of fear is that which we actually fear or the trigger that sends us into fear.

Because most of us do not distinguish what we fear from the feeling of fear, we have a tendency to resist fear and make it our adversary rather than embrace fear as an ally. And if you as the manager are doing this, it's a safe bet your salespeople are victims of fear as well.

We're all familiar with the three points in time: the past, the present, and the future. That which we fear is only the negative expectation or assumption of what may happen in the future (what we don't want to happen) and never what is happening in the present.

This is why you can't coach what you fear. That is, you can't coach the person on the fear they are experiencing simply because it hasn't happened yet. However, you can coach them on how they can upgrade their relationship with fear, which is what we are going to do with Michele.

If we are pushed to avoid consequences or what we don't want to happen, we are pulled toward what we do want, such as success or pleasure. Since fear is the negative assumption of the outcome, try shifting your focus as well as the focus of your salespeople when coaching them, to the positive outcome or what you do want to manifest, rather than the consequence you are looking to avoid.

The key point here is that our fears are just as real as our dreams. But as long as we give more power to our fears instead of our dreams, our fears will always seem as if they are more of a reality and in turn will get the better of us. If you stop and think about it for a moment, we construct dreams and fears in our minds. Both our fears and dreams are visions of a future point in time and are created using the same tool—our imagination!

Most of us spend more time focusing on what we fear rather than on the goals or dreams we want to create. Let's face it: We're all pretty good at articulating what we don't want to happen in our lives yet fall short when trying to come up with a vivid picture of what we do want or our goals and dreams.

If you know what you don't want yet don't know what you do want, then where do you think you are going to continually be directing your thoughts and energy? Your goals and dreams don't even stand a chance.

Imagine what would be possible if you embraced fear and considered it to be one of your greatest teachers? If you resist fear or react when you feel fear, then you can't learn from it or even recognize any lessons that would contribute to your continued evolution. And if you aren't learning from it, then you can't look at the fear as something that can be reframed into a positive opportunity to grow and change.

## UNIVERSAL PRINCIPLE OF MASTERFUL COACHING NO. 1: *MAKE FEAR YOUR ALLY*

What if fear was more your ally than your adversary? Consider fear to be your emotional feedback loop or internal barometer for learning. In other words, when we are in physical pain, our bodies react and let us know. It's a sign of danger or that we may be sick or injured. That's our body's physical feedback loop. Quite often if we ignore the pain, it gets even worse. By acknowledging the pain, we can choose to do something about it.

Embrace the belief that if and when you experience fear, it is trying to teach you something. Responding to fear in a healthier way will provide you with an opportunity to grow and learn, which leads to greater wisdom and unprecedented results.

Remember, that which you fear will happen is always happening in the future and, as mentioned, never in the present. If you can stay in the present moment as opposed to worrying about the negative assumptions of the future, you will notice that your fears will lose their powerful edge.

### ❧ FROM THE SIDELINES ❧

If you make decisions based on your fears, it will cloud and distort your judgment.

The rest of this story will illustrate how you, as a coach, can identify the limitations in Michele's thinking and how you can coach others with the same way of thinking that puts a ceiling on their fullest potential and the results they can achieve. The most effective coaches and managers have assimilated the following six universal principles into their philosophies and beliefs. Four of these principles will be the focus of the coaching I do with Michele; the other two will be discussed at the conclusion of Michele's story.

1. Embrace fear as your ally and tap into a healthier energy source to drive results.
2. Get out of your own head by shifting your focus to the moment.
3. Detach from the outcome and from your agenda.
4. Become process driven rather than driven by results.
5. Be creative. Create and coach new possibilities rather than expectations.
6. Become fully accountable for everything.

### FUELING THE FLAME OF SELF-DESTRUCTION

After listening to Michele's concerns, I asked, "If we were to go a few layers deeper, to be more specific, what do you most want to happen?"

"For my salesperson, Jennifer, I want her to:

- Develop a better, positive attitude.
- Start performing again and hitting her monthly sales quota.
- Consistently engage in the activities that bring in more sales.
- Start listening to me!
- Enjoy her work and be successful here.

For my company, I have very specific results and measurable goals I want to achieve this year. I want to grow a minimum of 15 percent this year. For me personally, I have my own income goals to meet. And I would like to find someone to take some of the operational responsibilities off my plate."

"I have an idea," I continued. "Let's list in detail the concerns you have, and then together we can pick each one apart and strategize on what needs to be done to eliminate them. How does that sound to you?"

"I like that idea," Michele agreed. "Let's do it."

The tone of the call became much heavier as Michele began sharing her fears of the future that contributed to her daily level of stress. After several minutes, I had to direct this part of the conversation to its conclusion, or run the risk of allowing this coaching session, and Michele, to be engulfed with feelings of terror and hopelessness. What follows are the top concerns and fears that Michele and I were able to identify at this point during our coaching conversation.

- What if I don't hit my numbers? How does that make me look?
- What if I fire Jennifer and she goes to work for one of my competitors and becomes their top salesperson?
- What if I keep Jennifer, invest my very limited time coaching and supporting her, and she still can't turn it around?
- What if I can't find another salesperson to replace her and in the meantime, we're losing market share to the competition?
- What if I fire her? How will the other salespeople feel?
- What if I keep her on board? What will the other salespeople think? Am I breeding mediocrity?

When I sensed that Michele had finished sharing the cause of all her distress, I jumped in. "I'm curious, Michele. Now that you've shared your concerns with me, do you notice any similarities within these concerns?"

"Yes, they are all paralyzing me from moving forward and sticking to one strategy that I can see through until completion. I keep second-guessing myself and my decisions."

I paused for a moment, just in case there was more that Michele felt she needed to share with me. She then continued: "And that it all focuses on the negative. My thoughts are consumed with all the bad stuff that could happen," Michele insightfully and honestly admitted. I knew a breakthrough was imminent.

"Michele, I admire your courage and your ability to look at and address these concerns head-on," I acknowledged, wanting to let her know I was with her, connected, engaged, and listening.

I continued, "Since we've come up with all of the worst-case scenarios, let's have some fun for a minute and come up with some best-case scenarios, okay?"

"Sure, but what's the point if these issues are still present?"

I suggested we complete this exercise before I responded. She agreed. "So, what would be the potentially positive possibilities that could also occur?" I asked.

Michele began, sharing with me the potential positive outcomes that could also come to fruition. With every plausible outcome she listed, she did so with a different demeanor. I sensed a weight being lifted off her shoulders; she sounded lighter. Her tone changed to one that was more like someone singing a favorite song rather than reluctantly reciting some dissertation in school in order to earn a passing grade.

Here's what she shared.

- We hit all of our targeted sales goals.
- I succeed in motivating my staff to achieve their goals and helping them win.
- I let Jennifer go and find another more competent salesperson to replace her.
- I keep Jennifer, invest my time coaching and supporting her, and she becomes a loyal employee who has turned her performance around for the best.
- I'm no longer concerned about what others think of me and do not allow that to get in the way of making the best decisions for my company.
- I've realized that there are no failures or mistakes, just options and opportunities to learn and better my situation. Rather than being paralyzed by fear, I allow fear to teach me something that contributes to my growth.

We continued this exercise for several minutes. When Michele felt that she shared with me the last possible optimistic outcome she could think of, I asked her to take the two lists she developed and write them out so she could compare them.

Curious about what she would see next, I inquired into what feelings or insights were coming up for her. "Did we thoroughly identify every conceivable feeling or outcome in each list?"

"I think we did, Keith."

"And what commonalities do you see? Are there any universal truths that apply to both of the lists you've created here?"

Michele studied each list for a couple of minutes, searching for similarities. Not recognizing any on a basic level, she stepped back from the lists and made a general observation that fueled her next breakthrough.

"Nothing that I see specifically, other than the fact that, at this point, none of these outcomes have even transpired as of yet."

I continued guiding this conversation and rephrased in my own words what I heard Michele say. "So, you're saying that each potential outcome or possibility you shared with me is, at this point, only a possible reality. The outcome is still an unknown and conditional of your behavior, actions, current way of thinking as well as the choices you make today. Is that accurate?" I wanted her to confirm and agree to this assessment before we continued our conversation. If I didn't, I would run the risk of creating a hole in our dialogue that could later affect the impact of this coaching session.

Michele agreed. I continued. "So then, we can say that each of these items, feelings, and expectations you shared are happening in the point in time we refer to as the future. And what about the other two distinct points in time?"

"Are you referring to the past and present?"

"Yes, in what point do you live, Michele?"

"The present."

"Are you sure?" I inquired.

After thinking about my question, she was surprised by her own answer: "Well, actually in the past. And in the future!"

It was during that very moment that Michele opened herself up to another breakthrough.

## UNIVERSAL PRINCIPLE OF MASTERFUL COACHING NO. 2: *BE PRESENT*

"Consider the three points in time: the past, present, and the future. Sure we physically exist in the present, but is that where you are truly living and responding, moment to moment? Consider that practically 95 percent of your waking hours are spent either living in the past or in the future. In other words, you're either reacting from a past experience or worrying about an expectation of the future. Where is the focus of your energy and thoughts?" I asked.

Michele thought for a moment. She reviewed the two lists she created during our meeting. The first list included all of the problems, fears, and worries that consumed much of her day.

"Well, given the list we created today, it looks as though my thoughts are clearly directed to the future point in time and one that I'm not too keen on reaching. So, I'm definitely living in the future.

"But then again, if I analyze the things that I think about and worry over what might happen, a few of those worries are things that have already happened to me before, which I certainly don't want to experience again!" Michele paused for a moment as she began combing through her first list. "I've certainly hired the wrong salespeople before. And have been known to invest way too much time trying to help turn them around. So much time, money, and effort wasted. And I've definitely waited too long to let an underperformer go."

I lowered my voice before delivering a tough message, yet one that I knew Michele was ready to hear. "It sounds to me that you're living in the past *and* in the future. We often live, listen, and react from the past or are pushing for something to happen in the future. And we do so at the expense of the present and the quality of our life."

The truth is, many managers are stuck living in the same deceptions they believe are true, which keep them from performing at their best and being fully present and engaged in the moment.

## MASTER EACH MOMENT IN TIME

Although planning for a great year is healthy and productive, during our quest to accomplish more we often lose sight of what is occurring today.

Are you focused on making today great or on wishing you said or did something differently at different points in your life? If you are living in or reacting from the past, that would sound like:

- "If only I (stayed with that company, was in a rewarding relationship, took better care of myself, opened my own

business, and so on), I would be so much happier/success-
ful today."

- "I should have done that years ago because I would have
  reached my financial goal by now."
- "I should have taken that promotion when I had the chance."
- "I remember the last time something like this occurred. I'm
  sure it will happen again."

These examples illustrate how you are responding to and living in the past.

Conversely, are you trying to get somewhere in the future? If
you are living in or reacting to the expectations of the future, that
would sound like:

- "Once I make a certain amount of money, then I will be
  able to have true peace of mind."
- "As soon as I own my own house, I'll feel more established/
  secure."
- "If I can just find my soul mate, my life will feel complete."
- "Once I finish this project and eliminate these problems, then
  I'll be happier and have more time for myself and my family."
- "When I lose 10 pounds I'll become a lot more confident
  and less self-conscious."
- "Just let me get to that point where I can create my ideal
  career. Then I'll feel totally fulfilled and satisfied."

We often live, listen, and react from the past or push for
something to happen in the future. To be fully present means you
are able to focus on a single person, idea, or topic. It means not
having any preoccupations with the past or future—the two points
in time we have no control over.

Being fully present takes practice, effort, focus, and a willingness to exclude all that is not directly relevant to what you are currently engaged in, especially while speaking with someone. Living
in, responding to, and thinking in the moment is both healthy and
more productive. It will enable you to embrace the magnificence
life offers today without sacrificing what is most important to you
(friends, family, health, career, etc.) in an attempt to get somewhere. Learn to master each moment in time, realizing that what *is*
always takes precedence over what *was* and what *will be*.

If you can practice this, the quality of your communication as well as the impact of your coaching efforts will greatly increase.

You will experience significant results when you open up your thinking and detach yourself from the outcome. During a coaching session or a conversation,

- You will notice your energy level will naturally increase.
- You will experience less stress.
- You will uncover new and greater possibilities, solutions, and opportunities that you would otherwise miss without having to push for them.
- You can now focus on mastering each extraordinary moment in time without worrying about yesterday or tomorrow.

## UNHOOK YOURSELF FROM YOUR AGENDA

I waited until Michele finished digesting the importance of this concept. She then exclaimed, "Keith, I totally live in the future!"

"And much of what drives us to live in the future is our unquenchable thirst for results, especially in business," I explained. "Ironically, it creates the very thing that, as a coach, you need to avoid: attachments to the outcome. So, what do you think you might be attached to, Michele?"

"I don't think I'm attached to anything." Her response was too quick to dismiss and move on. Michele thought for another moment, internalizing what we had been discussing thus far. Her next comment confirmed my observation that this was an area that demanded more focus, investigation, and attention.

"I just never realized that while living in the future, I'm also hooked on having a certain outcome or result that I want achieved in the future. I thought being mindful of the future and knowing what I want to create was just good business practice."

I knew we needed some evidence to support this concept and solidify her buy in. "While counterintuitive, being hooked on your goals can actually sabotage your efforts, especially when it comes to coaching your salespeople. Just think about the questions you ask your salespeople on a daily or weekly basis. What do those questions sound like?"

"What do they sound like?" Michele thought for a moment. "You know, the typical questions managers ask their salespeople." She then listed several questions she asks her team. "Are you hitting your numbers?" "How many follow-up calls did you make today?" "How much good volume did you book this month?" "How many cold calls did you make?" "How many appointments did you have this week?"

I continued, "And you have good reason to relentlessly drive these questions into your salespeople's heads, yes? After all, there's the pressure on them to reach quota or a certain level of acceptable performance. And then, as their manager, there's the pressure you experience to get them to perform and reach their numbers."

"But if I'm hearing you correctly, if I'm attached to the results, then I can't be engaged in the present moment. Is that correct?" Michele insightfully asked.

"You are so right," I continued. "Just think about how your conversations typically flow with your salespeople. Are you ever attached to an outcome or an expectation during a conversation with someone?"

"Wait. That feels like it may fit for me. Can you explain?"

"Just consider this scenario for a moment. You have the expectations of your salespeople outlined in your mind. And to support them in achieving their goals, you want to provide some coaching and discuss a game plan for them to achieve their year-end goals. The weight of these demands and the anxiety you feel when attempting to get them to close more sales inadvertently puts undue pressure on every salesperson you speak with, fostering an unhealthy relationship. And the worst part is, that added burden you put on your salespeople is then passed along to every prospect they speak with. Moreover, it puts a strain on each new relationship your salespeople are attempting to forge with the more qualified prospects.

"The irony is, this constant push to reach sales numbers keeps you and your salespeople hooked on the goal, diverting your efforts away from refining the selling process needed to generate more business. The quandary then becomes, "I'm too busy to work on my process. I have numbers to meet!"

"I see that now!" exclaimed Michele.

"Congratulations on recognizing this!" I applauded and acknowledged Michele's willingness to look at and own this newly surfaced truth, which created a new opportunity to improve upon how she's currently coaching and supporting her salespeople.

This is one example of how managers can get hyperfocused on their objectives to the point where it actually becomes counterproductive. However, there's more to learn about detachment. Our third universal principle of masterful coaching will reveal the reasons why managers continually fall into this trap and the collateral damage that follows.

## UNIVERSAL PRINCIPLE OF MASTERFUL COACHING NO. 3: *DETACH FROM THE OUTCOME*

If you were ever in a situation where you've walked away from a conversation feeling drained or exhausted, chances are there was something you were attached to or attempting to control in the conversation.

When coaching someone, here are some attachments to be aware of that can grip you and limit your potential.

- The need to be right or look good.
- The need to produce a desired result or achieve a certain objective.
- The need to be understood or prove your point.
- The need to have people agree with you.
- The need to avoid being wrong, looking bad, and hearing "No."

When speaking with your salespeople, if you find that you are repeating yourself, pushing to get someone to see it your way, or creating evidence to strengthen your side, you may be caught up in the ego of the situation.

The conversation then turns into a struggle for power and control. Being attached to the outcome during a conversation achieves the following undesired results:

1. Limits the ability to recognize or create a new or better solution.
2. Creates a barrier in your listening that prevents others from contributing to you.

3. Invalidates the other person by not respecting his feelings or point of view.

4. Prevents you from adjusting your approach or strategy so that it is more aligned with the other person and her style of communicating.

5. Inhibits your flexibility and adaptability.

6. Diminishes the impact of your coaching, since you can no longer listen purely, openly, and authentically for the real issue or problem.

Ultimately, attachments are based in fear and a strong desire to control the situation, even other people. Quite often in situations like these, managers put themselves and their own personal agendas ahead of the team's needs and goals, often resulting in a need to micromanage. This micromanagement creates a sense of mutual distrust between managers and their salespeople, weakening the integrity of the relationship between management and staff and fostering a mentality of "I" versus "we." Conversely, managers who are more trusting of their team, as well as their own ability to effectively coach them and drive growth, offer more autonomy to their salespeople. These managers are not driven by fear or the desire to control their people or the outcome but by the bigger vision of what is possible for them and for their team to achieve.

Managers often fall into the trap of being attached to the outcome when attempting to coach their salespeople, because their focus is fixed on a future outcome (the need for consensus, to be right, to be understood, to avoid a consequence, to be needed, etc.). Meanwhile, their salespeople are speaking to them in the present moment.

In order to let go of your expectations or attachments, especially during a coaching conversation, focus on the present. This will enable you to detach from the outcome, as all attachments are based in the future rather than in the present moment.

Keep in mind, I'm not suggesting that you abandon your goals and expectations of acceptable performance. There needs to be a healthy balance between holding someone accountable to the expected level of performance while, at the same time, being detached from the outcome. This is one of the most challenging concepts for any coach to master, especially if you are also a manager.

I have found one approach to achieving this delicate balance that works exceptionally well when coaching someone or having a conversation. Focus more on creating possibilities rather than being hooked on your rigid expectations.

We are now going to continue with what transpired during the remainder of the coaching session I had with Michele, beginning with this upgraded way of thinking.

## CREATE POSSIBILITIES, NOT EXPECTATIONS

"Michele, instead of being hooked on the *expectation* of generating the result you are seeking during a conversation, what if the intention was to create a new *possibility* through your collaborative efforts that would generate a desired result?"

I sensed confusion in her silence. I then shared with Michele the distinction between a possibility and an expectation.

"A *possibility* is something that may exist or what could happen, whereas an *expectation* is a rigid agenda or an attachment to a specific outcome. A subtle, yet powerful distinction. When you are open to possibility, you are inspired to innovate and create something new while being present in a conversation or an activity. You feel a sense of choice in the pursuit of your goal.

For example, you can be gripped with a certain *expectation* about something (in this case, having to get your salespeople to produce something measurable, do something specific, or agree with something). Or, you can simply enjoy the *possibility* of creating a new outcome with your salespeople (determining how you can best support them and provide value to them), without being attached to the specific agenda that you had at the beginning of the conversation."

"I hear what you're saying, Keith," Michele said with some skepticism. "But what if some people on my team are about to lose their jobs unless they start bringing in more consistent sales? After all, I *do* have certain *expectations* of performance. Or should I make those just possibilities?"

"If you have an attachment to certain outcomes during a conversation, then you might as well have that conversation by yourself. If you are so focused on having the other person see your point of view, if you're attached to creating a specific result, you are going to miss out on the ability to cocreate a new and better outcome as a result of listening deeply and openly to what the other person was actually saying."

I continued. "Sometimes we get so attached to having others see our point of view that we exhaust all our energy just to prove a point. We might do this with our salespeople, prospects, coworkers, boss, family, or friends. The problem is, if you are so attached to your own agenda inside a conversation, then how can a new or better possibility ever surface? How can you listen to your salespeople's wants and needs or create an effective, long-term solution for the problems they face daily? How can you coach them around the concerns they have about a prospect or their approach, which might get in the way of the sale? It just can't happen."

Michele's skepticism started to fade as she became more receptive to this idea. "You know, I can remember a few instances where I've allowed myself to open up my thinking and, as a result, the other person actually came up with a few really good ideas that I would have never considered. I guess as a manager, there's an underlying expectation that we must have all the answers. From what I'm hearing, that really isn't the case at all. It sounds like it's more of a collaborative approach."

I confirmed her observation. "Now, imagine what would be possible if you brought this same line of thinking with you into each coaching session with your salespeople. What if you believed that every conversation you had with your salespeople allowed for the creation of a new *possibility* rather than a rigid expectation that would elevate them to greater levels of success? This way, if you don't generate your desired result, then the possibility is still just a possibility."

Once Michele digested this, she replied, "Okay, so if I'm hearing you right, expectations are based in the point of time we refer to as the future, whereas possibilities are happening or being created at any moment in the present."

"Yes, you've got it, Michele."

## UNIVERSAL PRINCIPLE OF MASTERFUL COACHING NO. 4: *BECOME PROCESS DRIVEN*

"Let's kick off this part of our conversation with a question. Would you say you're someone who is very driven for results?"

"I'm definitely driven by the results," Michele responded without hesitation.

"Consider this paradox: The result is the process. In other words, what if you shifted most of your attention away from your goal or the end result and to the process?"

Michele challenged me on this. "Now, wait a second, Keith. I've been pretty open to what you've shared with me so far. As it is, you've turned my thinking around and upside down, all for the better. However, I have sales numbers to meet that I need to keep my eye on."

"I am not surprised. Often people who are attached to the outcomes in their efforts or during conversation are typically people who are very results driven. Just think back to the questions you shared with me that you continually reinforce with your salespeople. What if I told you that by continually focusing on the end result of your selling efforts, it will actually prevent you from reaching your sales goals?"

"I can't say that I agree with you, at least at this point."

"Let me drive this point home with a question. What's the point of eating a bowl of chocolate ice cream: to get to the end or to savor every bite?"

"To get to the end!" Michele responded, jokingly. I could tell she was receiving this message.

How about the goal of a self-care or an exercise regimen? Unless you're in it to compete professionally, it's to maintain a level of health, vitality, and personal satisfaction. The same holds true for measuring productivity, maintaining your peace of mind, and experiencing a sense of achievement at the end of each day.

Besides, you don't *do* the result; you execute the process, which *produces* the result as a natural by-product of your efforts. That's the paradox. By honoring the process, you can enjoy the benefit of knowing that you will attain your goals, since it's the process that will get you what you want. (Imagine building a house without a blueprint, the contractors, and the tools and materials needed.)

As discussed in Chapter 1, to generate better results, you must either change what you do or change how you think. To continually develop a high-performance team, exceed your sales goals, and better manage your mindset, change your thinking to become process driven rather than results driven.

"But Keith, at the end of the day it's the results that matter, right?"

"Of course, that's one measure of success. However, the anticipated results are just not where you're going to focus all of your time and energy. Even though having a monthly sales goal keeps your eyes on the prize and your focus on the end result, it may actually do more harm than good. Salespeople and managers are always telling me how results aren't showing up fast enough. Then, at the end of each selling month, fear and worry run rampant as salespeople scramble to do their best to close sales and meet their numbers.

After all, once you've set your goals, they are not going anywhere. They are still out there, living at a designated point of time in the future, whether the future is one month away or one year away. So, once you step back from your goal or the end result that you seek, at what point in time do you need to take the actions or steps to achieve this goal?"

"Today."

"Here's a situation where being results driven means you are living in the future. And if you're living in the future, you are not engaged in the moment. How does this line of thinking ultimately affect your activity?"

Michele sounded a bit frustrated at the realization of how true this was for her. "Great, here we go again. If you're referring to how I'm pushing more for the result to happen rather than focusing on the process that will make it happen, I guess I can't argue with you there."

"That's why it's critical to become process driven," I said, wanting to continue this momentum. Ask yourself, 'Do I have a sales, prospecting, follow-up, time management, or even a customer service process in place that I can trust?' When you look at your daily schedule, does it outline the specific and measurable tasks and activities you need to engage in that will move you toward your goal? What about a 30-day new hire orientation you follow for each new salesperson you recruit into your sales team? Or a process to determine whether to turn around or terminate an underperformer?"

"Nope. Well, we do have a customer service process in place but that's about it."

"Then you can see that it makes total sense as to why you are so hooked on the result. Chances are, people who are solely focused on the end result don't have a process they have faith in. As such, they concentrate more on trying to control the outcome: pushing for what they want rather than managing their process. After all, you can't trust and manage the process if you don't have a process in place to do so! Trying to achieve more without a process to guide you would be equivalent to driving from New York to California without a road map while wearing a blindfold. Not only can it be stressful but you're bound to wind up somewhere other than your intended destination."

Michele began to lighten up and become more receptive to the changes she knew she had to make. I proceeded to bring this portion of our conversation to its natural conclusion. "Once you have outlined a path and a success formula to follow as it relates to the systems you need to put in place, allow the doing or the process to be the reward and where the pleasure resides, not just the end result. This way, you can be responsible for your future goals without having to worry about them. If you continue your quest with your eyes focused on the finish line, you'll miss out on the journey. Therefore, be careful not to hook yourself on to the future so you can enjoy the process of reaching your goals today."

## TRUST THE PROCESS

It's essential to know when enough is enough at the end of each day. Trust the process you've put in place. After all, there's always more to do. There's always more that can be done at the office, at your home, or in your life—another call that can be made or another e-mail that can be read and responded to.

Meeting your goals will be the result of the cumulative efforts you make and the activities you engage in every day. When you're mindful of the process, you now have the opportunity to recognize, enjoy, and celebrate your accomplishments on a daily basis. Some of these achievements may feel very small or insignificant, but celebrate them regardless, instead of waiting until you've achieved your *final* desired result. (And when does *that* occur, anyway?)

"Now I'm going to get a bit more cerebral on you, Michele. One of the most important capabilities of an effective coach is to be creative. The greatest coaches have harnessed their creativity to offer the most powerful alternative solutions for their clients—solutions their clients, as well as the coaches, couldn't see on their own. Here's my question. At what point in time does creativity occur?"

Michele thought for a moment, then responded. "Hmmm. I guess in the moment."

"That's right. Which means if you're not engaged in the moment and in the process, you can't truly be creative.

If you're hooked on the future or on the result, there are several other key coaching disciplines you cannot be effective at carrying out.

- First, you can't be listening. Active listening happens in the moment.
- Second, you can't ask better questions. That falls under the realm of creativity. That is, you create the most pertinent questions in the moment.
- And finally, if you're not fully present, you can't be engaged and connected with the person you are speaking with, which, by the way, that person will be able to sense."

"Okay, Keith," Michele began. "You made a believer out of me. I get it. It looks as though I have some work to do, starting with redefining and documenting all of my systems and procedures, as well as clarifying my personal vision of what I really want to create rather than continually focusing on what consequence I'm looking to avoid. Doing this will keep the fear at bay. This was a very productive call, and I appreciate you supporting me through this tough transition because I don't think I could do this alone. So, thanks, and I'm looking forward to talking with you next week."

Michele and I spent the next several minutes recapping our call, especially what new breakthroughs or insights were created.

The next section of this chapter will focus on the two remaining principles that the most successful coaches have adopted.

## UNIVERSAL PRINCIPLE OF MASTERFUL COACHING NO. 5: *BE CREATIVE*

Those people whom you consider to be highly effective and influential, masters of networking and referral generation, or sales champions, share one common denominator that makes them so great at what they do. These people are highly creative and leverage their creativity to the full extent in everything they do.

The most effective managers and coaches on the planet realize that coaching is the art of creating possibilities and opportunities that didn't exist before.

After all, when you are helping one of your salespeople solve a problem, refine a skill, bring in more sales, or develop a more effective way to perform a task, think about what it is you are actually doing. You are creating a new possibility or outcome. Keep in mind the story of our friend Michele and the barriers she was up against that prevented her from becoming a more creative manager for her team. Living in the future, being driven by fear, and being attached to your own agenda are the adversaries of creativity.

Think about the possibilities you can create today as the manager of a sales team. Although the opportunities are boundless, there are still managers out there who may feel confined or restricted when it comes to making the necessary changes desperately needed to maximize the performance of their sales teams. These managers feel that they are pushing up against what they perceive to be a ceiling of limitation, which robs them of their abilities and drive to foster positive change. These managers feel powerless to become the catalyst they need to be in order to modify, let alone transform or revolutionize, their existing sales culture.

Unfortunately, this strategy of justification falls outside the confines of sound coaching principles, and here's why. Being creative is the conduit to taking full responsibility for everything that shows up in your life, which is what the world's greatest coaches do. For managers, this equates to being fully accountable not only for reaching their sales goals but also for carving the path, creating the momentum and desired environment, as well as accelerating growth and progress, even if they're not the CEO.

## UNIVERSAL PRINCIPLE OF MASTERFUL COACHING NO. 6: *BECOME FULLY ACCOUNTABLE— FOR EVERYTHING*

One universal principle that the most successful coaches adhere to is this: You are fully accountable for everything that shows up in your life. If we apply this to our communication, then a masterful communicator is fully accountable not only for the message that is delivered but for the message the other person is hearing. Therefore, we must own the responsibility of the entire communication process and adjust our communication style accordingly.

Now think about how this principle applies to your salespeople. If a salesperson that you are managing fails, whose fault is it?

Over the last several years, the media has focused our attention on some of the most devastating business failures of our time. Millions of people lost their life savings and were financially ruined by the fall of corporations such as Enron. In the wake of these ethical disasters of mind-numbing proportion, the integrity of business leaders has been forced back into the limelight.

Some noteworthy companies have risen to the occasion or at least have made an attempt to do so, starting with taking full responsibility for their failures, specifically JetBlue and Southwest Airlines. During the winter of 2007, devastating weather conditions combined with dreadful mismanagement and the poor deployment of resources caused the delays and cancellations of hundreds of flights, which left thousands of passengers stranded.

These two companies clearly screwed up. But here's what they didn't do. They didn't run and hide. They didn't spin their story. They didn't blame everything on the weather, as bad as it may have been. Conversely, here's what they did do. They took responsibility; they apologized to their passengers, their families, and the general public. They did their best to come forward and honestly explain that they made big errors. And in the spirit of good business practice and customer care, JetBlue offered their passengers refunds on their tickets, and, in some cases, Southwest Airlines actually gave their passengers their flights for free. While it may not have been their fault entirely, these companies still took 100 percent accountability for this debacle. They took full ownership of the problem even if the cause of the problem was outside of their control.

This is the type of mindset that leaders and executive sales coaches must adopt. How does this apply to you and to the question I posed earlier regarding where the ultimate responsibility rests if a salesperson fails? Whether your team consists of 1,000 salespeople or just one, the simple fact is that avalanches roll downhill. They start at the top. That's why you are 100 percent accountable for the success and failure of your sales team.

## THE TOP 19 EXCUSES MANAGERS USE TO JUSTIFY WHY SALESPEOPLE FAIL

Now, when I share this truth with my clients regarding full accountability, I expect some pushback from managers and executives. I hear things like, "C'mon, Keith, don't managers get a little bit of a break here? How can we be fully accountable when we're already stretched thin and still expected to achieve higher sales goals with fewer resources. Don't salespeople have some role and responsibility in this? After all, it's their careers and it's what they were hired to do. I mean, what if . . . ?"

No, I didn't cut this person off. I heard their entire rebuttal. That's why we're going to list all of the what-ifs (also known as excuses) that I've heard from managers when I challenged them to be fully accountable. Here are just some of the reasons I've heard as to why managers feel they should not be fully responsible for their salespeople.

1. I just got promoted and inherited my sales team. I didn't hire these people.
2. We don't do background checks. Sometimes you just don't have all the information to make the best hiring decision.
3. Some of these veteran salespeople have been here forever.

4. We don't have time for a sales training and coaching program.

5. That's normal in my industry. Turnover is something we just have to deal with.

6. I don't have the authority to make hiring and firing decisions.

7. We can't offer competitive packages like other companies can. It's straight commission. No salary or benefits. We do our best to play the hand we're dealt.

8. We don't have an evaluation process.

9. There's just this one person who, no matter how hard I try, I just can't get along with. That just makes my job tougher.

10. The salespeople are really independent contractors. So if they need help, they should get help on their own.

11. If they fail, then they really weren't cut out for this position.

12. We've given them training. Two weeks of training that covers all of our product line. Soft skill development? No.

13. Needed help? Then they should have come to us. We would have helped them. That's their responsibility. How can I read their minds if they're having a problem?

14. My sales team is awesome. It's the other divisions we have to interact and work closely with that are bringing our numbers down.

15. I need quick studies. If they don't pick it up fast, then chances are this position isn't for them. I don't have time to babysit them. That's our qualification process: The strong survive.

16. I worked with that guy for three weeks of solid, on-the-job training. And still nothing.

17. You can't make any headway in this company. They're opposed to doing that sort of thing.

18. The President and her board already feel that things are going well, and this is not a priority. So why change? And if that's how they feel, what can I do?

19. It's hard to find good sales talent out there now. Our market is supercompetitive, and this is what I have to work with.

Interestingly, in each of these excuses, problems, and situations, there is one common denominator present—the manager. Here's how I respond to these excuses:

"Ultimately, you have a choice, yes?"

These excuses are a declaration for these managers, as if they are etched in the stone writings of their predecessors that must never be challenged or questioned. And each one of these justifications is backed up with the evidence of experience to support its truth. Regardless, at the end of the day, these managers are still dealing with the same problems or are stuck with a team of underperformers. These managers have surrendered. They've given up. They've lost. The instant you begin to buy into a justification, you've started to surrender your personal power.

Here's an alternative. You can be weighed down with excuses or empowered by the ability to make better choices. Either way, you're accountable for these excuses, just as you are accountable for your sales team. Since you are evaluated or compensated by how successful your team is, then tolerating these excuses will come at a heavy price. Ultimately, you will be the one responsible for breathing life into these excuses or pioneering innovative solutions in order to eradicate them.

Once you take full accountability for yourself as well as each person on your sales team, you will be able to empower others to be fully accountable for themselves.

Therein lies the ultimate source of power. When you take ownership of full accountability, you get to choose what you are holding yourself accountable for. It will be your choice to use your personal power, your talents, your vision, your values, and your integrity in a way that moves you and your team forward. If you stop for a moment and think about it, this isn't your practice career or simulated sales team. Nor is it our abilities and intentions that show the world who we truly are. Instead, it will always be our choices and our subsequent actions that define us.

CHAPTER

# Six Fatal Coaching Mistakes and How to Avoid Them

M istakes happen. They're part of life. Openly embraced, mistakes are the greatest impetus in our continued evolution and the primary contributor to lifelong learning. Resistance, as it has been said, is futile, for any mistake that is ignored or rejected is bound to be repeated until the lesson has been revealed and a change has been made.

If we were to move beyond this line of thinking, the real problem comes when we fail to recognize the mistakes we make. Sure, it's challenging enough to find the lesson in every experience, especially the painful ones. But what if you aren't aware of a problem that needs your immediate attention? What if you can't recognize the mistakes you're making, especially as they relate to coaching your salespeople? This can be very costly. The quest to continually search out opportunities for improvement is now replaced with "Well, that's just the way it is" or "I guess that's the best it's ever going to get;" a mentality of mediocrity.

This chapter exposes the six most elusive coaching errors so you can recognize and avoid making them. Here's your chance to expand your peripheral vision and learn about the six universal, and often fatal, mistakes that managers make when coaching their salespeople.

## COACH THE RELATIONSHIP WITH THEIR STORY

The burden that Lauren was carrying around as the team leader for her business development group was glaringly obvious to Joan, her manager. "I'm just so stressed out," Lauren said in desperation.

"Where's all that stress coming from?" Joan inquired, searching for what was behind the stress that triggered this reaction.

"It's just the accumulation of all the projects I'm working on right now. It's a bit daunting with all the growth we've experienced this past year. Unfortunately, our staff has not grown in proportion, to offset and balance out the workload. I know it's something we're working on. It's just not happening fast enough. I'm worried that the quality of my work will suffer."

"Has the quality of your work suffered?" asked Joan.

"No, not yet at least. The only thing that's really been affected is my schedule. I'm not able to get out of the office until eight o'clock and I'm starting my day here at around seven in the morning."

"Lauren, I certainly don't want to see you burn out or have this negatively impact your personal life," Joan began. "I've noticed an imbalance in the workload among your team. It seems that some of the people on your team aren't putting in the hours you are. As the team leader, it looks as though you have an opportunity to further utilize your account manager to support you and take on some of the tasks that are keeping you here late."

Lauren seemed a bit uncomfortable listening to Joan's observation. "As we've discussed, one of my goals within the next year is to take on more of a leadership role within the company and move toward becoming a partner one day. I can't afford to have one of my account managers make a mistake on any of these projects. That's why I'm not letting go of some of these tasks as much as I have in the past."

"I tend to think that in order to be an effective leader, I need to be the best doer in all or most of the areas under my supervision," continued Lauren. "Not that I need to be doing all the work, but I need to know that others know I can do the work. Besides, how would that look through the partners' eyes if I start making mistakes on client projects? There goes my chance for promotion. And at that point, a promotion is the last thing I'd be worrying about since I'd probably be canned and on the streets looking for a new job. I have no idea how marketable I am, since I've been here from the time I graduated college! The next thing I know, my family would have to move elsewhere, because we wouldn't be able to afford our home and lifestyle. What a disappointment I would be to them."

Joan wanted to make certain she understood what Lauren was saying. "So, you're working at this extreme level out of the fear of not fulfilling client expectations, meeting a deadline, or reneging on a promise which to date, has not happened. And if you don't meet these expectations, it would lead to many disappointed clients, which would be bad for your career trajectory. You would lose the respect of the people on your team, your peers, the partners, even your family. You will be passed over when the time comes for promotions and would earn the reputation of being a second-class producer who's just making it in her role. You'll wind up losing your job and find yourself unemployed and living on the street. Did I get that right?"

After further coaching, Lauren realized how ludicrous and irrational her thought process was. Her state of mind was drowning in an ocean of overreaction around her story, which I refer to as a S.C.A.M.M.

## FATAL COACHING MISTAKE NO. 1:
## BELIEVING THE S.C.A.M.M.—A MANAGER'S
## MOST ELUSIVE ADVERSARY

Lauren did a wonderful job constructing her own personalized fable. I'd like to introduce a more comprehensive acronym for this type of damaging thinking. When you stop and think about what a story truly is, it's a diversionary tactic or a S.C.A.M.M. Not only are you conning yourself with untruths that validate your situation or yourself but you are also enrolling others in this creative deception. The acronym stands for words that encourage personal propaganda and fund your campaign for unnecessary noxious drama.

S.—Stories

C.—Cons

A.—Assumptions

M.—Meaning

M.—Mindset

A S.C.A.M.M. is an action, excuse, or belief you hide behind that justifies your circumstance, behavior, and performance, even your position on something, that provides you with an excuse so you do not have to be accountable for your responsibilities, goals, or the situations you put yourself in. The one commonality that each of these five words share is *choice*. At the very core, your stories, cons, assumptions, imposed meanings, and mindset are ultimately a choice.

Other examples of S.C.A.M.Ms that you can begin to recognize in your salespeople are as follows:

- An excuse for the behavior you really don't want anymore.
- An action, a lack of action, or a belief that keeps you from being accountable or looking at the real truth in a situation.
- A persistent or constant complaint.
- A source of energy. Even though it may be a negative energy source, human beings tap into any available energy source, even if it causes additional problems, stress, and difficulties (e.g., adrenaline, playing the victim, thriving off chaos or drama, making other people wrong, taking on the Mother Teresa role, being a martyr, striving for perfection that paralyzes movement, etc.).
- A justification for the situation you're in today, the one you were in yesterday, even the one you may be in tomorrow (fears, assumptions, excuses, anticipated outcomes, etc.). For example, "C'mon, be honest. Look at who's selling the most. Who do you think is getting all the preferential treatment and better quality prospects handed to them? If it were me, you would see a big difference in my sales numbers."
- A reason for being who you are today. That might sound like: "I'm not very trusting of people because when I was eight years old. . . . " or "If you really want to know why I

am so reluctant to prospect it's because during my first sales job. . . . " or "The first manager I ever had was a tyrant. His management style really took a toll on me, on my confidence, and on my ability to perform."

- A rationalization for doing something you are better off not doing which isn't aligned with your goals and objectives.

## ❧ FROM THE SIDELINES ❧

Your S.C.A.M.M. holds the power to manipulate and shape your attitude.

Just ask salespeople who have to prospect to build their businesses. They can justify practically any activity that will take them away from prospecting, allowing them to major in the minor activities that act as diversions to doing what's truly needed.

To further illustrate the importance of identifying and eliminating your personal S.C.A.M.Ms, especially the ones that your salespeople fall victim to, consider the costs you incur by not recognizing and defusing them. In addition to having an effect on your overall quality of life, it will also have an effect on your ability to coach. For example, if your salespeople's incomes depend on bringing in new business, yet they are reluctant to cold call or prospect due to some stories they've told you (and themselves), what is the greater cost? If salespeople don't prospect, it not only affects their professional satisfaction, selling opportunities, peace of mind, greater financial security, even their careers, but in the end, this burden falls on the shoulders of the manager.

## UNCOVER YOUR BLIND SPOTS

How can we fall into the trap of believing our own stories, fables, and illusions? Because they are *blind spots*. We're just so used to them, we become blind to them. Although we can more easily see the challenges and S.C.A.M.Ms in others, where they are stuck, what their core issues may be, and what might be an obvious solution for them, we are always the last person to be able to see them in ourselves. This is true regardless of your age, profession, wisdom, or experience.

What further drives the investment we make in our stories and the fables we create about ourselves is that we fall in love with our stories and the things we think are true. We love our stories and S.C.A.M.M.s! The more we tell them, the more engrained they become in our thinking and our being and the more we believe them. The problem is that we give our stories way too much power over us. The more we believe our fables, the more factual they seem to us, further adding to the challenge of distinguishing between what is reality and what is not.

Like the rest of the human race, managers need an objective person to peer inside their lives and help them identify and rewrite the stories they tell themselves, the ones that hold them back from greatness, prevent them from living life the way they want, and subsequently inhibit them from becoming a fully self-expressed, masterful executive sales coach.

Whether you're an athlete, a coach, a manager, or a salesperson, you still require a coach on the sidelines to observe you and uncover the confining behavior or thinking that you cannot. There is a tremendous value to having someone on the outside looking in and pointing out the things that you are unable to recognize on your own, especially when you're in the thick of the game.

## STORIES MANAGERS BELIEVE THAT THEIR SALESPEOPLE TELL

Salespeople are a creative bunch, especially when it comes to the stories they tell themselves. These are also the same stories they tell their managers during meetings, conversations, or performance reviews. Unfortunately, managers find themselves getting sucked into the stories, which wastes their valuable time and resources on a well-fabricated issue that has no real resolution.

Once you're able to uncover a salesperson's S.C.A.M.M., the tactical coaching strategy would be to coach the person to rewrite the story. This is a key point. In other words, you don't coach the story or feed into the story. If you do, you are coaching someone around a lie, something that doesn't even exist. Instead, you coach the person on his relationship with the story in order to uncover the real truth of what's going on.

What are some stories you hear from your salespeople? I've listed a few of the more popular fables that you can recognize the next time a salesperson tells one to you.

1. *Fear of failure (or success)*. "I'm afraid of failure, yet I won't take the steps to ensure my success. Therefore, if I sit back and do nothing, then I can never fail at anything!"

2. *Perfectionism/either-or thinking*. "Either I create the perfect (prospecting, time management, goal setting, management, coaching) system to use or I don't do it at all. A similar perfectionism type of story is created by the type of sales-people I refer to as knowledge junkies. Their story can sound like this: "I'm still not ready yet. Just a little more training, research and due diligence, then I'll be ready."

3. *Taking it all on*. "I can't delegate these tasks that other people may be able to do because they will never do it as well as I can."

4. *Been there, done that*. "The last time I attempted to build my business through prospecting, it was a waste of time. Therefore, I know that prospecting won't work for me."

5. *Playing it safe*. "Sure, I've been prospecting. I mean, I've been targeting my current accounts to see if there are any service issues that need to be handled and whether I can get more business from them. After all, you need to take care of your current customers, right?"

6. *The accountability trap*. "Of course I have a to-do list. I check things off as soon as I can fit them in." Do you have a deadline associated with each task on your to-do list? A task without a deadline is another S.C.A.M.M. Writing down a long list of tasks or activities that are not scheduled and have no timelines or completion dates associated with them is another way to avoid accountability. Since you are keeping the timeline open ended, you don't have to be re-sponsible for completing the tasks by any specific date. No schedule, no commitment.

7. *Not having a schedule*. "I'm so busy that I don't have time to create my routine!" The absence of a routine frees you from being accountable for certain things you're responsible for

or you may not want to do but have to do in order to reach your goals.

8. *Everyone comes before me.* "I can't say 'No' to my clients. I have to take care of them or they will go elsewhere, right?" Do you have a salesperson who has a hard time saying, "No" to clients and drops everything at their request? Either you are going to run your own life, or other people and circumstances are going to run it for you. Honor the commitments you make to others as well as the commitments you make to yourself. Besides, you cannot effectively take care of others if you do not take care of yourself first.

9. *Interrupt-driven.* "I can't focus on any task for very long because I am constantly being interrupted by people, situations, problems, and new tasks I'm suddenly responsible for. It's hard to get things done." This easily distracted salesperson probably has a long list of tasks that never get completed. This person may also be an adrenaline junkie who loves the rush of working on overdrive when trying to do it all and juggle many unfinished and ongoing tasks.

10. *Playing the victim.* "I can't believe I wasn't able to schedule an appointment with Mr. Prospect today. I feel so dejected and frustrated, too frustrated to do anything else productive today." Rather than moving on and forging ahead, this person allows one bad experience to affect the rest of his day.

You may find that one or two (or more) of these behaviors describe some of your salespeople's S.C.A.M.Ms (maybe even some of your own), and this is actually good news! I never said that you would like bringing these truths to the surface. Although it takes a conscious effort to uncover other people's diversionary tactics, it takes a lot of courage to admit that you use them, too. However, now that you have a greater understanding and awareness, you can do something about them. When you notice yourself or your salespeople falling into any of these traps, you can choose to either continue engaging in the S.C.A.M.M., or make a better choice that will generate the results you really want.

> ### ❈ FROM THE SIDELINES ❈
>
> If a salesperson is reluctant to take the necessary actions to achieve the results that matter most, there will always be some type of confining belief, story, or S.C.A.M.M. at the core that is getting in the way.

## FATAL COACHING MISTAKE NO. 2: WANTING MORE FOR OTHERS THAN THEY WANT FOR THEMSELVES

Yes, you can actually want too much for your salespeople and your clients, more than they, in fact, may be ready for or even want for themselves. Jake learned this lesson quickly as a new coach starting out.

To this day, Jake's unwavering commitment to every one of the salespeople on his team is to help them make the long-term changes they want and need in their careers.

When Jake first started coaching his salespeople, he made a personal commitment that he would not just be a sales coach but an exceptional coach that every salesperson in his company would call on first. And in the spirit of becoming this person, he put action behind this commitment. He carefully prepared, researched, and practiced prior to every coaching session he had with a salesperson.

"Coaches deliver value while challenging their clients to achieve more through the utilization and development of their natural skills and talents so they can live up to their fullest potential" was Jake's firm belief. He was insistent, practically obsessed with the notion that his salespeople must walk away with measurable value from every interaction and coaching session they had with him.

This manifested itself in a variety of ways. For example, if salespeople were coming to Jake ready to review their targeted objectives, he challenged them to reconsider their goals and make them even loftier, encouraging them to reach for even bigger, more rewarding results. Or, Jake might suggest that they identify a timeline in which they wanted to attain their goal or, better yet, shorten the timeline they initially developed for achieving this milestone.

If a salesperson was struggling to bring in an acceptable number of appointments each week through referrals and was considering putting together a cold calling campaign, Jake would be right there ready with the call template, opening statement, and process she needed to be effective at cold calling, including the number of dials she should start making today in order to achieve her sales goals.

Whatever objectives and goals his salespeople would have, Jake was ready to act as their primary source of support, encouragement, knowledge, structure, and insight needed to achieve what mattered most to them.

You name it, and Jake was ready for every conceivable question, goal, or challenge his salespeople threw at him. And, boy, did he push and push and then, when he was finished pushing, he pushed some more. Just think about what happens when you eventually keep pushing without gauging the resistance level? You get pushback.

But why should a coach sense pushback from a salesperson, when the salesperson was the one who set the goals in the first place? What Jake wasn't aware of was the flaw in his strategy. Look at the word *client*. Now, look at the word in the middle of the word. That's right, you'll notice the word *lie*. To be clear, Jake's salespeople weren't intentionally lying to him. It's just that people often lie to themselves and believe the lies to be true.

These lies come in a variety of shapes and forms. For example, a lie could be an unwillingness to look at the truth, or a lack of awareness around the real issue. People can deceive themselves about the way they process information or may be unrealistic as to how fast they could move in order to reach a goal. In some cases, people don't like the solution because it wasn't what they expected or wanted, or they weren't comfortable with it. This can cause pushback.

Sometimes, salespeople won't admit that they lack the skills they know are necessary to achieve their goals. They aren't sure they can put in the time and effort to master the skills. This new awareness may cause resistance. Rather than pushing through and forging ahead without knowing all the facts, coaches need to take the salesperson's pulse to avoid causing further damage.

To prevent forcing your agenda and expectations on those you coach, it's critical that you find out what your salespeople's expectations are from your coaching, the value they expect and how they want to be coached.

## TAKE THEIR PULSE, NOT YOURS

Even though Jake's salespeople were telling him they enjoyed and benefited from his coaching, he felt something was off. At the end of every coaching call, Jake felt like he'd just run a marathon. He was exhausted and deflated. His energy was all used up. Jake poured his heart and soul into every coaching call, believing this was what a coach was supposed to do. Not exactly.

As a new coach, Jake didn't have enough experience to recognize that how he felt at the end of a coaching call was a telltale sign that something was indeed off. So, he did what every new, intelligent, insightful coach would do. He called his mentor coach.

Here's what Jake came to understand. Sometimes we want so much for our clients and staff to be happy, satisfied, and successful that we have a tendency to instill our own agenda into the coaching process. If it sounds similar to having an attachment, you're correct. However, the attachment in this situation is about wanting more for your clients or employees than they want for themselves or are ready for.

Sure, you're committed to being a resource and delivering value to each of your salespeople, especially when coaching them. This is certainly the right mindset to have when coaching. However, the pendulum of extremities can swing even further. In this situation, you become so committed to delivering value when coaching your salespeople that you're now making it about *you* and how much value *you* must deliver. In turn, the coaching call is now being driven by your agenda instead of an agenda created by the person you are coaching. It's a subtle yet vital distinction.

In truth, the real measurement of value derived from the coaching relationship is determined by the person you are coaching and how that person defines value, not how you define it. While this may sound counterintuitive, you need to surrender your attachment to delivering value and let it be co-created organically during each coaching session.

## ❈ CHECKPOINT ❈

If you're feeling drained or tired at the end of every coaching session, you're probably bringing your own agenda into your coaching.

There is a big difference between being committed to your people and wanting to support them, and giving them more than they are ready for. An example could look like this. You may have a salesperson who is very content and satisfied making a yearly income of $150,000. However, you also have salespeople on your team making twice that much, which tells you that the opportunity exists for this salesperson to make an income of $300,000; it can be done because others are doing it. You may look at this salesperson as an underperformer, someone you feel you need to coach so he can be more successful and make more money. Or maybe you have your own sales goals to hit and this salesperson, although a consistent performer, could make your life easier if he just sold more.

This is a blind spot for many managers and executives. Maybe this salesperson is making more money each year than he ever thought possible or more than he thought he would ever make in a lifetime. Maybe he isn't driven or motivated by money the way other salespeople are and feels content with his income without having to sacrifice his personal life. His career currently supports his lifestyle, gives him a personal sense of fulfillment, and enables him to contentedly achieve his goals.

In a different situation, you may discover that a goal one of your salespeople initially shared with you is no longer applicable. Sure, it may have been a goal she thought she wanted at the time but when she explored what it would take to achieve that goal, she realized it wasn't what she really wanted after all. Whether it had to do with the additional resources needed, time investment, skill development, realistic results, or what she would have to give up in pursuit of this dream, this salesperson now realized that abandoning the goal would be in her best interest. Having this realization during a coaching session is the real value that you have delivered. For her, it was a breakthrough regardless of whether you feel it was valuable enough.

Even though coaching is about stretching and challenging people to attain more than they would be able to on their own, sometimes what they can achieve, what they want to achieve, and what is in their best interest are in conflict with each other. Therefore, when coaching people, it is not always about what is possible, realistic, or attainable. Instead, it becomes more about what your employees want, what they need, and what is most aligned with their personal and professional vision. Subsequently, this determines the focus of your coaching and helps define the right priorities for them.

In other instances, some coaches are so driven to provide value that they often give the person they are coaching the answers prematurely or feel they have to jump in and fix something in order to demonstrate their value as a coach. Here's an example. It is very common for me to have a coaching session with a client where I do nothing more than listen. Maybe I'll ask the client two or three questions to drive the conversation forward, but that would be all the talking I would do during a 40-minute coaching session. The rest of the time is spent listening. Inevitably, at the end of the call I would hear, "Thanks for a great call! I got so much value from our time today. I really appreciate all the help you gave me."

What did I actually do here? All I did was ask three questions, and spend the majority of the session listening. As a new coach, it may be hard to believe that simply being a sounding board is a powerful part of the coaching process. Think about this concept for a moment. How many people do you have in your life that you can talk with openly and honestly and share your innermost thoughts, fears, and dreams without worrying whether you are going to be judged or evaluated? Some people are very fortunate to have friends and family members who can act as sounding boards. Yet, they too may have their own agenda. Keep in mind that sometimes all a person wants is to be listened to and understood. Everyone needs a safe place to share what's going on in their heads. In turn, they come to their own solutions or conclusions. Creating a safe place during a coaching conversation where your salespeople can talk openly and freely without feeling vulnerable is one of the most powerful coaching strategies. It promotes self-exploration and facilitates additional insight.

> ### ❧ FROM THE SIDELINES ❧
>
> The amount of value received from coaching will be determined by the person you're coaching, not by you.

Just as your clients and staff will come to you with different goals, needs, problems, expectations, and objectives, every person you coach will move at a certain pace. Individuals will have their own ways that make them comfortable in which they process and internalize information as they travel down their path of personal discovery and achievement.

As a sales coach, you want to deliver value when working with your sales team. To do so, you must first establish what value means to them and what they are expecting from the coaching experience.

Align your coaching around the person's goals and personality, rather than trying to fit their goals and individuality into your style of coaching. If you don't, you risk setting your salespeople up for failure. You may also find yourself passing judgment on the people you coach.

## FATAL COACHING MISTAKE NO. 3: ARE YOU COACHING YOUR SALESPEOPLE OR JUDGING THEM?

It's not my place to pass judgment on anyone. You may feel that as the manager you need to judge your salespeople since you are responsible for their performance. There are two different types of judgment: the healthy kind and the kind that gets in the way when coaching. I'm not referring to the type of judgment call you make after looking at the last six months of a salesperson's pitiful performance and his lack of effort to turn his sales numbers around. In this instance, it may be a sound judgment call to let this person go.

A coach needs to suspend the kind of judgment that comes from ego. Judgments in a coaching conversation take on the form of *shoulds*. And a *should* judgment, as we discussed in Chapter 1, is defined as the coach's agenda. This includes placing our values, integrity, strengths, passions, goals, work ethic, mindset, way of doing things, and expectations directly on the people we are coaching. This type of judgment is guaranteed to create tremendous resistance. It blinds us from recognizing the individual personalities, aspirations, and talents of the people we coach.

When coaching managers and I hear any of the following comments, I suspect that they are passing judgment on the people they are coaching.

- They should be farther along.
- They should raise their monthly goals. I remember when I was selling and . . .
- They should have closed that sale by now.
- They should be happy to come to work every day.
- They should have known that by now.
- If they've been in the industry for as long as they say they have, they should already know these specifications.
- I wouldn't conduct a sales call the way they do. They should do it this way, which is how I would do it.
- They should be making more outbound calls each day if they want to hit their quota this month.
- I already know why they're not selling. I don't need to ask them. I can just look at their numbers.

### ❀ FROM THE SIDELINES ❀

When passing judgment on others, you are really passing judgment on yourself.

We pass judgment on the very things we want to create for our salespeople. We want them to have greater success, to eliminate a problem, to reduce stress, to make more money, to achieve bigger goals, to be happier and healthier. Yet, who's responsible for defining these goals? They are. While you may set certain performance expectations, it's up to your salespeople to determine what success and satisfaction mean in their world, in their life. Coaches must coach based on the expectations, needs, and agenda of the people being coached.

Learn to suspend your judgment. Otherwise, you will make another common coaching mistake, which is to make the coaching process about you.

## FATAL COACHING MISTAKE NO. 4: COACHING ISN'T ABOUT THE COACH

It's not about you. I wish I could make this statement and move on to the next topic, but I can't. Not just yet. This one needs more attention.

On a very basic level, there are two people involved in a coaching relationship: the coach and the person being coached. Although many managers know the coaching process is about the person being coached, they still make it about themselves. Knowing this and getting it to the point where it's being reflected in your coaching are two different things.

Here's the type of thinking that limits the effectiveness of your coaching and makes the process about you:

- I don't want to say the wrong thing.
- I don't want to look bad.
- I don't want to push too hard.
- I don't want to be rejected.
- I don't want to be the bad guy.
- I don't want to blow it.
- I really want them to win.
- I have to deliver value.
- This has got to work. I don't want to have to recruit again.
- They have to turn it around. I have numbers to hit!

Do you notice the one word that is used in each statement above? I, I, I, I, I! Making the coaching process about you is the number one roadblock to successful coaching.

Instead of making the coaching process about you and how much you can gain by having your salespeople achieve their objectives, make it about them and how much value you can co-create with them, without any attachments to the outcome.

If you are experiencing any resistance to your coaching or if you find yourself pushing your people too hard during a coaching session, look at the subject of your process. Chances are, your process is about you!

Once you shift your focus toward the person you are coaching, you will immediately be relieved of the unnecessary pressure to look good and perform.

After all, if you are making the coaching process about you and are primarily concerned with your own performance, you won't have the mindset, focus, or energy to capture the salesperson's interest, respect, and trust.

Make the coaching process about the salesperson, about your sales team, and the value you can deliver rather than about what you can gain if your team starts performing better. Once you do so, the benefits for all that follow as a result of your coaching become the natural by-product of your selfless efforts and good intentions.

## FATAL COACHING MISTAKE NO. 5: SHARE IDEAS, NOT EXPECTATIONS

I'm reminded of a story one of my clients shared with me that took place at a recent company retreat. Gary was a senior partner in one of the top three accounting firms in Texas. The purpose of this retreat was for the partners to discuss the corporate vision, new ideas, and growth strategies as well as year-end goals. It was an opportunity for all of them to get together, removed from the daily stresses of the office. This year's two-day retreat was at a resort built around a majestic 30-square-mile lake.

The first day and a half consisted of meetings, outings, and exercises, all of which were going well. Ken, the managing partner who helped coordinate the event, was pleased to see that people were enjoying themselves and benefiting from the experience. That afternoon, he was on his way to a small, invitation-only breakout group with several of the senior partners in the firm.

The meeting was going smoothly, given the diversity and dynamics of the group. Ken was doing a great job facilitating the conversation and moving from one topic to the next, all of which had been approved by the senior partners and placed on the agenda prior to this afternoon event—all except one person. It seemed that

Buck, the founder of the firm, a gray-haired, well-respected, sharp elderly gentleman, never saw the e-mail that contained the agenda.

Although Buck is no longer involved in the day-to-day operation of the firm, something on the agenda not only caught his eye but stirred up quite a strong reaction in him. Even though Buck had been carefully directed by Ken to be more of an observer or facilitator, Buck delivered an edgy opinion on this particular topic. It was a line item listed in the meeting's agenda that dealt with new business development initiatives. Specifically, the firm was considering hiring an outside marketing firm to assist with their public relations and advertising campaign. "After all these years of sustained double-digit growth, you think we now need to go out and hire someone to do what we've always done naturally and quite successfully on our own? I remember about 10 years ago, we retained the services of a PR firm with very poor results. Since when are we no longer competent enough to handle this internally?"

After Buck shared his thoughts on the matter, the conversation just stopped. No more open forum. No more safe, open sharing, no more flowing dialogue. An issue that, less than 10 minutes ago, had full buy in and consensus from the team regarding the direction to go had now gone full circle, right back to the beginning. It was as if a new topic had just been introduced, which had no current buy in or solution. No one said a word until Ken redirected the conversation to the next item on the agenda.

It is a fact that if you're a boss, manager, or executive responsible for managing people, you are their superior. And, therefore, you have a certain degree of influence over how your staff feels about certain subjects. Buck didn't make any decisions. He basically said, "This isn't the way it used to be. Why is it different now? Agree with me or experience my wrath."

Managers and executives have the power to shut down a conversation or open up a dialogue. Quite often, they don't realize how much of an influence they have over their staffs and how influential they can be without even trying. When a manager takes a strong stand or position and makes a statement like, "Here's the solution" or "Here's how it is," it removes any opportunity for others to contribute a different and potentially better idea.

There's a difference between sharing an opinion or idea and sharing an expectation. It's one thing if the manager or boss shares an opinion that allows the dialogue and flow of the conversation to continue moving in a positive, collaborative direction. It's entirely different when the manager shares an expectation with a strong agenda or ultimatum behind it. An opinion or idea from the boss opens up further conversation. An expectation shuts it down.

Buck could have kept the collective conversation moving forward with an approach like this. "Here's one thought that I want to put on the table. It still has some wet paint on it and needs some further development. I would love to hear your responses and how you feel about it so that we can incorporate everyone's ideas and create something even better." With an approach like this, it is likely that bosses will get a response that encourages unfiltered collaboration and multiple contributions.

Now that we have uncovered several traps that coaches find themselves in, I hope you're feeling more confident and prepared to launch your team into the next stratosphere of success through your sales coaching. However, before you put your coaching hat on, there's one more trap worth discussing. Even though this book provides *you* with the platform and process to evolve from manager to coach, what steps are you taking to prepare your sales team for change?

## FATAL COACHING MISTAKE NO. 6: MISMANAGING EXPECTATIONS: ARE YOU PREPARING YOUR SALES TEAM FOR CHANGE?

Maria was a new sales manager hired by Media Pros, Inc., a sports management consulting firm. She was recently introduced to the coaching model at a seminar for senior managers in her company.

Maria went back to her team pumped up and ready to begin implementing some of the coaching methods. However, it seems that Maria missed the section of the seminar on how critical it is to prepare your team for coaching by managing their expectations.

Compound this with the fact that Maria has only been in her position for less than five weeks. It's difficult enough for a sales team to adjust to a new boss, but further changes without proper preparation and communication will cause a rebellion.

❈ **FROM THE SIDELINES** ❈

Question: What could a manager do to his team that would cause an uprising?
Answer: Make a dramatic change without preparing his team for it.

Maria's boss set up a meeting with her and an outside executive coach to discuss the resistance Maria was running up against when attempting to manage and coach her team. Maria told the executive coach that she felt she had assimilated herself into her team and prepared them for any changes she was making. Since Maria's sales team worked remotely, she introduced herself to the team via a conference call and let them all know she was there to support them and help them become even more successful in their careers. Sounds pretty good so far, right? However, after further exploration, the executive coach uncovered the breakdown in Maria's new manager orientation process.

The executive coach asked Maria the following questions to help discover why Maria failed to manage her team's expectations as well as develop a strategy to communicate her objectives in a way her team would understand and embrace.

1. Did you conduct one-to-one meetings with each salesperson on your team?
2. Did you ask each of them how they like to be managed? Are they coachable?
3. Did you inquire about their prior experience with their past manager? Was it positive or negative?
4. Did you set the expectations of your relationship with them? Did you ask them what they needed and expected from their manager? What changes do they want to see?
5. Did you inform them about how you like to manage and your style of management? This would open up the space for a discussion regarding how you may manage differently from your predecessor.

6. Did you let them know you just completed a coaching course that would enable you to support them even further and maximize their talents?

7. Did you explain to them the difference between coaching and traditional management?

8. Did you enroll them in the benefits of coaching? That is, what would be in it for them?

9. Did you let them know about your intentions, goals, expectations, and aspirations for each of them and for the team as a whole?

10. How have you gone about learning the ins and outs of the company? Are you familiar with the internal workings, culture, leadership team, and subtleties that make the company unique? Have you considered that your team may be the best source of knowledge and intelligence for this? Did you communicate your willingness and desire to learn from them as well, so that the learning and development process can be mutually reciprocated?

With each question, it became more evident that Maria did not plan or prepare her staff for change. She did not prepare her team for a new boss or for her new approach to management.

At the end of the conversation, it was clear to Maria what she had to do. She would start with a team meeting to address many of the questions posed to her by the executive coach. Maria would use this meeting to explain the changes she wanted to make and the benefits each person on the sales team would realize. Maria also knew that she needed to address any gossip, rumors, or negativity that could poison the team. She would acknowledge that with any change in management there is an adjustment period. Maria wants her team to know that she is sensitive to what they are going through during this transition, as well as to each of their individual needs. She needs to reinforce her role and the fact that even though her style, personality, and approach may be different from what they are used to, she is there to help them thrive in their careers.

Once Maria finished facilitating this team meeting, she scheduled one-on-one calls with each salesperson on her team to discuss these questions. More specifically, the questions that relate to their specific needs and goals and how they want to be managed and coached. This experience was a huge lesson for Maria and would be for any manager. If you fail to inform your salespeople of your good intentions, they have no idea what they are, thus leaving it up to each salesperson to form his or her own opinion.

A situation where a salesperson had a less than favorable experience with the old manager can be made worse and repeated if the new manager does not take the steps to create a new experience between her and her salespeople.

If management does not break the cycle, they may encounter situations where their salespeople are not engaged at all, especially in the coaching process. New managers would then have to form their own conclusions, thinking that either the coaching doesn't work or it just may be the salesperson who doesn't work. In truth, what isn't working is the exchange of communication and as such, a critical message goes undelivered perpetuating conflicts, communication breakdowns, distrust, and underperformance.

Ironically, you may be doing everything else right when managing your team. That is, your heart is in the right place, your intentions are pure and sound, and you truly want to be the best coach you can be for your team. But without defusing any faulty assumptions, gossip, or beliefs, resistance from your staff will be imminent and your coaching will be unsuccessful.

Whether you're a new manager or a manager who's a new coach, informing your team about any new initiatives or changes you plan on making and the enrollment process you will use to initiate buy in needs to happen prior to actually implementing the change.

To recap, first take that step back and assess your team's needs as well as the unique needs of each individual on your team. Let them know how you plan on supporting them. Then manage these expectations with surgical precision. This will foster a strong, healthy relationship which you can build on right from the start, creating the nurturing and open environment that will enable you to earn your salespeople's respect and trust.

CHAPTER 4

# Tactical Coaching

## WHO DO YOU COACH?

"Who should I be coaching?" I've been asked this question hundreds of times by both internal sales and corporate coaches as well as those looking to build a career as a coach and develop a sustainable coaching practice on their own.

The short answer is that not everyone is coachable.

You can determine if people are ready to be coached by who they are—the degree to which they are receptive to making positive, long-term change both in their thinking as well as in their behavior. This determination is less about what the people do or their position, age, industry, experience, education, knowledge, or intelligence. Remember, coaching is about building sales champions from the inside out.

The following six qualities need to be present in the person and the coaching relationship in order for your coaching to have a profound impact. I've identified these attributes by the acronym A.G.R.O.W.T.H.

# A.G.R.O.W.T.H. SUCCESS INDICATOR TO DETERMINE PERSONAL COACHABILITY

1. *Actionability.* A combination of both action and ability. The word represents both the actions that will drive success as well as the person's actual proficiency and aptitude. Without action, nothing happens. And without the person's innate ability and intelligence to carry out the task as intended, the action becomes an exercise in futility. As I tell my clients, "If you're only willing to do today what you did yesterday, then what do you need me for?" This holds true for both action in your thinking and in your doing. Coaching is based on forward movement by engaging in activities you either haven't tried, haven't done consistently, or haven't modeled on established best practices. (You may have been engaging in the activity in a less than effective manner.) In addition, action is the effort you put forth to change your current beliefs, your attitude, and how you think.

2. *Gap.* Simply put, the gap is the space between where the person is now and where they want to be. It is the space where new resources, beliefs, skills, strategies, and dialogues are cocreated by you and them. This gap stands in the way of the person's goal and where the magic and power of your coaching occur. We will spend some time later in this chapter discussing how to uncover and coach the gap.

3. *Responsibility and ownership.* I connect these two characteristics because there is a symbiotic relationship between these traits: One cannot exist without the other. If the person you are coaching is unwilling to take full responsibility for her life, career, or for the outcomes produced throughout the coaching process, your coaching will be ineffective. The coaching sessions can quickly turn into an environment for excuses. What's worse, coaching someone who is unwilling to take total ownership of her success creates a situation where the coach can easily become the scapegoat and validation for the salesperson's lackluster results, failures, and inefficiencies.

4. *Willingness.* How badly does your salesperson want to achieve the goals she has laid out? Is this person willing to go above and beyond what her peers are doing to achieve what matters most to her? How has she demonstrated evidence of her commitment and desire to achieve the outlined objectives? Determination and drive are the fuel that propels the coaching forward. Without an unconditional willingness to forge ahead, even in the face of adversity and doubt, you may find that these meetings quickly turn into a prodding or pushing session. The danger is, you may start pushing harder than the person is ready for and then you are dictating the agenda rather than the salesperson.

5. *Trust.* Trust is the backbone of any relationship, especially a coaching relationship. The foundation of trust is even more essential if the person you are coaching is your employee, peer, or coworker. As with respect, trust is earned. What have you done to earn the trust of the person you are coaching? Or, what have you done to destroy the trust between you and a person you are coaching? Can it be repaired? Can you trust the person you are coaching? Do you have evidence that makes them untrustworthy? Listen to your instincts on this. If you can't trust them, don't coach them.

6. *Honesty.* Honesty is distinct from trust. Honesty refers to the ability of the person you're coaching to be open and vulnerable with you, the coach. Honesty relates to the degree in which the salespeople not only share with you pertinent information about themselves, their situations, challenges, upsets, and inspirations but also their willingness to look inside themselves and embrace the truth in every situation, whether they like it or not. Part of the role of a coach is to hold up that proverbial mirror so that people can see the truth of what's going on, what's getting in their way, and what they need to do to achieve unprecedented results. A defensive attitude creates an unhealthy coaching environment.

## DON'T COACH THE SQUEAKER

For whatever reason, managers experience momentary lapses of sound business judgment. Maybe it's due to desperation or old fear-based reasoning, or maybe it's a result of falling victim to any of the excuses I listed in Chapter 2.

As a result, many managers reward the toxic people and ignore their top achievers.

They reward the wrong people by giving them their time via coaching and one-to-one attention. They reward the uncommitted underperformer rather than the talented new hire, veteran superstar, or the promising up-and-comer. Managers invest far too much time trying to salvage the needy salesperson, the consistent complainer, the ongoing confrontation creator, and the problem maker.

Become more vigilant about who you invest your time in. It's not about putting all of your time and energy into every person on your team. But it's certainly not prudent to continually invest your time into the "C" players who are not fully committed to turning themselves around or taking the steps that would demonstrate the evidence of their good intentions.

Although it's often true that the squeaky wheel gets the grease, more of your time should be spent rewarding the people who contribute to you and help your team thrive, the people who consistently reach and exceed performance goals, the people who are going to be around for the long term and who want to grow with you and with the company. Honoring the guiding principles listed in the Coachability Indicator we just discussed will enable you to identify the people on your team who warrant an investment of your time that will be sure to produce a measurable return.

## COACHING THE WHOLE PERSON

Here are three factors that prevent people from bringing in more sales with less effort.

1. Lacking the selling skills and core competencies needed to be a sales champion.
2. Inability to develop the right strategy and system that consistently generates the desired results. This includes not

only the sequential steps that need to be taken in a selling system but also the right language or dialogue used in their communication.

3. Failure to create and embrace the right mindset to achieve unprecedented breakthrough results. That is, people must identify and eliminate the limiting, negative, or faulty thinking that's getting in the way of achieving more. Consider this universal law. "How you think determines what you get." Therefore people need to change their thinking first in order to change their behavior. Unfortunately, practically every training program I've ever seen falls short on delivering this missing component that completes the full development of sales champions.

Chances are, your salespeople are doing things right now that you want them to avoid the most. And you probably already know what some of these limiting and detrimental activities are!

## DEVELOPING SALES CHAMPIONS FROM THE INSIDE OUT

The most productive people master the art of abandonment: the ability to let go of old stuff that no longer works. We all want better results but in order to generate these desired results, we must do what precedes them: change. We have to change something first.

Sydney J. Harris once said, "Our dilemma is that we hate change and love it at the same time; what we really want is for things to remain the same but get better."

In my experience, generating extraordinary results requires changing two things. You must be willing to change what you do and change how you think.

The fact is, successful people not only do things differently they also think differently. They are wired differently.

Ironically, most people focus solely on the doing side without focusing on how to best manage their mindset and their beliefs.

If you focus solely on the skills you need to develop, then you wind up developing only half the salesperson you can be. Take a salesperson who only focuses on following a certain step-by-step selling process. Now, if success in selling depended only on what you did, then every salesperson who followed this process should perform at the exact same level. After speaking with thousands of salespeople and sales managers every year, I know this is certainly not the case.

It's like upgrading a computer. When you get coached by an expert, part of the process is similar to taking an old 386 processor and upgrading it to a Pentium 5. To continue the analogy, we're upgrading your operating system—how you think, how you're wired—so you can think better. We are removing any corrupt files or thinking, so you can operate at maximum efficiency. Sales coaching is about coaching the core, the inside, the essence of who you are, which then affects what you do and who you become—a sales champion.

## WHAT DO YOU COACH? COACH THE GAP

The most common question I hear from managers who are just starting to shift from manager to coach is, "How do I recognize where it is they need and could benefit from coaching most?"

Actually, covering the specifics of what you can coach from a tactical perspective is the easy part. It's uncovering the *who* or the limiting thinking or outlook people have that ultimately shows up in their actions and behavior that is elusive. Only gifted, exceptional coaches can do this, and I'm going to share with you how to develop this ability on your own.

Regardless of what you've identified as a possible focal point in your coaching, there is one model that's applicable in every coaching scenario. It also happens to be the very thing each coaching opportunity has in common: the gap. The gap is the space that exists between where the client or salesperson is today and where she wants or needs to be.

The gap is the space that exists between:

- What people know (current knowledge, philosophies, assumptions, stories, outlooks, beliefs, etc.) and what they don't know or don't realize is possible.

- What people do and what they need to do (the activity that supports their goals).
- The resources, strategies and skills they have and the ones they don't have.
- The results they are currently getting and the improved results and goals they really want to achieve.

Imagine a bridge for a moment. Picture yourself standing on one end of a long bridge, concentrating and focusing on the other side, which is where you want to go. Think about what you need to do to get to the other side. Consider the resources needed to arrive at your desired destination in the shortest amount of time and with the least amount of risk. Reaching the other side is your goal. What might you need to fill in this gap—the void that exists between you and your goal?

What is needed? You need a car if you want to get to your destination as fast as possible. You need fuel as the resource needed to get your car moving. You need a clear path that would help you arrive at your destination with the least amount of delays, obstructions, and diversions. Identifying these resources (which we did through the use of inquiry, just as you do in coaching) provides definition, structure, and an executable strategy that will collectively evolve into an actionable and comprehensive solution to this situation that brings your goal to fruition.

Instead of assuming what you think your staff already knows, start determining what they need to know in order to fill in this gap and ensure clear communication. You'll increase your awareness and become more sensitized to what they need to learn and what opportunities there are for coaching. Instead of sharing what you perceive to be the solution to a problem before understanding the person's needs, recognize the gap in every coaching conversation.

A teacher shows you how to do something—something you've never done before or tried before in a consistent manner. The teacher or trainer provides you with a foundation, a process, or a benchmark of best practices to give you a starting point in relation to where you would begin on your path of development.

A coach, however, shows you how to do what you are doing even better. First the coach would need to see how you perform now. So the coach would watch you to see the things that you cannot and gently advise you on how you can refine your approach to the point where you can do it on your own. Coaching is the discipline management uses to leverage all of your salespeople's individual strengths and talents to keep them living up to their fullest potential today, rather than being seduced by what tomorrow could potentially bring.

## ❋ FROM THE SIDELINES ❋

Sales training is what you need to become a salesperson. Sales coaching is what you need to become a sales champion.

## DO I COACH THEM OR TRAIN THEM?

Keep in mind that part of the reason why identifying the gap is such a critical starting point in coaching is to first determine whether the issue at hand is, in fact, a training issue, a coaching issue, or an advising or consulting issue. If you have salespeople who have never been trained in the art and competencies of selling, how can you coach them? The gap in this scenario is the lack of a personal selling foundation and core ideology that training would have provided.

In such a case, you would fill the gap initially with a training component before coaching can take place. Remember the distinction between training, coaching, and consulting in Chapter 1. In the following three scenarios, I've identified where each competency and approach would come into play by first recognizing the gap that you would need to uncover and assess in every coaching situation.

### Scenario One

*Situation:* Tim, a rookie salesperson has been hired to generate appointments on the phone for the outside sales team.

*The Gap:* Since this is Tim's first sales job, he's never cold-called before nor has Tim ever been trained in how to cold-call effectively. Therefore, the gap is the training, skills, knowledge, as well as a step-by-step tactical approach and dialogue that he needs to perform his job effectively.

*Training Solution:* This is a training issue, because Tim first needs to develop some strong habits to solidify a healthy foundation on which he can build. Learning how to do something for the first time such as selling or cold-calling is not coaching but training, consulting, or advising. Tim needs to be shown best practices, the how-to's, and the mechanics of selling and cold calling as well as the philosophy behind them.

## Scenario Two

*Situation:* Nine months into her training, Samantha's (Sam's) boss was questioning whether she would make it for the long haul. Out of the initial 10 new recruits that completed the week-long training, practically nine months ago, Samantha was one of the only two who had made it this far. She had been told that if she could make it a year, and build up her book of business, chances are she could start developing a successful career as an executive recruiter.

Eight months ago she had secured three top accounts. But she had been relying too heavily on them to make her numbers each month, and her promising start was now coming to a slow and painful halt. One of the three large clients left her, and the other two were slowing down their recruiting efforts. However, Samantha was on the phone practically every day making the calls she knew she needed to make in order to survive her first year.

*The Gap:* Samantha proved early on she could be successful at cold-calling for new clients. Her initial four month's book of business provided her with the volume to make her monthly sales quota. Although Samantha was still making her daily number of cold calls, she was no longer getting strong results from her new business development efforts. Moreover, her boss noticed how worried and stressed out Sam was as a result of this. For these reasons, the gap is actually a combination of training and coaching.

*Training* and *Coaching Solution:* In a case like Samantha's, the solution may be a multifaceted one that would approach her situation from a few different angles. Here are four different ways you could coach and support Sam.

First, if Sam's approach was working when she started nine months ago but it's no longer working today, then something changed. Her boss noticed Sam didn't have a templated process that she was following and more or less made up her approach on the fly. Thus, having Sam work off a proven template so she could create a level of consistency in her selling efforts is one part of this solution.

Second, this fine tuning of her approach and putting it in an actionable, step-by-step process would eliminate any inconsistencies and allow her to best manage what approach works best.

Third, Samantha appears to be driven by fear and consequence, that is, the loss of her job. Being driven by consequence and scarcity (i.e., what you don't want to happen) is a negative source of energy that dilutes not only the impact of your selling efforts but also the quality of your life.

Here, Sam needs to be coached on developing a new way of thinking—one that empowers her, lifts her spirits, and focuses on her goals and dreams.

Finally, is Samantha in need of some new resources? That is, where is Sam mining for new business? Does she need to look at alternative ways to prospect? Does she need a revised call list? These are just a few of the components of her sales engine that need to be looked at more carefully to diagnose exactly what is going on and where the gaps are.

### Scenario Three

*Situation:* Bob, a successful, established, and well-seasoned insurance salesman, had been a long-time top producer for his company. Since the company merger, restructuring, policy changes, and compensation plan revisions, Bob needed to start generating new clients to fill up his sales funnel again. Even though Bob used to spend half his days cold-calling, he hasn't done it in a while, relying more on referrals and the income he generated from renewal business. Bob was great on the phone and generated a significant amount of new prospects as a result of his recent cold calling efforts. However, it seems that Bob was not able to close these prospects the way he would a referral or an existing client. He was used to people saying, "Yes" without him even asking for the sale. Objections? The only one Bob was used to hearing among his clientele was whether or not they should write him a check or hand him their credit card.

Now, it seems that every time Bob met with one of the new prospects, he was walking out with a note to follow up rather than a sale. Bob wasn't used to hearing, "Thanks, let us think about it," or "You're the first person we've spoken with regarding a policy," And he was certainly not used to hearing, "Wow, that sounds awfully expensive." Even though Bob did his best to try and convince these people to buy from him, he felt his rebuttals were falling on deaf ears. To make matters worse, Bob forgot how to actually ask for the sale.

*The Gap:* Have you noticed the gap here? The gap in this situation is in Bob's closing technique and in his attitude toward closing. Bob is holding on to some limiting beliefs. Moreover, his tactical selling approach and natural selling acumen need to be polished to address the new selling situations that he has not had to face in a while.

*Training* and *Coaching Solution:* This is a coaching and training issue. We've identified that there are some limiting beliefs getting in the way of his taking action. Specifically, salespeople don't overcome objections, prospects do. Rather than convince prospects, which it sounds like Bob was attempting to do, he needs to respond with questions rather than statements so that prospects can overcome their own concerns. As such, the coach needs to use well-crafted questions and a process of inquiry to explore deeper into Bob's perception of closing and asking for the sale. Does closing mean dumping more information? Is he not asking for the sale in fear of rejection? Finally, Bob needs some hands-on tactical responses the next time he hears these objections. The training will take care of this, providing Bob with the dialogue and the steps to defusing objections that will turn more of his prospects into customers.

Remember, if salespeople aren't willing to take action or refuse to change their behavior, it's because they've developed a *belief barrier* around it that's preventing any forward movement.

## WHAT EXACTLY *CAN* YOU COACH?

I have found that the gap represents several key indicators or areas of opportunity that you can coach your salespeople around. The opportunities for coaching someone are vast. Here is a detailed list of what you can coach.

1. *The who.* Values, passions, standards, boundaries, integrity, and so on.

2. *The attitude.* Belief, mindset, philosophy, outlook, or assumptions.

3. *The lesson.* What have they learned? Why are the same lessons repeating themselves? Are they getting it?

4. *The ideal characteristics.* The ideal qualities you have defined that encompass a sales leader or manager. (Extroverted, actionable, honest, strong communicator, process driven, accountable, curious, organized, strong integrity and presence, knowledgeable, comfortable disposition, smart, responsive, etc.)

5. *The skill.* Is there a missing discipline or one that needs further development?

6. *The activity.* Are they engaging in the activities that support their goals?

7. *The strategy.* How do they plan to achieve the intended result? What resources are needed?

8. *The commitment.* Observe their energy level, consistency, enthusiasm, and motivation.

9. *The communication.* The language, dialogue, or communication regarding style, delivery, presence, and disposition.

10. *The relationships.* The relationships they have with intangible concepts and feelings as well as with their stories and S.C.A.M.Ms, which we discussed in Chapter 3.

## THE TOP 10 CHARACTERISTICS OF HIGHLY EFFECTIVE SALESPEOPLE

Apollo Commercial Real Estate and Investments has finished mapping out the core characteristics and competencies they will now use as a guide for all new hires as well as for their internal sales coaching and training programs. They have determined that salespeople with the following skills and characteristics tend to be top producers. Sales champions:

1. Are constantly learning and continually invest in themselves and their professional development.
2. Are masterful communicators.
3. Are creative. The art of selling is the ability to create new solutions and possibilities.
4. Develop a positive and healthy attitude.
5. Are passionate about what they do and deliver unconditional value to their customers for the joy of it.
6. Create an experience that allows for the sale to occur.
7. Are responsive, proactive, highly adaptable, and flexible rather than reactive.
8. Exemplify what their customers want most (leading with integrity and honesty; they are resourceful, solution driven, responsive, reliable, etc.).
9. Are process driven. They know where they are going and have a path to get there, including specific measurable goals and a selling system to manage their selling process (step-by-step documented process, tools and templates, a prospecting system and a personal vision).
10. Are masters of time management and organization.

While some qualities you may deem as non-negotiable are not included in this example, use this as a starting point to create your own master list. Keep in mind that to achieve peak productivity and get your sales team to leverage their strengths and abilities, a good sales coach creates the possibility for them to develop and refine *all* of these core competencies and traits. At the same time, an outline like this can be used to develop your own training and coaching initiative and a gauge to uncover what each one of your salespeople need to be coached on. Finally, identifying what a sales champion looks like in your company enhances your capabilities as a sales coach.

As you hold your people to these higher standards, you will find there are some top producers who may not possess every single trait. For example, they may not be truly passionate about their job or their product or service. Then the question becomes, "Is this an essential characteristic for success? Will it put a ceiling on personal potential?" The answer, of course, is a resounding and absolute "Yes."

CHAPTER

# The Seven Types of Sales Managers

## THE SEVEN Ps

It was 8 A.M., Thursday morning, approximately one hour into the delivery of my newly revised Executive Sales Coaching program to a team of 16 senior managers and directors of GreenCorp. After identifying the essential qualities of a leader, we shifted the focus toward the cornerstone of the day's program.

Throughout my years of coaching managers and executives, I've been able to identify seven types of sales managers. Using these seven types of managers as examples, we are going to cover some of the methodologies and critical competencies necessary to become an effective sales coach. It all starts with the way we communicate.

The disparity between a great leader and a mediocre one is in how they communicate. The way we communicate is what determines how other people choose to relate to us or engage with us. They decide who we are by what we say and how we say it.

Even though you may find characteristics in the seven types of managers that you see in yourself, you will be able to identify your one dominant style of management.

The following three chapters cover the lessons these managers learned. For the ones who executed these new strategies, these lessons directly impacted their bottom line. We begin by identifying each of the seven types of managers.

1. The Problem-Solving Manager
2. The Pitchfork Manager
3. The Pontificating Manager
4. The Presumptuous Manager
5. The Perfect Manager
6. The Passive Manager
7. The Proactive Manager

Regardless of which type of manager you are, one thing is painfully apparent: Something has to change in each of these management styles. According to The Gallup Organization, "Only 20% of employees working in large organizations feel their strengths are in play every day—that means that most organizations operate at 20% of their potential and capacity!"

In all of my years of training and coaching managers, one thing is certain. Each manager has a unique communication style and approach. That's a great thing and something I certainly encourage each manager to develop, based on his or her personality, unique skills, strengths, and talents. Conversely, there are some communication styles that you should avoid.

Keep in mind that the communication styles I am referring to are those that focus more on how to communicate for results, including the use of language that the world's greatest coaches use during normal daily conversation. This is the same phraseology, as well as the mindset, that becomes part of your coaching process and strategy. (We discussed the mindset of the coach in Chapters 1 and 2.) What you will learn in this chapter is the *how* piece of the coaching equation: the tactical stuff.

Even though each management style encompasses qualities that seem to produce results, each one also incurs a cost. This cost can place limitations on your performance as a coach and the results you can expect from your salespeople. In the end, there is only one management style you will uncover that is worth modeling. If any of these styles resonate with you or if you feel that a certain type of manager describes you, here's your opportunity to adjust your communication style for maximum impact.

Before we identify new habits and strategies to use, we must first let go of what will get in the way of our ability to follow through with this new coaching model. Therefore, we're going to begin by exposing the perception that managers have about their role by learning more about the first of the seven managers we are going to examine—*The Problem-Solving Manager.*

## THE PROBLEM-SOLVING MANAGER

In a typical workweek, what do you spend most of your time doing?

Managers most often respond: "Impromptu meetings, handling problems, putting out fires, dealing with requests from salespeople and customers."

Managers and business owners often tell me they believe their primary role is problem solver or firefighter to their employee's challenges, a role probably learned from their predecessors or mentors. These problem solvers are constantly putting out fires and leading by chaos. (I don't suppose you know anyone like this?)

The paradox here is this: It is often the manager who creates the very problems and situations that they work so hard to avoid. Continually providing solutions often results in the lackluster performance that they are working so diligently to eliminate.

Stop for a moment and consider the message you send to your salespeople every time they come to you with a problem and you fire back a solution or fix it for them. The message "I have the answer you're looking for" trains your employees *not* to become accountable or self-motivated. Instead, it creates a greater level of dependency on you, the manager, which prevents your staff from sharpening their problem-solving skills or discovering solutions on their own. To make matters worse, think about what happens when the solution you give them isn't the best one or doesn't achieve the desired result? Whose fault is it then?

And as counterintuitive as it seems, your next response in this atmosphere of dependence you've created is to further travel down this rabbit hole and continue to get even *more* involved to the point of micromanaging—taking on more control and responsibility: a poor use of your time. The results can be catastrophic: exhaustion of resources and the depletion of a manager who has now far exceeded his or her capabilities, further diluting the productivity of the group.

In order to create a staff that is internally driven and self-motivated, as well as develop a culture of accountability and ownership, your job is to:

- Get your salespeople to continually improve.
- Empower your salespeople to solve their own challenges.
- Develop other leaders.
- Motivate people without pushing or exhausting your energy.

Leaders accomplish this through coaching. And coaching uses a process of inquiry as opposed to the dissemination and broadcasting of facts, figures, and solutions. Coaching allows people to access their own energy or strength to solve a problem or create a solution. Doing so builds their level of awareness, confidence, mastery, and achievement. Tapping into people's previously unused strengths and talents advances personal growth and learning, challenging them to discover their best.

We learn best through our own personal experiences and by doing, which is why coaching is so effective. It is modeled around this very principle. Coaching moves away from training (telling someone how to do something or giving someone the answer) to more of a process of inquiry. The very core of the coaching strategy is asking more and better questions, in which we help people find their own answers rather than simply telling them what to do, the way to do it, or being their solution provider.

Why do managers struggle so much when it comes to letting this behavior go? After all, a considerable amount of research shows that people learn faster, produce more, and are highly motivated when coaching methods are employed that tap into the collective wisdom of the group and each individual. The challenge for management is how to continually use this powerful resource. Even though the participative or collaborative coaching approach to management is widely agreed to be effective, it is seldom put into practice. So why do managers feel so compelled to continually solve their salespeople's problems rather than offer more powerful, thought-provoking questions that shift the responsibility of the solution back to the individual?

Here are some of the excuses I've heard, all of which are real mental barriers to letting go of a perceived role as Chief Problem Solver. The new management style will be to respond to situations and problems with better questions rather than more answers.

1. *Habit.* "I don't know another way to handle it. It's simply just a habit for me. It's how I've always done things."

2. *I'm the boss.* "I thought providing them with the solution was my responsibility, especially if I know the right way to handle it."

3. *Following the predecessor.* "I learned this from my manager. That's how she did it."

4. *Gives me purpose.* "Problems provide a sense of purpose. They're a reason to go to work. They are an energy source for me, albeit a negative energy source. I thrive on problems and chaos."

5. *Avoidance behavior.* "I'm not certain I can pull off this coaching thing. Besides, this isn't the best time to try something new with all of the current initiatives we have going on right now, compounded with a strong push to reach our sales goals. So, let me keep managing my people the way I have been, just until we get through this tough period. Then, when I have more time, I can focus on implementing these new techniques. And if that means having to give my people the quick solution in order to save some time, then so be it."

6. *Justification.* "It's just easier sometimes to give them the answer rather than having to stop what I'm doing, pause, give the problem back, wait for them to answer, then uncover what's still missing in their solution (the gap), identify and remove any inconsistencies, assumptions, and, finally, add the additional support, resources, methodology, or strategies needed to execute their solution."

Coaching is about having the clients grow on their own. And questions broaden their peripheral vision so they can best respond to the events or things that are coming at them. To drive this lesson home, I will share with you the three fundamental rules of sales coaching.

Rule Number One: Let your salespeople do all the work.

Rule Number Two: Let your salespeople do all the work.

And finally, Rule Number Three: See rules one and two and let your salespeople do all the work.

If you ever feel like you're working way too hard to drive performance, this may come as a shock; just let your staff do the work required of them to succeed at their job-not you.

Management is about managing and controlling known, measurable resources whereas coaching is about creating something new: a new possibility, a new insight, a new way of thinking and doing that didn't exist before. Managers who work with known quantities are simply recreating the same results over and over again. However, now that you are going to start tapping into the true abilities of your people through the better use of questions, coaching allows you the ability to create new opportunities that will yield new, improved results.

When you are coaching your team, you are setting the direction, guiding and positively influencing them in a way that drives them to produce more. You are acting as the facilitator and innovator of new ideas as opposed to a manager who works with tools, resources, and strategies already in existence. To manage is to control, protect, or coordinate what you already have. When you are managing, you simply attempt to keep what is occurring under control, which isn't necessarily a bad thing. However, we are looking for areas we can improve upon and what we can do differently to get to our goals faster, which is accomplished through coaching.

Managers do not want to train employees to become dependent on them. Managers want their employees to sharpen their own problem-solving skills and solve their own challenges according to the three rules of coaching. How do we accomplish this on a tactical level? We leverage the first of the two most important skills of coaches, that is, the effective use of well-crafted questions.

## THE QUESTION IS THE ANSWER

The greatest managers know how to respond to their salespeople's requests, problems, and challenges with a question rather than a solution or statement. These managers actually *listen* the solution out of the salesperson by asking the right questions.

On the surface, it's apparent what questions accomplish. A question is a tool of inquiry you use to gather information. While this might seem fairly obvious, questions actually accomplish much more. (In the appendix, I share with you dozens of powerful coaching questions to use during a coaching session.) Here are some benefits you can realize by asking the right questions.

1. Questions raise awareness when people stop to rethink something and challenge current perceptions, assumptions, or behavior; they stimulate new answers and possibilities.

2. Questions encourage ownership by empowering someone to come up with his own solutions that are a perfect fit for him, rather than being told what to do.

3. Questions create more of a pressure-free environment. Forget the shallow, superficial conversations that transpire daily that fail to foster any connection or loyalty between people. Questions motivate a person to share more information and ideas, promote more meaningful conversations, and cultivate deeper, richer relationships with your employees.

4. Questions help people clarify their thoughts, while uncovering their needs, goals, problems, fears, values, objectives, attitude, assumptions, or opinion on something.

5. Questions encourage people to get clarity of the truth, the real truth, on their own (as opposed to a story, excuse, assumption, and S.C.A.M.M.). This reduces their resistance to acknowledging the real issues or core truths. People become uncomfortable when their issues are pointed out to them by someone else.

6. Questions encourage the kind of disciplined and active listening that a coach needs to further develop, especially during a coaching session.

7. Questions enroll, convince, and persuade people to do something they may normally be resistant to doing. Instead of attempting to change someone's mind or convince someone to do something, questions will give people choices (rather than a direct order) and encourage people to help themselves.

Questions are what we use to get information that we wouldn't have gotten otherwise. All the answers we ever get are responses to questions. However, since our society has become so answer oriented and everyone is looking for the quick fix, we often wind up with ineffective solutions because we fail to ask the right questions that would generate greater results or possibilities. Unfortunately, managers focus more on the solution than on the question.

## SOLUTION-ORIENTED QUESTIONS

Questions precede change. Therefore, it's important to be aware of the words you use in the questions you ask. I want to direct your attention to one very common trap when it comes to asking questions.

Problem-solving managers have a natural predisposition to focus on problem-oriented questions. It's important to be aware of the words we use in questions we ask because our reality is created by the language we use. This is true for the external questions we ask others as well as the internal questions we ask ourselves.

For example, when something goes wrong or we don't get the outcome we expected, what does our internal dialogue sound like?

"Why do bad things keep happening to me" or "Why can't I do this?"

And how about with other people? What questions do we ask our salespeople in situations when things go wrong?

- "Why can't you get this right?"
- "What's wrong with you?"
- "Why do you feel you keep running into the same problem?"

- "Why can't you just follow the process we've laid out for you so you can do this properly the first time around?"
- "Why do you continue to show up late to every meeting?"
- "Why didn't you close that sale?"

And what are the answers to these questions? What do these questions focus on? They focus on the problem.

Yes, problem-focused questions do support or collect evidence as to why we can't succeed at something, or they confirm negative beliefs about others or ourselves. Both internal and external questions shape our reality, stimulate learning, and promote transformational breakthroughs. That's why it's so crucial that you transform your questions to become solution-oriented questions rather than problem-oriented questions. Solution-oriented questions are forward moving questions that focus on the solution and a positive outcome and don't dwell on the problems that keep you stuck in the past.

Let's identify some typical problem-focused questions and the solution-oriented questions you can ask instead that will keep you going forward.

Now that you have these tools available, the next time you're confronted with a challenge posed by one of your salespeople, remember to give it back by asking a question. You'll notice the problem-solving manager in you start to fade away, as you develop a team of

| Problem-Focused Questions | Solution-Oriented Questions |
|---|---|
| What's wrong with me/you? | What's the lesson here? |
| | What did I/you do well? |
| | How can I/you handle this better the next time? |
| Why do I/you keep messing this up? | What needs to change? |
| | How can I/you get this right the next time around? |
| | What strategy or solution can we put in place to achieve the results you really want? |

*(Continued)*

| Problem-Focused Questions | Solution-Oriented Questions |
|---|---|
| Why didn't I/you get this right? | What's needed to succeed the next time? (actions, strategy, tools, resources, etc.) What new possibility can be created here? |
| Why can't you just turn in the weekly reports on time? | What system can you put in place to get this done each week on time? |
| | What resources might you need? How can I help you accomplish this? |
| Why do you keep running into the same problem on every sales call? | What is the lesson here that you can take away from this experience? |
| | Where's the opportunity to improve on your process? Who do you need to be to prevent this from happening again and become the sales champion you know you can be? |
| Why are you always late? | What needs to change/happen so that you can arrive on time, stress free? |
| | What system can we put in place that would eliminate this problem permanently? |
| | How can you change your thinking around the way you manage your time that will make you a master of your day? |

people who are less reliant or needy and more self-driven and proactive. This is a surefire way to create more time and space in your day.

In Chapter 6 we will discuss the manager whose general idea of motivation is a frontal assault of fear and consequence followed by the proverbial push off a cliff into the rocky waters below. That manager would be the Pitchfork Manager.

CHAPTER

# Ignition On! *Now* They're Inspired

## THE PITCHFORK MANAGER

During one of my seminars, I recall one manager calling out, "Just reading down the list of the seven types of managers in the order you wrote them, I don't think any of us manage using a pitchfork, even if it is a metaphor for using force or coercion to manage."

She was correct. It is a metaphor for that, and more. People who manage by a pitchfork are doing so with a heavy hand: demanding progress, forcing accountability, prodding and pushing for results through the use of consequence, threats, scarcity, and fear tactics. This style of management is painful for salespeople who are put in a position where they are pushed to avoid consequences rather than pulled toward a desired goal.

Given the shocking statistic I shared with you in the last chapter, the question now becomes, Why are companies incurring such a high cost from a failure to leverage each person's full talents and potential, especially since this cost could be avoided if the manager were better trained to become an effective leader and coach? Because all too often, management doesn't see the problem.

They don't accurately diagnose the source of the problem—themselves. Too often, management is quick to blame the failure to achieve their strategic goals on the inability to attract new and better talent, a tough labor pool, a downturn in the economy, a rise in operational costs, a surge in competition, a shortage of resources, and an increase of their daily responsibilities and duties. Some of these things may be contributing factors, but the real issue that prevents salespeople from living up to their fullest potential has everything to do with the tactics managers use to motivate and empower them.

*Empower* means "to give strength or power to." Ironically, instead of giving power, managers do the opposite: They take power away from their salespeople, even though they don't intend to.

There are many ways to empower people, and one of them is through effective delegation. It's empowering for the person you're delegating to because it demonstrates the trust and respect you have for them and in their abilities. Managers also attempt to motivate their people by providing incentives, setting goals, acknowledging top producers, even using consequences or threats.

Managers use these tactics in an attempt to stimulate some level of interest and forward movement from their staff. And when all else fails, managers often try to coerce or push them into action. The question is, how much time do you invest in motivating your staff through empowerment?

Often managers spend time pushing people into action when trying to get them to perform. It's like you are pushing something uphill, right? And you can certainly feel the resistance. As a result, when you stop motivating or pushing your staff, think about what happens. They stop moving and the momentum that was there comes to a screeching halt because it's no longer being fueled by you.

Your staff is no longer being motivated by an external force and therefore slips back into their old ways. When that external stimulation is no longer present, people have a tendency to revert back into their old habits. All momentum is lost unless someone is there to push them.

Now, your model of motivation may work at some level but how do you feel after continually having to push and motivate your staff? Tired, drained, frustrated, exhausted.

The biggest difference between traditional management and coaching is their philosophy of how to motivate or empower people, which you may find to be a bit counterintuitive. You see, there's a paradox here when it comes to facilitating professional growth among our salespeople. That is, too much force creates pressure that will backfire. Those managers who continue to push because they think they are facilitating progress, are in fact, blocking progress.

As we move ahead, I will share with you a few ways to get and keep your salespeople motivated that won't consume or exhaust you in the process. I will also identify specific examples of language you can use to empower others using our sales coaching model.

## PUSH VERSUS PULL—A SIMPLE MODEL OF MOTIVATION

Within the first several minutes of my seminars, I ask all participants to list their challenges and concerns as they relate to managing a sales team. Inevitably, a few of their concerns relate to motivating salespeople in a positive way to increase their productivity.

So, how do we accomplish this? There are two types of motivational philosophies. One is based on an attraction model, and the other is a push structure. A pull type or attraction model empowers people, whereas a push type structure robs people of their power and potential.

Managers try to motivate people by force or by pushing because they are attached to the outcomes. Other push structures include using fear, consequences, or threats when trying to get people into action or motivate them to complete a task.

Attraction-based strategies used to motivate people include things like pleasure, support, and coaching. Another way to motivate is by tapping into that person's personal vision or goal, that is, helping people gravitate toward a specific goal or outcome that they want to achieve rather than prodding them with a consequence to avoid.

The major difference between the two is that the attraction model requires much less effort over time and has long-term effects whereas the old-school push strategy of motivating requires a lot of effort and is temporary.

Ultimately, the goal is to get your employees to become internally driven as opposed to having to be externally motivated through an outside force—your precious and limited time and energy. Let your employees tell you how they want to be motivated, which will lead to the development of a self-driven team of salespeople.

If you are ever curious about why your incentive programs or motivational strategies don't work, perhaps the *real* issue is not tapping into what might drive your employees to motivate *themselves*. So, tap into the individuality of your team.

## LET YOUR SALESPEOPLE TELL YOU WHAT MOTIVATES THEM

John, a client of mine who owned a mid-sized security company, discovered this solution. His staff of 25 had a tendency to deviate from company procedures that continually resulted in production delays. We uncovered the source of the problem; they were unclear about their responsibilities. As part of the solution, we asked his staff to write up their own job descriptions and career goals.

The results were surprising. Telemarketers wanted flextime and opportunities for career growth. Salespeople cared more about job stability and positive acknowledgment for good performance rather than commissions.

In response, he adjusted the job descriptions and procedures, creating individualized incentive programs geared to each employee's goals and strengths.

After doing this exercise, he reported that there was less friction and communication breakdowns. People were taking ownership of their responsibilities. This exercise provided a greater sense of accountability and direction. John also found his staff to be much more responsive to changes in his company that supported the corporate vision that he and his team could all be pulled toward, rather than pushed to achieve.

He empowered his staff by acknowledging their natural abilities, while supporting their individual personal visions, goals and needs.

Tap into the individuality of your own team. For example, a 10-person sales team is not just 10 salespeople. These 10 salespeople are 10 individuals who just happen to be salespeople and perform the same job function. In other words, focus on their individualities, their personal and unique needs and goals, as well as their natural strengths and talents to uncover what drives each person. Not everyone is motivated by the same proverbial carrot or technique to drive performance. Truly great managers are sensitive to the fact that each person on their team is unique and as such, these managers appreciate these differences and do not try to fit each team member into a "one size fits all" incentive program or selling strategy.

The unfortunate reality is that most management techniques and sales cultures prevent or discourage individuality. Now, please don't misinterpret my point here. I still believe in developing a universal culture and the systems that drive it. That is, I believe that you can take best practices, essential selling competencies, certain key strategies, and chronological steps to the sale, and weave them into what has been referred to in various sales cultures as *the right way to sell*. Then managers would say, "Here's our selling methodology that if you follow you'll be successful." And I believe the same can be done for a coaching and management system—from how we recruit and hire to how we retain, develop, and motivate people.

However, managers fail to go beyond the foundation of the system to complement the personality and style of each salesperson. That's when the system begins to break down. Eventually, managers end up pushing for results because they are pushing against the inherent individuality that their salespeople desperately want to express.

Many managers assume that every salesperson is motivated by money. This is not always the case. As a matter of fact, it can be demotivational when the carrot dangling in front of salespeople is not only distracting but also promises a reward they don't even want.

A Maritz poll reported the following: "The degree to which employees felt compensated for their work had little to do with how they felt about management. The perception that a company genuinely listened to and cared about its employees was *nine* times more important to employees than satisfaction with their pay, in rating the relations between labor and management."

It isn't always about the money. Trust, loyalty, motivation, and commitment must be earned by managers. And you earn them by demonstrating that you care about them as individuals and that your attention is on managing and coaching each one of them as a unique person rather than as a commodity.

## ASK YOUR SALESPEOPLE HOW THEY WANT TO BE COACHED

How do managers uncover each salesperson's internal drive? By using one of the most valuable coaching tools—asking better questions. To uncover each person's internal drive, the strategy to achieve what matters most to them, and the way they want to be coached, schedule one-to-one meetings with each member of your team and invest the time asking questions to uncover what is important to each of them. Listen to their responses and ask more questions as you uncover what they most want.

Here are some suggested questions you can use during your one-to-one meetings in order to tap into each person's internal drive, while uncovering exactly how you can best coach and manage them.

1. What do you want to be doing that you aren't currently doing? (What would get you excited to come to work every day?)
2. What areas do you want to strengthen, improve, or develop?
3. What is most important to you in your life and/or career? (What does a successful career and/or life look like to you?)
4. What are the three most important things you would like to accomplish right now that would provide you with a deep sense of fulfillment and satisfaction?

5. What is your action plan to achieve those goals?

6. What obstacles might prevent you from reaching those goals?

7. How can I best support you to achieve those goals?

8. How can I best manage you and hold you accountable for the results you are looking to achieve?

9. How can I hold you accountable in a way that will sound supportive and won't come across as negative or micromanaging?

10. How do you want me to approach you if you don't follow through with the commitments you make? How do you want me to handle it? What would be a good way to bring this up with you so that you will be open to hearing it?

Questions will assist your employees in uncovering what internally motivates them based on their beliefs and values, so they can use their own energy to achieve it. You are also uncovering the style of management they respond to best. Moreover, you are setting up the expectations on both sides as to what to expect from one another. It certainly beats using your energy to push or stimulate interest or action based on your assumptions or beliefs of what may work for you.

If you rely on pushing to get someone into action, you already know that they won't move unless you're there to push. It's more effective to help them articulate what they want so they can begin to self-motivate. Empowering people by tapping into their internal drive doesn't drain your energy. Pushing for results is exhausting.

## MOTIVATE THROUGH PLEASURE RATHER THAN CONSEQUENCE

Motivating through fear and intimidation results in the other person pushing to avoid something they don't want (loss of a job or a measurable consequence) rather than gravitating toward something they really do want.

If people are governed by a fear of being punished or of losing their job if they don't perform, how do you think this affects them, their attitude, and their performance? How about the morale of your team? And, ultimately, how does this affect your clients? I think it's safe to say that there's clearly a measurable cost associated with using these motivational tactics. You cannot inspire others when you are afraid, and you can't be inspired when your mind and soul are full of fear and worry.

Now, imagine what it would be like if you and your staff came to work every day feeling happy, fulfilled, committed, and supported? How much would your bottom line increase? I promise substantially.

The good news is that you have the power to create this environment by taking full responsibility for the morale and culture of your team. After all, if we are all responsible for our communication, which also includes the message being received, then we can conclude that we are then responsible for the barriers, breakdowns, and problems that are a result of faulty communication. And if we are responsible for these problems that stem from poor communication, then we must also be responsible for the culture and morale within our company because, ultimately, a corporate culture is manifested through communication.

Imagine what our days would be like if we were motivated by pleasures instead of attempting to stay one step ahead of consequences? We're pulled by pleasures; we're pushed by consequences. Pushing requires effort to continue the momentum. Being pulled toward something is a by-product of natural attraction and magnetism. The shift from using consequence to using pleasure to motivate your people requires a change in your beliefs about how to motivate people and also a change in your communication strategy.

## COMMUNICATE FROM ABUNDANCE RATHER THAN FROM SCARCITY

If you listen to children talk, they often talk about what is present or what was pleasurable for them. If you ask a child, "How was the park?," you'll hear things like, "It was great! It was so much fun!" Children communicate from a place of pleasure, from abundance, from what is present for them. Now, ask an adult how dinner or a movie was and you'll hear, "Not bad." If you ask someone to do a favor for you, a typical response might be, "No problem" or "No worries." Adults often communicate from the point of view of what isn't there, what is lacking or missing, what will not be present, or the consequence and fear that are being avoided by their action rather than what will be present as a result of their efforts.

Instead of focusing on what is not present or focusing on the potential consequence, talk about what benefits will be present. For example, the following statements are fear-based threats. "If you don't make your quota this quarter, then you won't have a job" or "If you can't get this project completed within the time frame we discussed, then you won't be able to take that vacation you wanted at the end of the month." These statements are consequence-driven statements that focus on what will be missing or what the person will not be able to do or have if they don't do what is expected of them.

Your communication style says a lot about you and where you are coming from in your thinking. So if you're communicating from scarcity, then where do you think your focus is when it comes to managing others as well as your mindset? Chances are, you are being driven by fear and consequence instead of your own goals and visions. And if that's where your focus is, what exactly do you think it is you are going to create? If there's one universal law worth remembering, it's this: How you think is exactly what you are going to get.

What about these statements? "If you reach your quota this month, then you will be eligible for the quarterly bonus" or "Once you complete that project, then the only thing I want you to focus on the following week would be planning your vacation and the fun you're going to have during your week off, especially knowing that it's a paid vacation week." Notice how these statements imply the benefit or pleasure that will be present in the person's life rather than what will be missing.

Here's another example of communicating from scarcity. "If you don't get more organized, your stress level as well as your workload will continue to increase to become even more unmanageable and overwhelming."

Now, here's the same message but this time it's being delivered from a place of abundance. "If you keep following through and honoring your daily routine, then you will eliminate the overwhelming workload that's been weighing you down. This way, your stress level as well as your workload will become more manageable so that you can feel in control and start enjoying your job again."

Now, when it comes to selling, uncovering the pain or the cost of not making a change is a strategy I certainly endorse when motivating prospects and customers to make a purchasing decision. However, it's not the typical method of communication you want to use in the office, even though there are those people who respond to it. Closing a sale for the most part is a one-time event. And even if you are constantly selling or upselling to existing clients, it's not something that typically happens on a day-to-day basis with the same customer.

On the other hand, developing a positive atmosphere within the workplace is something that requires daily reinforcement, often more than once a day. Since we do not want to breed a negative culture, consider this instead. If a consequence needs to be driven home, then you are better off asking questions that will help the salesperson articulate the cost of not changing, for example, "What is it going to cost you if you don't make any changes?" or "If you don't make prospecting a daily activity, how is that ultimately going to affect your sales funnel as well as your income?" or "I understand you've never worked off a structured routine and still have achieved some great success. However, as you get busier, what might eventually happen if you keep overcommitting yourself?"

This subtle, yet powerful change in your language and communicating from abundance can set the tone of not only every meeting or conversation but the culture of your company. As we have already discussed, the right language can create and reinforce the positive environment you want and one that people desire to work and thrive in. It also makes talking with you a pleasurable experience.

## MAKE ACKNOWLEDGMENT UNCONDITIONAL, MEASURABLE, AND SPECIFIC

What do people want most in their careers? Statistics show that people want the positive reinforcement and acknowledgment that lets them know they are doing a good job.

The number one issue people have in the workforce today is, "Will I be valued and will I have a job in the future?" You want the people who are working for you to want to be there. Otherwise, what do you think they are going to spend their time doing?

Yet many managers do not acknowledge their people's value and do not appease their concerns. Instead, managers focus more on problems rather than on their team's achievements or solutions to drive continued, sustainable growth. These managers are continually putting out fires and jumping from one problem to the next.

The by-product of acknowledgment is you build morale, which breeds the type of culture that you are looking to create. Ask yourself, do you get acknowledged for something on a daily basis? Chances are, if you have not been the recipient of consistent, positive, and authentic praise, then you may be conditioned to believe that acknowledgment is not all that critical or effective. After all, we learn from our predecessors. Just ask yourself, how often do you authentically acknowledge people on a daily basis?

Why don't we praise our employees enough? Why are we so stingy with our acknowledgment? What are we afraid might happen? Do we feel that we only have a limited supply of acknowledgment and we don't want to use it up?

Oh, I can see it now. You are in your office one day and one of your salespeople comes in and says, "I just want you to know that I've noticed you are taking more time and interest in my work and your positive reinforcement is generating some worthwhile results. I'm getting the sense that you are appreciating what I'm doing here more and more. Well, I just want you to know that you are making me feel just too good about myself and the company, so this has just got to stop!"

Of course this is an obvious exaggeration, but the real truth is, we don't acknowledge others more often because:

1. We don't know how to and are reluctant to do so;
2. We are afraid that if we acknowledge people too much they'll start to slack off;
3. We simply don't think it's really all that important; or
4. We are afraid that it won't come across as genuine.

The key to using positive reinforcement and acknowledgment as a powerful, motivating tool is to use it authentically, measurably, and unconditionally. Do not issue generic, hollow statements of praise that sound like "Good work!" Instead, recognize when something specific has occurred. Notice what people do or how they have improved. Praise them for who they are and who they are becoming.

General recognition such as, "I love the work you're doing" or "You did a great job," is not enough. It can actually backfire to work against you if the person you're delivering the acknowledgment to feels it's not genuine, conditional, a manipulative strategy, or believes you have attached your own agenda to it. Give genuine and honest acknowledgment and make sure it's specific and measurable.

Reinforce a behavior, activity, change, mindset, or technique that you noticed that made a profound impact on their success and the results they've achieved.

By acknowledging a specific behavior, the person will know what to do next time. In essence, you are reinforcing best practices while the person is doing them.

Here are three examples:

> You really demonstrated your ability to effectively follow up with Mary Johnson, the last sale you made. Your persistence, the way you specifically approached the conversation with Mrs. Johnson, and the steps you took when honoring your selling system turned that volatile prospect into a happy customer. This is certainly an accomplishment to feel proud of.

> I really appreciate you honoring this deadline and turning this proposal around for me so quickly, even with all of the other priorities that are on your plate. Your work through this process is a testament to your commitment to doing what it really takes to effectively manage an overwhelming workload.

> I knew you could do an exceptional job on managing that new project and getting the team involved in completing it—and you proved me right! There were many opportunities to lose your cool or dump this project on to someone else but you maintained a positive attitude and a steadfast work ethic. I just want you to know I truly admire that in you and your commitment to see this through to completion.

If your appreciation of a person's efforts is truly authentic and sincere, you have the power to make an employee's day. Besides, how else will your employees know if they are doing a great job? When they *don't* hear about problems? I have yet to hear about someone who left an organization because they were appreciated too much.

Since your salespeople know what behavior to reinforce, your recognition will further sharpen their ability to self-generate results and solutions on their own rather than expecting you to do it.

## MAKE YOUR PEOPLE RIGHT, EVEN WHEN THEY'RE NOT

This principle makes a huge impact on people's productivity and attitudes.

I refer to it as The Code of Rightness. In my 20 years as an executive sales coach, I have yet to make any of my clients wrong. I always make them right! How do we make people wrong?

Often we don't even realize when we are doing it. Making people wrong or *make-wrongs* come in a variety of formats. Sometimes when we talk to each other—our friends, coworkers, spouses, or children—it certainly doesn't sound like we're coming from a place of love or kindness.

- "You are wrong. That's not how you should do it."
- "Why don't you follow up like I told you to? That person wanted to buy from you, and you couldn't turn them around."
- "This is not what I asked for."
- "You just can't seem to ever get this right."

Ultimately a *make-wrong* statement is anything that robs people of their positive source of motivation and power or puts them on the defensive. You will know it's a make-wrong by the response you get.

Here are eight examples of make-wrong statements and questions. These are the more elusive ones that take place in daily conversations. Read each one so that you can recognize a make-wrong when you are doing it.

1. *A comparative statement.* "You look so much better than last time I saw you!" "This is definitely better than the work you turned in last week."

2. *Blame statements.* "The fact is, if you had been paying more attention up front to the details about this company and had been more organized, you wouldn't have put yourself in this situation where you lost the deal for us."

3. *Focusing on what happened before.* "Now, do you remember what happened the last time you tried to network through trade associations? You spent a ton of time doing it with little to show in return. You don't want to repeat that again, do you?"

4. *Targeting the negative.* "I see you missed the mark in these areas." "I see you brought in this sale but what about the 20 other prospects in your pipeline that you haven't closed yet?"

5. *Negative, problem-oriented questions.* "Why didn't you get this done correctly?" "Why can't you get this project completed sooner?" "What prevented you from reaching your sales quota this month?"

6. *Always/never statements.* "You never seem to be able to get your paperwork in by the established deadline." "Why is it that you can never get to the office or to a meeting on time?" "Why are you always afraid to pick up the phone and make the calls you need to?"

7. *Negative acknowledgment.* "Nice work, but what happened to the list of referrals that you were supposed to get from them?" "Congratulations, that deal went through, but just remember, don't expect full commission on it because we had to lower our prices on this one to get the sale." "Great job on reaching quota this quarter. However, I did want to remind you that you won't be eligible for the bonus because of the deal you split with Alice last month." "You had a huge week this week. You should feel good about it. By the way, whatever happened to the reports you promised me over two weeks ago? You told me you were going to turn them in then. I need them tomorrow, you know."

8. *Condescending humor.* "Congratulations! You win the award for the person who is most consistently late to meetings."

Using these toxic communication strategies not only turn off people's listening but will be interpreted as a personal attack, whether you are telling people they are wrong, correcting people, or putting people on the defensive, thus forcing them to come up with reasons as to why they didn't meet your expectations or do what you thought they should have done.

So, why do managers act this way? Well, when people are busy making someone else wrong, they are making themselves right. (Think back to our conversation on attachments and the need to be right in Chapter 2.) Making other people wrong is a source of energy for some (after all, human beings don't do anything unless we're getting some type of payoff out of it).

Sometimes we get so attached to something, such as wanting to be right, that we sacrifice the opportunity to cocreate new and greater possibilities.

When you have a team of people striving to reach performance goals, it is not who is right but what is right that is important. Think about it. We often forget that everyone is working toward achieving the same ultimate goal.

Rather than making people wrong, you can make them right even if they are wrong. After all, through their eyes, they feel as if they're right. So, respect people's viewpoints and communicate that to them.

To see rightness in people, you must believe that people are doing the best they can at any given moment. If their best doesn't meet your standards, you always have the choice to make changes. I am well aware that, in some instances, there's a right way to do something and a wrong way. For example, in your company there is probably a right way and a wrong way to fill out an expense report or a weekly sales activity report. When an employee completes the report incorrectly, instead of saying, "That's wrong" or "That's not the way to do it," simply add another truth to their statement by asking another question or add more to what has been said to create a new possibility. Otherwise, while making yourself right, you run the risk of making the person you are talking to wrong and this can shut down open communication. The person becomes defensive, stops listening to you, and a confrontational atmosphere is created.

Here is an example of a better response in a situation like this. Notice how this approach still makes the person right and keeps the conversation focused on how to handle and resolve the issue at hand.

"Bob, thanks for getting this information to me on time. I know these reports are new to you and can be a bit tricky, so I appreciate your efforts in getting this done. Based on what I've seen after reviewing your reports, I think there's an opportunity for us to sit down and discuss how we can make this process easier, faster, and more worthwhile for you. Are you open to discussing how we can do this?"

Managers must develop a new language and approach to communicating genuine respect and concern to the people on their team in a way that would make people feel better about themselves and their performance.

## CREATE NEW OPPORTUNITIES RATHER THAN MAKE PEOPLE WRONG

Here are some more questions that gracefully correct someone and create a new opportunity without making someone wrong. To avoid confrontation, respond to a person's inaccurate statements with a question that directs the conversation toward creating a new possibility, belief, or solution. These questions allow you to correct someone without having an emotional reaction or telling them they're wrong. Instead, they enable you to respect the person's viewpoint and efforts by adding another truth to the situation. The following questions will enable you to create a new opening and outcome that would otherwise go unexplored.

1. What else do you feel might be possible?
2. Can you please share with me your thinking on that?
3. Is it possible that there may be another approach/solution here?

4. Is it possible that there may be more/other facts to consider?
5. How can I best assist you now?
6. That's interesting. Can you share with me why you feel/see it that way?
7. What else is true about that?
8. I'm not too sure what you mean. Can you say more about that?
9. May I ask where you heard/learned that?
10. What are you noticing that supports your feelings about this?

Rather than reacting to their remarks, these questions demonstrate your interest in understanding what they are truly saying, what motivated their comment or assumption, or the source of their information. Use this as an opportunity to validate and empathize with some aspect of their feelings. Saying things like, "I appreciate how you feel" or "I understand your feelings on that" lets the other person know that you are sincerely trying to understand where they are coming from. Respecting someone's point of view, whether you agree with it or not, demonstrates a willingness to continue with the dialogue rather than shut it down. Most important, learn to put your ego aside and let go of your need to be right.

# Assumptive Coaching and Dangerous Listening

## THE PONTIFICATING MANAGER

When I speak to a group of sales managers, one of the first questions I ask is, "When approached by your salespeople with a problem, are you talkers, interrogators, or listeners?"

Most agree they are talkers.

Let me introduce the Pontificating Manager. These managers will readily admit they don't follow any particular type of management strategy. Instead, they shoot from the hip, making it up as they go along. As a result, they often find themselves in situations that they are unprepared for. Interestingly, The Pontificating Manager thrives on situations like this. They use these opportunities to once again create new approaches on the spot.

Like many of the managers discussed in this book, the Pontificating Manager believes this approach actually works. And quite frankly, it often does, but not for the reasons the manager thinks.

This type of person is often fun to talk with and be around. The Pontificating Manager is the type of manager who can talk to anyone and immediately make people feel comfortable. This character strength becomes a crutch to their leadership style, often blinding them to the need to further systemize their approach. As a matter of fact, the only thing consistent about these managers is their inconsistency.

Pontificating Managers exploit their charming and gregarious personalities. They possess a strong belief in their company and in their career. Their conviction and passion about what they do and the value they can deliver come across in his communication. The excitement, energy, and exuberance these managers display are contagious! Their enthusiasm drives results. As a result, people love to work for them.

In a world full of many managers with great personalities who are engaging, friendly, and love to be in the spotlight, the Pontificating Manager is the most popular of all. And even though this approach seems to work for many, their lack of a strategic management system limits their success.

Pontificating Managers are famous for offering unsolicited advice to their salespeople, mostly because they do not take the time to fully listen to their salespeople or understand their individual needs and concerns. These managers enjoy getting up on their soapbox and telling their team what they need to do or what they need to change, without consistently following up with them or holding them accountable for those changes. Pontificating Managers hope that their words of inspiration will be enough to instill long-lasting change. These managers are in desperate need of developing the second most essential proficiency of a coach: masterful listening.

A Maritz poll revealed: "Only one in ten employees believed that their companies really listened to or cared about them."

Interesting how this statistic connects caring with listening. What blocks our ability to fully listen? Let's find out.

## EIGHT BARRIERS THAT PREVENT MASTERFUL LISTENING

What causes someone not to listen? Here are the top eight barriers to unrestricted and masterful listening.

1. Are you doing something else while the person is talking? Are you thinking about the next meeting or call you need to make, how much money you will make if you hit quota, or what you will be eating for dinner?

2. During your conversation with someone, do you wait for a pause so you can say something?

3. How difficult is it for you to stay quiet? Do you say something without thinking first?

4. Are you faking your listening just so you can get in your own comments?

5. Do you practice selective listening? Do you hear only the things you want to hear?

6. Are you aware of the message the person is sending not only through her words but also through body language such as facial expressions, physical gestures, eye contact, and vocal intonation?

7. Do you allow background noise or your environment to hinder your ability to listen?

   If any of these behaviors seem familiar, you are creating a huge barrier that limits your ability to fully listen. Although we have mentioned various factors that limit our ability to listen, there exists another barrier we have created in our listening that we aren't even aware of. That eighth barrier is the *filter* we've created in our listening.

8. Do you listen through filters? Whether you realize it or not, we all do. When you listen through a filter, you are listening based on a past experience or belief or some type of anticipated future outcome or expectation. When you pass judgment on people because of their age, success, or how they look, and when you invalidate people based on what you see or based on a similar situation with another

salesperson, you build a wall that prevents clear and unrestricted communication and understanding of the message being received.

## LISTENING THROUGH FILTERS—A MANAGER'S LETHAL WEAKNESS

Have you ever met someone and passed judgment, based solely on appearance? When you walk by a homeless person on the street, what do you say to yourself? Would you take the advice of this person as quickly as you would from someone you respect and admire? The information might be just as valuable, yet too often the situation and the person delivering the message determine whether we will listen to what is said.

Unfortunately, because we pass judgment based on what we see, perceive, or have experienced in the past what we *hear* is not always the message that is being *said*. People's age, their disposition, what they look like, how much money we think they have, how successful they are, their voice, the car they drive, or the house they live in all act as barriers to effective listening. When we validate or invalidate people based on these criteria, it prevents clear and unrestricted communication and understanding.

Here's an example that illustrates this point. Think about one of your prospects who, based on his appearance or attitude, you were certain was not going to buy from you no matter what you did. Maybe you felt that this person couldn't afford your product or service or was not the decision maker.

A week later you find out that this prospect purchased an inferior product from your competitor and at a higher price. Ouch.

The fact is we do listen differently to our spouse, our boss, a stranger, our children, our customers, a store clerk, our friends, and our salespeople, evaluating the messenger over the message.

That's why the greatest barrier to listening is the filter you have created in the way you listen. You are already listening to the message before you hear the message. You've anticipated what the other person is going to say or how the person is going to react based on a set of judgments you have that, for the most part, are grossly inaccurate.

"Treat people the way you want to be treated" is a common pearl of wisdom. Here's another version. "Listen to people the way you want to be listened to."

For example, have you ever spoken with a salesperson and, based on that person's appearance, race, sex, age, or disposition, realized you were listening from a past experience about another salesperson in a similar situation?

Let's do a quick exercise to uncover a few of the filters in your listening. Finish each of the sentences below. Pay close attention to your first reaction, the initial adjectives, thoughts, or assumptions (right, wrong, good, or bad!) that come into your mind. Pause briefly after each statement to give yourself some time to think about your responses.

- Politicians are:
- My prospects and customers are:
- My boss is:
- My family is:
- My salespeople are:

Take note of your visceral reactions to appreciate the value of this lesson. You are listening from a certain place and, as such, you have identified several filters in your listening. As a result, these filters are all you are going to tune into and hear. Your selective listening with these people will actually focus on what you *want* to hear, based on your assumptions, experiences, and beliefs, preventing you from listening to the intended message.

So if you want other people to change how they listen to you, you must first change how you listen to them. Imagine what would be possible if you applied this in every area of your life.

To take this concept to another level, I'm suggesting that you also assume what people will tell you, what they think, or what they will do, which gives you what you will hear and, as a result, you react accordingly!

During a conversation, has anyone ever said to you, "I know what you're going to say" and then cut you off in mid-sentence to deliver their rebuttal to what they thought you were going to say? If this is how *you* communicate, then why do you need the other person in the conversation?

Learn to focus on *how* you listen in order to open up your hearing to the full message. Destructive listening habits can lead to poor communication between you and your salespeople. In other words, these habits can cause people to *stop listening to you*.

Here are some questions you can ask yourself to determine when you are listening though a filter.

1. Do you give everyone you speak with the same respect and gift of your listening? Do you feel that you are supposed to value the message differently depending on who is delivering the message?
2. Do you listen differently to your spouse, your boss, a stranger, a prospect, a customer, a salesperson, or a friend?
3. Do you judge people when you are listening to them, based on perceived status, appearance, career, or age?
4. Do you stop listening when you think you know what the person is going to say?
5. Do you pass judgment based on regional or ethnic accents?
6. How good are you at remembering people's names?

Have you ever been in a situation where you were introduced to someone and two seconds later realized that you forgot her name? Why do you think that happens?

It's because you just weren't listening. And if you weren't listening, chances are you were doing something else, such as passing judgment and evaluating the person you were being introduced to. You were already forming a conclusion about her and the conversation without getting all the facts.

Because we judge people when we are listening to them based on what we see or have experienced in the past, it prevents us from embracing and learning from every interaction and giving everyone we speak with the same respect and gift of our listening.

If you are busy passing judgment or not respecting other people's opinions or points of view, then you can't learn from them.

At any point in time, you can be given a solution that would better your situation but because of the filter in your listening, because of your judgment, you cannot hear it.

To remove your filters and sharpen your ability to listen, here are a few things you can do immediately, starting with boosting your awareness and sensitivity to the truth or, I should say, the facts. (We confuse the two.)

## JUST THE FACTS, PLEASE

When salespeople need help in closing more sales, I ask them to list the objections they are hearing that are preventing the sales. When they start stumbling over their responses, I ask, "Are these the objections you are hearing directly from your prospects or what you're assuming is the reason they don't buy?"

Effective salespeople don't guess themselves into a sale, just like the greatest managers don't assume what their sales team needs without fully listening to them. To ensure you're operating with the facts, ask yourself this: "Do I have evidence to support my assumption or how I'm feeling?" Enjoy the peace of mind that comes from clarity in your communication by relying solely on facts rather than your perception of them.

## ENCOURAGE SILENCE

Many of us wait only a split second to respond to a person's comments, questions, or objections. And when we actually know the answer, it expedites our reaction. Unfortunately, we don't get any extra points for moving a conversation along faster. We actually create more problems this way.

If you are comfortable encouraging silence (and most people are not), then what do you think will happen? The other person is going to talk more. Chances are, if he talks more, he is going to tell you more: more about what is important to him, how he wants to be treated, what his core needs and goals are, as well as his fears or concerns.

Ironically, one of the easiest ways to tell whether you are listening to your salespeople is the most obvious. Become aware of how long you wait before responding to a salesperson's comments or questions. Most people do not wait long before their lips are moving and they begin to sputter something that is generic, shallow, insincere, and meaningless. These are the things you always wish you hadn't said.

Here's how to combat this. Get in the habit of waiting a minimum of *three to five seconds* before responding. You must consciously count to yourself to ensure that enough time has elapsed before replying. This conscious pause accomplishes five essential objectives and establishes you more as a sales coach. By encouraging silence, you:

1. Create a safe environment for that person to explore feelings and ideas with you.
2. Provide additional time to effectively process the information you have received.
3. Build trust and credibility.
4. Motivate the person to talk and share more information.
5. Resist the rebuttal.

## FOCUS MORE ON THE MESSAGE THAN ON THE MESSENGER

Another simple, yet powerful technique to improve your listening is to focus on the content or message the person is delivering, not solely on the messenger. The message needs to take precedence in normal conversation. This is one of the reasons why I find telephone coaching to be so effective. It forces my clients to focus predominantly on the auditory portion of our communication. There are fewer distractions to dilute our ability to listen and obscure the full message.

Many managers treat their sales team as a unit, all one person with the same goals, needs, strengths, weaknesses, and problems.

This is, in fact, another filter in our listening, and it gets managers in trouble, because it's where assumptions usually start developing. As such, this creates a barrier to learning about each salesperson as an individual and listening to their needs.

Another question I hear often is, "I can do my best to change how I listen but what about how everyone else, especially my salespeople, listen to *me*?"

Whose listening do you think needs to change first? Yours or your salespeople's? Yours, of course. So the benefit here is this. When you successfully remove the filters in your listening, you will suddenly notice that the way in which your salespeople listen to and communicate with you has changed as well.

Finally, to increase your spider senses and listen the information or solutions right out of a salesperson, let's draw a distinction that will further impact your ability to listen masterfully by focusing on the things you need to be listening for.

## LISTENING TO SOMEONE OR LISTENING FOR SOMETHING

Consider that most of the time, in the course of a conversation with our salespeople, we are *listening to* information. Simply, this is when we hear the words or the noise coming out of the person's mouth that we refer to as words. As you may have rightfully surmised, this is more of a passive and ineffective listening approach.

However, when you are *listening for* information, you are looking for the implied meaning behind the words. This type of listening prevents you from listening through a filter and wrongly prejudging or misinterpreting the message that the person is communicating to you.

There are five main things we listen for when speaking with or coaching a salesperson.

1. *Listen for their needs.* What are their desired results, goals, or expectations? It's often obvious what a salesperson may *want* (more money, better qualified leads, more time off, and so on), but what do they really *need*? A better qualification process and prospecting system rather than more leads? A stronger selling strategy that would close more sales rather than a higher commission? A more balanced routine and a system to efficiently manage their time instead of more time off?

2. *Listen for what is important to them.* Simply put, what do your salespeople want most from their careers, their selling efforts, and from you, their manager? What are their core priorities, goals, and dreams?

3. *Listen for the truth (and assumptions of the truth).* It is often up to the coach to help people distinguish between what they perceive as the truth and the actual facts. The more we justify our life, our behavior, our performance with excuses (S.C.A.M.M.), or the stories we believe, the more blurred that line becomes between our assumptions, stories, and the indisputable facts, until they ultimately overlap and become one.

4. *Listen for pain, concerns, and fears.* What aren't your salespeople saying that they need to share with you? What are they withholding from you? Do they have issues with the product, service, coworkers, clients, or selling strategy? Or, is the real issue with you?

5. *Listen for the gap.* As we've discussed in Chapter 4, listen for what is missing, or for what I call The Gap. This is the space of opportunity in which you will be coaching your salespeople. You present the solution which, in turn, fills the gap. So coach the gap! Through your coaching, your solution or your additional support, accountability, or insight become the bridge that takes your salespeople from where they are today (present state) to where they want to be (desired state). Keep in mind this gap is something that salespeople may not even be aware of. It could be a blind spot for them. For example, the gap can be their selling philosophy. How do your prospects buy? When dealing with underperformers, make sure that you're evaluating the selling strategy they are using in an actual selling scenario as well as the attitude and mindset that are fueling it.

I was hired to train a sales team at a manufacturing company. As I began the training, I discovered that the company was experiencing a large amount of turnover. There were many inconsistencies and breakdowns during the recruiting and hiring process.

There was no documented process that people could follow to attract the best talent, especially when it came to screening candidates and developing a strong retention plan to retain new hires.

I found that they were experiencing a 35 percent attrition rate. I proposed not only providing a sales training program but also creating a more in-depth solution to developing and strengthening their recruiting and retention strategy, to reduce the amount of attrition and complement the training.

The result was a comprehensive recruitment and retention strategy that ultimately reduced turnover within the company dramatically. By simply listening deeper, I was able to uncover what their true needs were, where the breakdown originated from, and what their core challenges were, challenges that they did not articulate because they weren't even aware of them. I listened for what they *weren't* saying: their needs, the gap, their blind spots and greatest point of pain.

### ❀ FROM THE SIDELINES ❀

Start listening to what you are listening to. Not only to what other people are telling you but also listening to what you are telling other people and, most important, what you are telling yourself.

There's a symbiotic relationship between the way we listen and the questions we ask. For example, if you're already listening from a certain place or through a filter, chances are you are not going to ask certain questions that can create new opportunities. After all, if you keep listening from the past and reacting based on a past experience or a future expectation, you will continue to create the same results as before.

## MAKE PEOPLE FEEL THEY ARE BEING HEARD

Finally, to become the Zen master of listening, follow this advice. If you do, you will create even more performance breakthroughs among your sales team. To become a masterful listener, make the person feel heard.

How do you know when you are heard? How does it feel? Feeling heard is a level above just being listened to, and few of us ever cause other people to feel as if they are truly heard. Sure, we may be able to increase the effectiveness of our listening but it is crucial to relay to your salespeople that they are being listened to and understood.

To make someone feel heard, respond to what the person says during the conversation by using *clarifiers*. Rephrase in your own words what the person said to show that you not only heard but also understood them. If you do not confirm the accuracy of what you are hearing, you are risking an unnecessary communication breakdown that will waste your time, money, and energy.

Here are some examples:

- For my own understanding . . .
- What you are truly saying is . . .
- What I am hearing you say is . . .
- Help me understand . . .
- Can you say a little more about that?
- Tell me more about that.
- It sounds like the criteria you're using to make your decision are . . .
- What do you see as the next step?
- Here's what I'm hearing . . .
- How do you mean?
- Can you say that in a different way? (Can you ask me that question in a different way?)

These clarifying strategies are effective in (1) establishing mindshare, (2) demonstrating your ability to fully listen, (3) stimulating the salesperson's thinking, and (4) encouraging the person to continue talking.

Using these techniques will accomplish two core objectives:

1. Clarifiers ensure that you received the message that was intended. If you did not receive the accurate message that was intended, the other person now has the opportunity to clarify the intended message. This prevents misunderstandings or placing the wrong meaning behind what's

being heard. Clarifiers ensure that you have accurately received the message the other person intended to send.

2. Clarifiers demonstrate to the other person that he is truly being heard and listened to.

Poor, ineffective listening can cause communication breakdowns, damage relationships, ruin coaching opportunities, and deteriorate the level of trust between you and your prospects, customers, family, and sales team. However, listening actively and deeply accomplishes the following:

- Active listening enhances relationships and improves your credibility. Listening creates a safe environment for a person to share and explore his or her feelings on a deeper level.
- The fact that someone knows that you are really listening produces trust and makes people you are communicating with more willing to listen to you.
- Pure, unconditional listening prevents prejudging or hasty, unsolicited problem solving.
- Active listening shifts you away from listening through your filters and giving out unsolicited advice so that you can listen with an open mind and an open heart.

People want two fundamental things in a conversation: to be listened to and to be acknowledged. Notice what happens when you give someone the gift of your attention and the gift of your listening. It's the principle of reciprocity; if you listen to me, I'll listen to you.

I hope that at this point you have a deeper understanding of how critical it is to your coaching efforts to become a master at listening. Take the time to fine-tune your listening skills so that you can hear more about what your salespeople need and want most. Soon, you'll be listening the solutions right out of them.

## THE PRESUMPTUOUS MANAGER

Presumptuous Managers focus more on themselves than anything else. To them, their personal production, recognition, sales quotas and bonuses take precedence over their salespeople and the value they are responsible for building within each salesperson on their team. Presumptuous Managers often put their personal needs and objectives above the needs of their team. As you can imagine, Presumptuous Managers experience more attrition, turnover, and problems relating to managing a team than any other type of manager.

Presumptuous Managers aren't too concerned about developing and fostering deep, richer relationships since they believe that once salespeople are hired, the burden of success should fall on them and whether they are going to make the cut and survive.

Presumptuous Managers are typically assertive and confident individuals. However, they are typically driven by their ego to look good and outperform the rest of the team. Presumptuous Managers breed unhealthy competition rather than an environment of collaboration and cooperation, so that their salespeople learn to be solely concerned with looking out for themselves. These managers are even reluctant to share their best practices with other salespeople for fear their sage advice will be used against them when there's a new account on the line that's open for anyone to grab.

Ironically, with all the confidence that Presumptuous Managers possess, their ego doesn't allow them to challenge the way they relate to and manage their salespeople. This is often fostered within a sales culture that has been a long-time promoter of one dominant management philosophy. At one point or another, the Presumptuous Manager was told, "This is how it has always been done. This is how we've always recruited and managed our salespeople. This is how the top executives do it and how it has to be done. And it seems to be working for us." As such, these managers sincerely believe that this is the only way for them to manage their team, thus revealing this manager's greatest weakness, his inability to distinguish the facts from the assumptions and stories. Unfortunately for the sales team, Presumptuous Manager's allow this line of thinking to dominate and dictate their career and how they manage their people.

## DON'T BELIEVE EVERYTHING YOU TELL YOURSELF

To illustrate this point I'd like to share a story with you. It's about a salesperson I recently started coaching named Presumptive Peter. You'll soon see why Peter earned this name. As we've discussed, there are certain assumptions (S.C.A.M.Ms) that we make during our selling and coaching efforts which become barriers to making more sales and reaching peak performance. As I share this story, here's what I want you to do. See how many faulty assumptions you can spot that Peter made throughout every stage of his sales process, starting with prospecting, all the way through the final step when Peter asked for the business and closed the sale. How many coaching opportunities for Peter can you recognize?

## GET OUT OF YOUR WAY AND OUT OF YOUR HEAD

Peter called me one day looking for help in increasing his sales. He wasn't getting the response from his prospecting and new business development efforts that he needed in order to reach his income goal or make his quota. After Peter shared with me his goals and challenges, we decided to spend the day together so that I could shadow coach him throughout a typical day. Following Peter around for a full day would give me the opportunity to witness first hand Peter's selling efforts as well as his capabilities, skills, and challenges.

A week after our initial phone call, Peter and I met early in the morning at his office. It was 7:30, and we decided to make cold calling the first activity of the day. Peter sold financial services and insurance-related products for Zeon Financial in a limited territory. Since the majority of Peter's sales take place face to face, the next step after uncovering a qualified prospect would be to schedule a meeting.

I sat next to Peter as he made several cold calls, listening to his approach. Curiously, I asked him what the initial goal of his cold call was. He responded, "To get the appointment."

> *When cold calling or prospecting, do you assume the objective of a cold call is to get the sale (appointment, demo, submit a proposal, etc.)?*

His approach was fairly simple. He would call up, say who he was and what he did, and ask the person if he could come and visit to demonstrate how they could benefit from his services. His approach sounded something like this. "Hi, Mary? This is Peter from

Zeon Financial. Did I catch you at a bad time? I was hoping to schedule a time to meet with you to discuss some alternatives to the high rates you're currently paying on your insurance, health care, and the benefits package you offer to your employees." After about 20 calls, Peter booked his first appointment.

> *When prospecting and moving your sales process forward (appointment, proposal, demo, etc.) do you assume that the prospect is in fact even qualified or a fit for your service/product?*
>
> *Do you assume that your prospect is the only decision maker (or is a decision maker at all)?*

Several calls later, Peter found himself in a conversation with a business owner who seemed to be interested in what he had to say. Before Peter could ask for the appointment, the prospect said, "Peter, I'm in a bit of a hurry. How about you send me some information that I can review. Then we can talk after I have a chance to review it." Excited to find someone willing to listen, Peter responded with a resounding "Sure, I'd be happy to. Would you like me to e-mail it to you or drop it in the mail?" Peter ended the conversation and quickly e-mailed his collateral material to his new prospect.

> *When sending out collateral materials, do you assume the materials contain the information that the prospect wants or needs? (What information are they looking for?)*

Peter felt he was on a roll now. The very next call, Peter was able to get the prospect on the phone without having to leave another voice mail. However, as soon as the prospect realized it was a cold call, she told Peter she was very busy and it wasn't a good time to talk. Peter responded with, "That's okay, I'll give you a call next week. In the meantime I'll send you out some information."

> *When speaking with a prospect, do you assume that you had permission to follow up and the time/day to do so?*
>
> *Do you assume prospects want your collateral material or are interested in reviewing it?*

After about three hours of cold calling, Peter realized that he had some people he needed to follow up with to whom he had already sent a proposal. There were five people to call on his list for today and another six to follow up with tomorrow. I asked Peter how he knew when he should follow up with each prospect. He said, "I just put them down on my calendar a week after I send them a proposal." Peter proceeded to leave four voice mails for the prospects he wanted to reach.

> *Do you assume how and when the prospect wants to be contacted when following up and the frequency of follow-ups? (phone, e-mail, mobile phone, etc.)*

As I reviewed his call list, I noticed that he had lines through some of the prospects' names—prospects that he had met with and sent a proposal to. "That's my dead list," he declared. "Those are the prospects that I permanently took off my prospecting list." When I asked him why they were on his do-not-call list, he said, "They weren't interested."

"Really?" I responded. "Why do you say that?"

"Well," explained Peter, "I've tried to call them on several occasions and was never able to get in touch with them. I've even left a few voice mails but they never did return my calls. Besides, if they were really interested, they would call me, right?"

> *Do you assume that just because a prospect doesn't return your calls or did not contact you again after your conversations with them, they bought from someone else, aren't interested, or are not going to buy from you?*

Peter continued making his follow-up calls. He was able to get in touch with one of the prospects he sent a proposal to last week. Since Peter thought that he was following up to get their confirmation that they wanted to move ahead with him, he was surprised when he heard this prospect say, "We still haven't had a chance to review your proposal. Our board meeting isn't happening for another two weeks, which is when we will put your proposal on the agenda for discussion."

Peter told this prospect that he would call them after their board meeting.

*Do you assume the process by which each prospect makes a purchasing decision? (Again, do you assume that your prospect is the only decision maker or is even a decision maker at all?)*

Peter had time to make one more follow-up call before we headed out to an appointment. The prospect answered the phone. It was Joan Edgewood, Vice President of Human Resources for Boiden Consulting Group, a large venture capital firm. Peter asked Joan if she had reviewed his proposal. She said she did and told Peter, "We decided to pass on using your services. But thank you for submitting your proposal. We'll keep you in mind if anything changes."

Peter thanked her for her time and the opportunity to meet with her. He then hung up the phone. When I asked what happened, he said, "They were going to stick with their current vendor. I think the price got in the way."

"Is that what she told you?" I asked.

"No," Peter replied, "but based on my experience, I'm pretty sure that's what it was. After all, my product is a commodity."

*Do you assume the objections or the reasons as to why your prospects do not buy from you?*

*Do you assume your product is a commodity? (If so, you haven't taken the time to research your industry and develop the compelling reasons that set you apart.)*

It was now almost noon and time for Peter's first meeting of the day. He was meeting with Dillon Barkley, the owner of Gennex, a chain of popular bars located mostly in the Northeast. He felt prepared to deliver a stellar presentation. We met Dillon in the lobby of his office building. When we finally got settled in his office, the first statement out of Peter's mouth was, "I've put together a PowerPoint presentation for you so that you can clearly see the benefits of our services and the options you have available."

*When speaking with a prospect or delivering a presentation, do you assume what's most important to them based on what you think is important or the most common features and benefits of your product or service?*

*Do you assume how the prospect wants the information delivered?*

*Do you assume that you already know what their expectations are and their objective of your meeting with them?*

Peter concluded his presentation by asking Dillon if he had any questions. He did not. Peter then informed Dillon that he would be receiving the proposal within the next few days. He shook Dillon's hand, and the meeting was over.

*After meeting with a prospect, do you assume the next steps that would bring the sale to its natural conclusion and earn the business of a prospect? Do you assume they even want or need a proposal to make a decision and thereby further assume how they go about making a buying decision?*

*After delivering a presentation, do you assume the prospect is still interested in moving the process forward? Have you uncovered all of their concerns, taken their pulse, and confirmed their level of interest?*

*Do you assume that the information in your proposal is the length and format and contains the information the prospect is looking for? How do you determine what information to put into your proposal?*

After the meeting, we talked in the parking lot, reflecting on the experiences of the day. It was now 2:30 P.M. on a sunny yet brisk autumn afternoon. I told Peter I had gotten all the information I needed at this point and that it was time for us to return to his office for a formal coaching debrief. I would share what I had observed as well as the type of coaching and training I would be doing with him to sharpen his selling skills.

When we arrived back at Peter's office, I told him with great assurance that, after implementing my suggestions, his sales would skyrocket. Peter smiled, thinking that I would be sharing a list of things he could do, action steps he could take, or strategies he could use that would assist in his selling efforts.

As I talked about my observations from our day and began working with Peter, he quickly discovered that he was mistaken as to what he thought he would be getting from me. Peter soon realized what was at the core of his problems. I shared with him the assumptions he made that created holes throughout his entire sales process and in the activities he engaged in. Ultimately, it was the assumptions that Peter had made throughout his sales cycle that overshadowed what needed to be done. His assumptions contributed to the lack of questioning that Peter needed to be doing in order to better understand and qualify each prospect.

Peter realized how critical it was to ensure that he was managing his mindset effectively. To think like a top producer, you not only need to adopt a new way of thinking but you also need to uncover your current limiting or negative thinking or assumptions that you don't even know about. Only a skilled coach would be able to help.

So, how many costly assumptions did Peter make?

How many did you notice and what assumptions are preventing him from selling more? There were seventeen unique costly assumptions and two of them showed up twice in this story. If you couldn't find the seventeenth assumption, it was this. Peter even assumed that he knew what I would be coaching him on that would dramatically boost his sales! Peter thought I would be sending him things to do or tactics to change, rather than showing him a new way to think.

After talking about each assumption in detail, Peter finally understood the relationship between the costly assumptions he was unintentionally making and how they affected his productivity. Most important, Peter was now well aware of how this also affected the questions he asks his clients and prospects. We continued our work together, creating a strategy that would eliminate these costly assumptions permanently.

Peter kept this list of costly assumptions in front of him every day. Now that I had raised his awareness about these costly assumptions, he can recognize them on his own. He invests time adjusting his approach and asking better questions to ensure he won't get caught up in this assumption trap again.

Four weeks later, Peter called me with wonderful news. Yes, Peter was finally able to get his sales and his income up. The best part was that Peter was not only able to reach his income goals but he did so working fewer hours each week. Peter is no longer wasting time on the wrong prospects. He's no longer scheduling appointments and meeting with prospects he shouldn't be meeting with in the first place. He is no longer drafting up proposals for people who really aren't interested or even qualified. Finally, Peter is no longer following up with people who have no intention of ever working with him.

Think about the assumptions you make when managing and coaching your salespeople that get in the way of asking better questions and probing further to uncover the real problem.

Here are a few.

- You may assume your salespeople know what you're talking about during a training session.
- You may assume your salespeople have the ability and determination to perform their job function.
- You may assume your salespeople understand the solution you provide them or the task you've delegated to them.
- You may assume that your salespeople's level of knowledge, experience, and technical know-how is the same as your own or better than you surmised.
- You may assume your salespeople are using the most effective selling strategy.
- You may assume your salespeople's level of loyalty and commitment to the company.
- You may assume your salespeople are consistently engaging in their required selling activities.

As a manager, after uncovering the costly assumptions you are making, the only surefire strategy to prevent them from getting in the way of your salespeople's next selling opportunity is to ask well-crafted questions. Do you know what gets in the way of asking well-crafted questions? The number one barrier: costly assumptions.

New universal selling laws challenge conventional selling wisdom and dispel the most common selling myths and assumptions:

- Closing is not something you do to a person. It is something that happens naturally with them.
- The greatest salespeople are not great closers. Rather, they are skilled openers of new selling opportunities.
- Salespeople don't overcome objections, prospects and customers do.
- Salespeople create many of the objections that prevent them from closing more sales.
- Well-crafted questions, rather than statements, defuse objections.
- Dropping the price will often result in the loss of the sale.
- The old adage of putting yourself in the prospect's shoes is really a costly assumption that destroys many a selling opportunity.

When coaching your salespeople, be mindful of these new universal laws, as well as the assumptions Peter had made in the story I shared with you. I can assure you, your salespeople are making these costly assumptions as well.

## BE CURIOUS

Be curious; just two simple words to assimilate into your thinking and your coaching that will keep your assumptions at bay.

If you're naturally curious then you will question everything. Since you're in the business of providing support and solutions for your salespeople, invest the time to uncover each person's specific need or problem, as opposed to providing common solutions that you assume may fit for everyone. For example, the words "Happy, frustrated, successful, satisfied, affordable, quality work, organization, integrity, and committed" can be interpreted in a variety of ways and often carry a different meaning for each of us.

Think about your visceral reaction when you hear a salesperson make a comment like, "I'm feeling stressed out and overwhelmed with my workload."

You may assume you know what she means based on a previous experience with her or with another salesperson. And because you have an answer ready, you don't even take the time to look behind the words and find out what the statement she shared with you means to her. Consequently, you just blurt out your trite response.

A better approach would be to use this opportunity to explore deeper into what she wants or needs most. Ask questions such as, "How do you mean?" "Can you say more about that?" "What is contributing to your feeling of stress and being overwhelmed?" "What needs to happen to reduce your sense of being overwhelmed?" or "What does being overwhelmed look and feel like for you?" Questions allow you to clarify what you've heard or go into a topic in more depth so you can become clear with what they are really saying. Moreover, questions will challenge your core assumptions and turn off your automatic thinking and responses to your salespeople's requests. Finally, if you are someone who is naturally curious, this change in your way of thinking will naturally encourage the use of more questions.

Be prepared for the answers you hear to the questions you ask, including the ones you ask yourself.

As we continue to build upon the lessons we've covered, the ability to truly become a strong influential coach rests on your vulnerability threshold. The next chapter will focus on this, as well as the three remaining types of managers: the Perfect Manager, the Passive Manager, and the Proactive Manager.

CHAPTER 8

# Vulnerability-Based Leadership

I t is the very drive for perfection that many leaders obsess
over that ultimately exposes our next manager's greatest
weakness: his inability to welcome himself to the human
race. Vulnerability is taboo in many business cultures and
causes panic and trepidation in the hearts of managers who are
afraid to be exposed.

While counterintuitive, it's critical for managers to be willing
and able to express their vulnerabilities in a way that enables them
to connect with their people and establish the type of trust that
motivates a person to go above and beyond the call of duty.
Although this is a concept that is easy to resist, no one is more
alarmed by vulnerability than the Perfect Manager.

## THE PERFECT MANAGER

Perfect Managers are masters of their trade, product, and profession. If you need to know technical data, statistics, and how the
product or service works, they are the people to call. In fact, their
perfection overflows throughout every area of their lives. In their
world, failure and mistakes are unacceptable.

This manager's perfection also shows up as an expert of industry knowledge. They can tell you the who, what, when, where, why, and how as it relates to their product and how to best sell and position it in front of their ideal prospects. Perfect Managers can even discuss in detail information about their competitors' products and how they differ. It seems as if these managers know more about their competition's product than the competition does!

Chances are, Perfect Managers have been called upon by management to help with product training and to provide the industry knowledge necessary for all new hires to possess. It was the technical ability and industry wisdom of Perfect Managers that prompted their promotion to management in the first place.

This manager is a talking spec sheet. After all, Perfect Managers want their salespeople to be able to present all of the relevant information to their prospects in order for them to make an informed and educated purchasing decision. Even though this selling strategy may work for Perfect Managers, it comes at a greater cost to their sales team. Their emphasis on acquiring more facts, figures, features, and benefits has overshadowed the ability of Perfect Managers to recognize the critical need for soft skills training around the areas of presenting, listening, questioning, prospecting, and the importance of following an organized, strategic selling system.

Perfect Managers rely on their vast amount of product knowledge and experience when managing and developing their salespeople. Because of this great imbalance, these managers often fall short on developing their interpersonal skills that would make them more human than machine.

While product and industry information is certainly crucial for salespeople to assimilate into their bank of knowledge, this approach has been known to backfire on Perfect Managers. In their quest to educate their salespeople, they actually overeducate them by providing too much information. The more information these managers provide to their salespeople, the more information that needs to be processed and considered by the prospect. The more information the prospect needs to consider, the longer the selling cycle becomes.

Perfect Managers possess some wonderful qualities. These managers are open to change, innovation, training, and personal growth with the underlying commitment to continually improve and evolve as sales managers, almost to a fault. However, this wonderful trait often becomes their weakness. In their search for the latest and greatest approach, like Pontificating Managers, Perfect Managers never get to experience the benefit of consistency.

### ❀ FROM THE SIDELINES ❀

Focus more on being human than being perfect.

Interestingly, these managers have a very low risk threshold and are reluctant to try anything new that hasn't already been proven to work. The creed of Perfect Managers is, "If you want something done right, you have to do it yourself." Delegation is not one of their strong points, so they wind up managing a heavier workload as a result. The term *control freak* is often used to describe this type of manager; they are less inclined to delegate tasks for fear they will not get done perfectly. As you can imagine, Perfect Managers often become the bottleneck to making positive change, as they have a tendency to obsess about making certain their solution, idea, or new approach is nothing less than perfect before executing it. (And when does *that* ever happen?) Perfection then becomes paralysis which prevents this manager from taking the necessary actions.

By continuously refining their approach, they never get comfortable with one. Because of this insatiable quest for perfection, Perfect Managers have not yet become confident enough to trust their own leadership and communication style, natural strengths, and talents. Instead, they often rely on other people's proven methods to achieve their goals.

These managers are seduced by management tactics they read about, tactics that others have used with a great deal of success. As such, Perfect Managers often try to mirror these techniques exactly without considering whether or not they fit their management style or personality.

Unfortunately, Perfect Managers try to incorporate everyone else's style but their own. It's amazing that these managers get any results at all since they never stay with one approach long enough to gauge its effectiveness. The intentions of these managers are sound; they always want to better themselves by investing their time in professional development so that they can maximize the potential of their sales team. However, finding the perfect approach to do so becomes a never-ending exercise in futility and the very thing that dilutes this manager's effectiveness.

## EXPRESS YOUR AUTHENTICITY: BECOME VULNERABLE

What does it take to be truly authentic? What does it take to become invincible? What does it take for you to become more powerful than you could ever imagine?

What it takes is probably not what you think. Not training, further skill development, a better coaching system, a better product or service, not even a better team of salespeople. To become an invincible manager takes vulnerability. It requires you to become truly vulnerable.

Remember, the number one issue within the workplace is lack of trust, specifically between management and staff. A Maritz Poll states, "Only twelve percent of employees strongly agreed that their companies' leaders were completely ethical and honest. Only seven percent strongly agreed that the actions of senior leaders were completely consistent with their words."

The cornerstone of any worthwhile relationship is trust. Trust is the mortar that binds any relationship, and if diluted, will affect the integrity of the relationship. Without trust, you have nothing to build on that could be sustained over time. And you are certainly not able to create a healthy coaching relationship without trust. Contrary to the opinion of some managers, there are no tools, incentives, compensation packages, or strategies that can compensate for any lack of trust in a relationship.

The only way to build trust is to let go of your need to be invulnerable or perfect, that is, to actually allow yourself to be vulnerable.

## EMBRACE YOUR HUMANITY

Now, when I suggest making yourself vulnerable, I'm certainly not expecting any of you to start driving without your seatbelts, leaving your front door unlocked, or verbally sharing every thought that pops into your head, which could result in swift removal from your management position. I'm not suggesting you do anything that is going to put you or someone else in harm's way.

The type of vulnerability I am suggesting encompasses what you can do to cultivate a safe environment to earn trust, to build trust, to reinforce trust, and to demonstrate trust within your company and among your sales team. There are more obvious ways to go about building trust, such as honoring your word; following through with your commitments; being consistent with your approach to managing, coaching, and communicating; being respectful and supportive. While these are all healthy practices that build trust, they will only take you so far. To build the type of trust that carries teams on to win the championship, to develop the type of loyalty that's unshakable and deep, the only way to foster this type of culture is through vulnerability. And that requires managers to demonstrate their vulnerability in front of their salespeople. Ultimately, it requires the manager to be human.

The development of a high-performance, long-lasting team depends on the ability of the manager and the team to be vulnerable. The core intention is to encourage a deeper connection to one another. Vulnerability-driven trust allows people to more comfortably and confidently share their mistakes, failures, challenges, feelings, and concerns that are often kept bottled up inside for fear that expressing them will be misinterpreted as a sign of weakness.

### ❦ FROM THE SIDELINES ❦

Show me a manager who embraces her humanity and expresses her vulnerabilities, and I will show you a fearless manager who is invincible.

When salespeople possess the unshakable belief in their manager that her intentions are sound with no hidden agenda, the salespeople do not need to feel guarded or protective around their manager or even around their team. This promotes a stronger feeling of trust, knowing that their vulnerabilities will not be used against them in any way and instead will become a conduit for their own continued development.

While it may sound counterintuitive, being vulnerable does not equate to weakness but to greater strength. Keep in mind that in order to develop a team built on vulnerability-driven trust, the vulnerabilities need to be shared by both management and salespeople. However, in order to develop this level of trust, it is the manager who must model and encourage this vulnerability-based behavior first. You can't expect your salespeople to show any vulnerability (based on their past experiences) until their manager shows that it is, in fact, safe for them to do so.

The most powerful leaders are the ones who are willing to risk losing face in front of their team in order to encourage an atmosphere where their salespeople would be willing to take the same risks themselves. Of course, your display of vulnerability must be genuine and authentic or you will risk losing the trust that may have already been present. When you notice your salespeople finally beginning to model your behavior, it is critical to the emerging culture you are looking to create that vulnerability is not to be punished and the sharing of any weakness, problem, or failure does not result in any type of consequence. Even with all of your good intentions, chastising or even making fun of someone else's admissions of failure or declaration of a personal shortcoming or weakness will discourage trust.

## EVIDENCE OF AN EMERGING CULTURE

You will know your sales team is moving toward developing a culture based on vulnerability when you notice some of these telltale signs. Some vulnerability-based behavior comes in the form of taking ownership of certain problems and mistakes and a desire to learn how to prevent them from happening again. This includes requesting help and assistance from both management and peers, acknowledging deficiencies in a skill set or mindset that require further development and attention, even recognizing destructive and costly communication practices. Other behaviors that would indicate your salespeople's willingness to address some uncomfortable issues that would expose certain vulnerabilities include tackling unhealthy interpersonal relationships, working through their fears, and admitting a poor attitude or an unprofessional appearance.

It is only in this type of environment when salespeople aren't on the defensive that a high-performance sales team can emerge. Now individuals on the team can focus their energy and attention on their job and core objectives rather than be worried about who's out to get them or being political or superficial with one another.

## VULNERABILITY AND TRUST

Vulnerability-driven trust is not something that can be achieved in a matter of days but requires a long-term commitment to turning around an existing culture. This will be achieved over time through repeatable shared experiences, structured exercises and activities, meetings, and, most important, the continual modeling by managers of the level of trust and vulnerability that they want their team to emulate.

Holding certain meetings with the sole focus on establishing this type of trust will prove to be an effective method of establishing this type of sales culture. For example, one exercise you can have your salespeople engage in during your weekly meetings could focus on learning more about each individual. Each person could share something personal, whether from childhood, personal hobbies, favorite activities, or favorite family stories.

Barry Kane, the Director of Recruiting for a large restaurant chain and a client of mine, facilitated the following exercise as an ice breaker during the last regional meeting he held for all of his recruiters. He had his entire team of recruiters come to the meeting prepared to share three different stories: their funniest recruiting experience, their most successful recruiting experience, and their most challenging or strangest recruiting experience. When he reviewed the evaluation forms that his recruiters completed after the meeting, they all reported this was one of the best meetings they ever attended.

This type of sharing encourages greater empathy, understanding, connection, and a higher degree of comfort that motivates people to share even more. Once this is established, you can move into the riskier types of exercises during your weekly meetings. In this second-tier type of meeting, each salesperson would have an opportunity to be critiqued by other people on the team. Working around the room, every salesperson would take a turn identifying one major contribution they feel the person they are critiquing has made, as well as one area the person could improve on.

A third approach to encouraging this type of culture would be to have your sales team members share one weakness they feel they possess. It would then become the responsibility of everyone on the team to support each other on how to overcome that weakness. This now evens the playing field, since every single player on your sales team has shared a weakness and will now play a very significant role in supporting each teammate overcome a specific challenge; without making the other person wrong.

To illustrate how I've used some of these programs in this context, Barry was encouraged by the director of HR to find an executive coach he was comfortable with to assist him on further developing his communication skills. After we uncovered some key areas to be addressed, I suggested that, depending upon the culture of the company, he might want to use one of the communication styles profiles to not only evaluate himself but also to ask some of the trusted executives he works with to use this assessment to evaluate his communication. This request was very well received and as a result of the responses we gathered, we were able to uncover a few more key areas to focus on that would further strengthen his communication skills and enhance his effectiveness as a manager; areas that would have otherwise gone unrecognized. Rather than an evaluation tied to his performance, we positioned this communication profile as a development tool that allowed this manager to even enroll others in this process. By doing so we further identified in a much more comprehensive way, Barry's strengths and opportunities for improvement without any repercussions.

It is impossible to build a high-performance team without trust to bind the relationship together. The cost of failing to do so is immense. The absence of trust leads to dissension, low morale, and high turnover. Teams that lack trust waste their precious and limited time and resources managing their behaviors and positioning themselves in the most favorable light. As you can imagine, sales meetings are certainly not something these teams look forward to. Distrusting teams are more reluctant to take the risks that are often required to maintain a company's competitive edge.

Vulnerability is a human condition as well as a discipline worth mastering. For Perfect Managers, it means welcoming themselves back to the human race and owning their role as mere mortals, rather than superhumans. For the team to achieve this, there must be daily follow-through so as not to lose momentum Perfect Managers begin, as inertia quickly leads to the erosion of trust.

Vulnerability is probably one of the hardest disciplines to master. But once achieved, it leads to the evolution of the fearless leader, and the rewards that follow are worthwhile: the development of a loyal, trusting, and top producing team. If you truly want to become fearless, become vulnerable. After all, when you have nothing left to fear, you then become invincible.

As you will see with the last two types of managers, not every manager has the challenge of demonstrating vulnerabilities; at least on a subconscious level. The next type of manager has a very difficult time distinguishing between the role of a manager and that of a parent, which is why I refer to this type as the Passive Manager.

## THE PASSIVE MANAGER

Also referred to as Parenting Managers or Pleasing Managers, Passive Managers take the concept of developing close relationships with their sales team and coworkers to a new level. These managers have one ultimate goal: to make people happy. While this is certainly an admirable trait, it can quickly become a barrier to leadership efforts if not managed effectively.

Because all Passive Managers want to do is please, they are more timid and passive in their approach. These managers will do anything to avoid confrontation, and collapse holding people accountable with confrontation and conflict. If Passive Managers hear a concern from a salesperson, rather than viewing this as someone reaching out for assistance or an opportunity to challenge a salesperson and help her grow, Passive Managers take the salesperson's side without exploring her concerns at a deeper level. The Passive Manager will do anything to appease people.

Persistence is not one of this manager's strong points. I'd go so far as to say this manager is the master procrastinator. Taking initiative? I don't think so. The Passive Manager's ideal strategy is, "Cross your fingers, avoid the problem, and hope it goes away." These managers have an office right on the beach, just to make it easier for them to stick their heads in the sand.

The Passive Manager's idea of making a strong suggestion may be sending an e-mail with a web link to an article for you to read, hoping that the support material does the managing. They are more inclined to watch over and protect their salespeople, rather than challenge and empower them.

Passive Managers have a very difficult time holding people accountable for doing their job and, more specifically, reaching their monthly sales quota. Because of their fear of doing so, Passive Managers are reluctant to ask salespeople the tough questions, hold them accountable for the things they said they would do or need to be doing, or attempt to talk to them about their damaging behavior for fear of losing them. Instead, Passive Managers keep it all inside and unexpressed, while watching the unacceptable behavior manifest and tolerating the mediocre performance that spreads like wildfire throughout the entire team. Then comes the greater cost: the decay of a once healthy culture due to the poisoning of the very foundation the company was built on.

Subsequently, these managers make excuses as to why their team isn't reaching their goals. You'll often hear them saying things like, "There's not enough time." "We don't have the resources and support we need." "This is the fault of (accounting, marketing, operations, etc.)."

Leadership isn't a popularity contest. It's about getting results. And in the spirit of continued improvement and achieving more with fewer resources, that means it's not always about the manager looking good or avoiding confrontation. To reinforce this message, I tell every client who's ever hired me that I am not being paid to be popular. Instead, they are paying me to coach them to do what they haven't been able to do on their own.

Passive Managers are certainly master practitioners of problem solving, fire fighting, and delivering solutions to any of the problems or challenges their salespeople bring to them. Their motives for doing so are clear and make perfect sense to them. It creates a stronger dependence on the manager and, boy, does the Passive Manager love to feel needed.

## EMBRACE HEALTHY CONFLICT

Confrontation. Conflict. While some managers actually thrive on it, the majority of managers tend to avoid it at all costs. Let me stress the word *cost*. Sure, I can understand that conflict is uncomfortable for some people, especially if you're a Passive Manager who would have a hard time concentrating on your work if you knew there may be someone on your team who doesn't like you.

So, in their quest to keep the peace, Passive Managers tolerate people's toxic, negative, and damaging behavior. All in the name of avoiding confrontation and coming across as anything but pushy and aggressive to their team.

Imagine what would be possible if you could defuse any conflict in a way that would empower your salespeople and move them forward exponentially faster than the passive-aggressive role most managers step in when handling conflict and disagreements? What if you were able to get permission or a verbal buy in from people to have what appears to be a difficult but needed conversation? Would it remove the tension and the fear you have around conflict?

## CALL THEM OUT USING THE COACHING EDGE

You can dramatically increase the power and effectiveness of your communication by, in essence, getting permission to be pushy. It all begins with how you set up the expectation and tone of the conversation or your approach to redirecting what sounds like a heated conversation. The ability to handle and defuse any hostile situation begins with asking for permission to speak to the person strongly and sharing your intention and desired outcome, which is what I call *the coaching edge*.

Think about it, if people give you permission to continue with a conversation or permission to deliver a tough message, then they are naturally going to be more accepting and open to what you say, rather than being reactionary and defensive.

Imagine how much more productive and happier you and your salespeople would be and how much time you would save if you could defuse and even avoid certain controversy and conflicts that shouldn't happen in the first place. Consider how much more support you could offer your people if you could get to the root of an uncomfortable issue that everyone would prefer to avoid. Now you can resolve these dilemmas from start to finish in a professional, collaborative, and positive way.

You can use the coaching edge in a variety of situations. You can use the edge to deliver a tough message. You can use the edge to deliver an uncomfortable truth. You can use the edge to open up a delicate and potentially explosive conversation, and you can even use the edge during the course of a conversation that seems to be rapidly turning into a fight or caustic argument.

Using the coaching edge, you can take the stand you've always wanted to take for your people. As a manager, this coaching tool will allow you the ability to give your people the tough, edgy support often required to propel people to their next level of success, while being mutually supportive and empowering. Using this communication edge, you can eliminate the faulty interpretations that result in avoiding the issue, and you can ensure that your intentions are pure, while getting solid buy in and a commitment from the other person to find a resolution.

## TAKE A STAND FOR YOUR SALESPEOPLE

Some messages are just tough to deliver. The most effective managers realize the importance of working through these caustic predicaments and the advantages that follow when taking a stand for what is best and right for the salesperson and for the company as a whole. As we've established, how receptive people are to hearing a difficult message depends on how you approach them with it. Here are 14 different examples of how to open up someone's listening and prepare them for having what could be an uncomfortable conversation or for hearing a tough message. In addition, you will also find some questions that will enable you to probe deeper and uncover more information that could lead to greater breakthroughs.

1. Can I point something out to you that may be tough for you to look at right now?

2. Can I share with you what I see and then we can work through this together?

3. I have something I need to tell you that is going to sting a little bit, but I need you to know that I'm sharing this with you for your own good. I just need you to be open to hearing it, okay?

4. Can you commit to at least being open to what I have to tell you, even if you don't agree?

5. You may not be able to hear this, but my role is to speak the truth about what I see is going on. Can I share with you an observation that may be uncomfortable for you to see but is sure to cause a major breakthrough in your performance if you can embrace it?

6. There's something that I see that may be a little uncomfortable for you to hear, and I just want to make sure that you are ready to hear it. Is it okay if I move forward in discussing this with you?

7. If you really want me to coach you on reaching this goal faster, then I need to know that you will be okay being challenged and stretched more than you're used to and held accountable for the commitments you make. Remember, it's all in the spirit of having you reach your goal. Is that fair?

8. Do I have your permission to say something to you each time I notice you reverting back to your old destructive habits or behaviors?

9. I'm clear that you don't agree with this new program, and I respect your opinion. Unfortunately, it's not helping either of us reach our goals. Since our goals are the same, then how about we focus more on what we have to do to successfully get past the next few months. Are you open to discussing how we can do so?

10. We can keep arguing about this or redirect our energy toward creating a solution that's going to work for everyone. Personally, I'd rather invest my time working on a solution with you now. Are you on board?

11. May I have permission to cut you off during the course of our conversations if I see an opportunity to coach you on something you could improve upon? More specifically, if I see you communicating from a place of weakness, I'm going to jump in and coach you to speak from a place of power which will double your effectiveness. Is this something you would be open to?

12. Can I push you a little harder to develop a better way to manage your schedule that will more than double your productivity each day?

13. The way you come across is keeping you from becoming extremely successful. Are you ready to abandon some self-defeating behaviors that would set you free?

14. I want you to know that whatever we discuss right now will be held in the strictest of confidence. I refuse to compromise on my integrity, and my word. I want this meeting to be a safe place for you to feel comfortable sharing with me how you're feeling and what you see as the real issue that needs to be addressed. This way, I can best support you in overcoming it/creating the right solution for you. How does that sound?

## DECLARE WHAT YOU REALLY WANT FOR YOUR SALES TEAM

Although the *wanting for* statement is a crucial component in the enrollment process, which we will be discussing in Chapter 10, it is also an independent, self-contained strategy you can use at any time during normal conversation. A wanting for statement can be used in a variety of situations. I've listed several different examples where it would be appropriate to use this coaching tool.

1. *You need to deliver a strong message to an underperforming salesperson about her need for a turnaround.* "Kelly, what I *want for* you is to be able to turn your performance around to where it used to be so that you can start enjoying your job the same way you did when you first started here, along with the financial rewards that follow."

2. *You need to prepare an individual or your entire sales team for some imminent changes; whether they are changes in HR, in your sales procedures, in your product or service, or in your administrative duties.* "What I *want for* each person on my sales team is to be able to walk into the office each day feeling confident you have all the tools and resources needed to reach your goals here, both personally and professionally. And sometimes, ensuring that these resources are readily available for you requires making some changes in our approach and how we do things."

3. *You want to reinforce your stand and commitment to the success of each person on your sales team.* "At this point, we have all been working together for some time now. And I truly hope that each of you is fully aware of my commitment to your continued success here. What I *want for* all of you is to be able to come to work feeling fulfilled in your career, motivated by the value you deliver to your customers, and supported by your management team. That's why I wanted to take a few minutes going around the room to identify some other areas we can improve on, things we can be doing better, or what I can be doing for you which would further support this ultimate objective."

4. *You want to provide some much-needed motivation by acknowledging and reigniting the personal power people may have forgotten they have.* "Jett, I know you've been in sales for a while now. And I know this isn't the first time you've felt a bit deflated when you saw your month-end numbers, especially with your work ethic and all of the effort you've put forth. Sometimes, with all of the things we have control over, there still exists those other market conditions, which we can't control. That's why I continually *want for* you to be able to manage and honor the process you've

put in place, which has always been proven to work well for you, but to do so without the additional stress and pressure you seem to be piling on yourself lately. In other words, it looks like there's an opportunity for you to shift back to being more process driven without pushing so hard for results, which, as you've seen, will come naturally when you honor your process."

5. *You want to open up the possibility to have a conversation about coaching someone around an area they have been struggling with.* "This may come as a friendly reminder to you but I felt it was important enough to mention. Due to the type of product we sell and the market we go after, you're going to find that it may take a little longer for prospects to open up to you and want to foster a relationship, especially when these prospects have been working with the same vender for as long as they have been. What I *want for* you is to feel confident that you have the resources you need the next time you are confronted with a hostile prospect, so that you can turn a potentially explosive situation into a new selling opportunity, similar to the situation you found yourself in last week."

Once you start using the wanting for statement more consistently in your communication, you will notice how much more open people will be to hearing and digesting your messages, especially the ones they may have a natural inclination to resist. A wanting for statement is a powerful communication tool for coaches. It reinforces the stand you have chosen to take for your salespeople in a quick and efficient way while simultaneously challenging them to bring out their best.

## THE "I'M SENSING THAT" STATEMENT

When talking with your salespeople, did you ever get the feeling that they were not being 100 percent honest and up front with you? Managers tell me they really don't have a foolproof approach for extracting the truth, the real truth, out of someone without sounding either confrontational, distrusting, or pushy.

Instead of confronting salespeople about their concerns, managers do not question what their salespeople say and try to do their best to work out a solution, even though they know that the salespeople are holding something back.

After all, what could you say to a salesperson who you feel is not being forthright? "I think you're lying to me or not telling me everything." This is certainly not an approach I would endorse. Aside from putting the salesperson on the defensive, there's a good chance that this approach will destroy any chance of getting this person to open up.

How can you tell when there's something else a salesperson may be holding back from you? Here are some signs.

1. A sudden change in performance.
2. A sudden change in attitude, disposition, or work ethic.
3. A sudden change in behavior around the office, among coworkers, or toward you.
4. A reluctance or unwillingness to do something that was typically done before.
5. A failure to honor certain commitments which were never a problem in the past.
6. A noticeable misalignment between intentions and actions (for example, you schedule a meeting to provide some additional coaching and training and the salesperson keeps canceling or delaying it).

Maybe you're in the process of screening a new candidate for a sales position. The person seems to have a clear interest in the position, and you have a keen interest in hiring him, but there are some inconsistencies in his resume that make you question his long-term commitment.

If you have ever run into a situation like this, there's a strong chance that there's something the person isn't telling you. Here's a great way to find out what's really going on.

*Use Your Sense.* If a salesperson makes a statement (or fails to confirm or do something for you), listen to your instincts. Remember that the real concern may be two to three questions deep. Here's an example of how you can use the "I'm sensing that" approach to bring out additional information from your salespeople that you feel is being held back.

You: "Rob, based on our conversation a couple of weeks ago, do you still agree that it would be to your advantage for us to meet one to one so that you can get the personalized coaching and attention needed to handle some of the challenges you're running up against?"

Rob, the Salesperson: "Yes. I definitely see the benefits."

You: "Well, we've been attempting to get together since then, but it seems that something always gets in the way of our meeting. I know you're working hard to bring in a few more accounts before the quarter is over, but *I'm sensing that* there may be something else that's getting in the way of scheduling this coaching session so that we can work through some of these challenges together. Is that true (or, is there any truth to this/how I'm feeling)?"

Rob, the Salesperson: "Well, actually . . . "

And now, let the truth be known! Rob may have had a bad experience with another manager, is reluctant to admit he is a little intimidated by this process, fears his job security, is worried what other people may think, doesn't want to hurt your feelings by saying "No," or wasn't motivated by a reason compelling enough that would make this a priority. Whatever his reasons, you will never discover what they are without digging deeper.

Notice the question I ask does not put the salesperson on the defensive. I'm not accusing him of anything or making him wrong. I'm not offending him by pointing my finger and playing the blame game. I do *not* say, "Every time we plan to meet, you keep rescheduling with me." "You told me that you were going to call me but you never did." "You said we would be able to get together for a few minutes." "I told you I was going to call you on Friday at 9 A.M. and when I did, you weren't there."

Instead, here's one of the very few times during a coaching relationship when you can actually make it about *you*: your feelings, that is. By beginning a statement with "I'm sensing," you acknowledge how you are feeling. Then ask the person for help in determining whether your feeling is, in fact, valid.

This approach gives your salespeople the space and permission they need to share their real concerns without feeling pressured. Of course, there are those occasions when the person is actually telling you the truth or simply isn't interested in having a one to one with you. That's why it's critical to tap into your intuition and trust your instincts to determine how deep you actually want to dig to uncover the truth about what is stalling your ability to create a breakthrough in your salespeople.

Finally, let me introduce the last type of manager we will be discussing and the icon of executive sales coaching worthy of imitating: The Proactive Manager.

## THE PROACTIVE MANAGER

These managers are models for what all managers should aspire to become as they move forward in their careers. The Proactive Manager encompasses all of the good qualities that the other types of managers possess, yet without all of their foibles and pitfalls.

Proactive Managers are the ultimate executive sales coaches, adopting the positive characteristics from each management type. For every manager who displayed a competency worthy of developing or imitating, Proactive Managers embraced each one, taking the time to collectively make these strategies and principles their own.

Here are the characteristics that this ideal manager embodies, as well as the ones for you to be mindful of and develop yourself. The Proactive Manager possesses the:

- Persistence, edge, and genuine authenticity of the Pitchfork Manager
- Confidence of the Presumptuous Manager
- Enthusiasm, passion, charm, and presence of the Pontificating Manager
- Drive to support others and spearhead solutions like the Problem-Solving Manager
- Desire to serve, respectfulness, sensitivity, nurturing ability, and humanity of the Passive Manager
- Product and industry knowledge, sales acumen, efficiency, focus, organization, and passion for continued growth just like the Perfect Manager

The Proactive Manager encompasses all of the positive characteristics and qualities that encapsulate the ultimate manager and coach, as well as the additional skills and coaching competencies that every manager needs to develop. The Proactive Manager is a truly authentic person. The Proactive Manager relinquishes all of the self-imposed pressure to perform or look good and manages a healthy coaching mindset (refer to Chapters 1, 2, and 3).

Proactive Managers take the necessary time with each salesperson during every coaching session. They have a path to follow that encompasses their entire coaching system. They take the time to craft the right questions in order to get the salespeople involved in the conversation. Instead of memorizing certain canned responses, Proactive Managers seek to deliver value in every conversation and honor what is in their salespeople's (and company's) best interests, regardless of whether their decisions are what would serve them best personally. As such, they encounter very little resistance and only minor pushback when it's time for them to hold their people accountable for the goals and results they are responsible for.

Most important, the Proactive Manager is a genuine, humble leader who embraces her vulnerabilities. She is driven by her higher self to deliver value and make an impact instead of being driven by her ego. The Proactive Manager is true to herself without attempting to become someone she is not. She uses the tools and approaches that complement and align with her personality, values, strengths, and talents from which the ultimate sales coach can emerge.

## A VIEW FROM THE SIDELINES

The last several chapters of this book have provided you with the tools and skills that will enable you to become a true Proactive Manager and coach for your sales team.

To truly assimilate, digest, and put into practice all of the content so that it becomes second nature to you requires consistent reinforcement over the entire life of your career. That's why I suggest starting out practicing and developing just one manageable strategy, principle, or skill at a time.

Keep in mind, persistence and discipline are the core characteristics in your success formula that will enable you to become the ultimate sales coach.

To develop some momentum in your career, start by listing just three things that you can do differently today that would impact your success and the success of your sales team. If you feel three is too aggressive, then pick just one strategy or principle you can focus on or skill you want to develop further. It could be something you haven't tried such as fine-tuning your listening or asking your salespeople better coaching questions. It could be a commitment to embracing some of the coaching principles we discussed. Or, you could begin by recognizing when you may be making your salespeople wrong and start making them right.

The communication checklist that follows contains a list of concepts and communication strategies that you can work on. This checklist is a guide to assess and track your growth and manage the areas you want to improve on in order to upgrade the effectiveness and power of your communication.

If you are still unsure about the type of manager that you most resemble, try this. Tape yourself (audio and/or video) conducting a sales meeting, delivering a presentation, or facilitating a coaching session with one of your salespeople. You can also ask your peers what type of manager they think you most closely resemble. I'm sure they would be happy to tell you. Regardless, you now have enough new material and areas of opportunity to help you develop and fine-tune your approach and management style that will lead to sales coaching mastery.

# THE COMMUNICATION STYLE OF THE EXECUTIVE SALES COACH

## 30 Days to Masterful Communication

FOUR-WEEK PROGRESS GRID

Week of: _____

| Category/Actions | Monday | Tuesday | Wednesday | Thursday | Friday |
|---|---|---|---|---|---|
| 1. LISTENING | | | | | |
| Uncovered the Filter in My Listening | | | | | |
| Encouraged Silence | | | | | |
| Resisted the Rebuttal | | | | | |
| Focused on the Message vs. the Messenger | | | | | |
| Made a Person Feel Heard/Used Clarifiers | | | | | |
| Began Listening *for* Certain Things vs. Listening *to* Someone | | | | | |

| | | | | |
|---|---|---|---|---|
| **2. LEARNING** | | | | |
| Allowed Contribution/Received Value in Conversation | | | | |
| Learned from Others during Conversation | | | | |
| Shifted Problem-Oriented Questions to Solution-Oriented | | | | |
| **3. COMMUNICATION ACCOUNTABILITY** | | | | |
| Took Full Responsibility for the Way the Message I Sent Was Being Heard | | | | |
| Avoided/Recognized Costly Assumptions | | | | |
| Identified the Coaching Gap | | | | |
| Questioned for Clarity/Checked Communication/Got Complete | | | | |
| Delegated Outcomes vs. Dump Problems | | | | |
| Created Ownership of Outcome and a Completion Date | | | | |

*(continued)*

| | | | | |
|---|---|---|---|---|
| **4. DETACH FROM THE OUTCOME** | | | | |
| Opened Up to New Outcomes/Possibilities/Ways of Doing Things | | | | |
| Shifted the Focus/Agenda from Me to Them | | | | |
| Focused On Being Present vs. Living in the Past or Future | | | | |
| Let Go of Controlling the Outcome | | | | |
| Respectful of Others and Trusted Their Abilities and Problem Solving Skills | | | | |
| **5. COMMUNICATION STYLE** | | | | |
| Asked Others How I Come Across and Learned from It/Accepted the Message | | | | |
| Paused before Responding vs. Reacting | | | | |
| Exercised Choice in Response to Events/Others | | | | |

| | | | | |
|---|---|---|---|---|
| **6. EMPOWERING OTHERS** | | | | |
| Motivated through Pleasure vs. Consequence | | | | |
| Gave Authentic Measurable Acknowledgment | | | | |
| Asked Questions vs. Provided Solutions | | | | |
| Honored People's Individuality | | | | |
| Made People Right vs. Wrong | | | | |
| **7. EXEMPLIFYING MASTERFUL COMMUNICATION** | | | | |
| What I've Modeled for Others | | | | |
| Took a Stand for People—Used the Coaching Edge | | | | |
| Managed Healthy Conflict | | | | |
| Set Boundaries and Honored Standards | | | | |
| Embraced and Modeled Vulnerability | | | | |
| Used a *Wanting for* Statement | | | | |
| Used an *I'm Sensing That . . .* Statement | | | | |

*(continued)*

| 8. RESULTS/SUCCESSES | |
|---|---|
| Monday | |
| Tuesday | |
| Wednesday | |
| Thursday | |
| Friday | |

**Directions:**

1. Make four copies of this sheet, one for each week.

2. Write down a goal that you want to accomplish and can control. Determine the appropriate actions to take or skill to develop in order to achieve that goal.

3. As you successfully work on a competency, strategy, or an action in thinking, check it off under the corresponding day of the week. Create a daily list of coaching habits that includes specific actions or strategies rather than trying them just once.

4. Each day, under number 8, list the surprise, result, or benefit from taking a different action to upgrade your communication.

5. Congratulate yourself for upgrading your communication! Consistency in thinking ⇒ Consistency in Action ⇒ Greater Results!

## CHAPTER 9

# Facilitating an Effective Coaching Conversation

## PREPARING FOR THE COACHING SESSION

Coaching is an organic conversation. The greatest coaching sessions often start with focus on a specific agenda, then can evolve naturally to a different agenda entirely, depending on the flow of the conversation and the root of the issues at hand.

When it comes to structuring a coaching session with someone, like anything else, the pendulum of preparation can swing both ways. Too much structure and rigidity inhibits creativity, flexibility, and the ability of the coach to quickly shift gears and expose a new opportunity that did not exist before, whereas too little structure can lead to unfocused conversations with little substance, especially with a salesperson who has a tendency to pontificate, dominate conversations, skirt or avoid certain issues or questions, and talk in circles.

If you recall from previous chapters, it is the client or the person you are coaching who creates the agenda, not the coach. This chapter covers the delicate balance of preparation and structure that you can use for every coaching session you facilitate. This proven approach will maximize the value that each salesperson will experience during every coaching session.

## THE ANATOMY OF A COACHING SESSION

The following steps to take in a coaching session are more guidelines than concrete, rigid laws. After you coach for awhile, you will find that the majority of your coaching sessions will follow this outline without any conscious effort on your part.

I've noticed throughout my coaching that the nine steps below flow naturally from the very beginning of the coaching session all the way through to its conclusion. Keep in mind that the majority of these steps can be accompanied by the questions listed in the Appendix.

1. *Opening*. Small talk. Casual conversation about their week and how they are doing/feeling.
2. *Confirm expectations*. Verbally set the expectation of the coaching call. What do they expect from you and what do they want to walk away with or learn?
3. *Review prep form*. Review the prep form and each question. Discuss their weekly progress in greater detail.
4. *The L.E.A.D.S. coaching model*. (See page 176.) The five steps to facilitate a coaching conversation. This phase also includes the direct coaching you feel is appropriate, the solution you can deliver that would solve the person's issue, or the resources you can provide.
5. *Identifying value and their take away*. Confirm that expectations have been met. Ask what new insight or way of thinking the person is leaving with, a skill that needs further development, a more positive feeling that has surfaced, a solution solved, or a problem eliminated.
6. *Take their pulse*. Conduct a brief recap regarding how they are feeling thus far. What do they want you to do more of or less of during the next call? Are you sensing excitement or resistance?

7. *Action steps and fieldwork.* Outline the measurable steps they are committing to taking, tasks they are willing to complete, conversations they say they will have, or results they plan on achieving by the next coaching session.

8. *Schedule next meeting.* Set the time and length for the next coaching session.

9. *Conclusion.* Wrap up the call or the meeting with any final thoughts or additional areas of opportunity to coach on during the next coaching session.

Now that we've broken down the steps to facilitating a coaching session, here's your introduction to a tool that your salespeople will use in preparation for every coaching session they have with you.

## THE COACHING PREP FORM

Managers are on a never-ending quest to leverage their time and efforts. Yet, ironically, I see many managers facilitate an hour-long coaching session with a salesperson that, with just a little more preparation, could have been shortened by about 30 minutes and still achieved the same or an even better outcome.

You can leverage the time you invest in each coaching session by using what I refer to as a Coaching Prep Form. This prep form is used as a way to help both you and your salespeople identify the areas they want to focus on during every coaching session they have with you.

Here's how it works. Each salesperson completes this prep form and sends it back to you prior to your scheduled coaching session.

There are several advantages to using this prep form. First, it provides you with a written update regarding the progress they are making, the areas where they are stuck, the opportunities they have in front of them, and, most important, the topic they want to address during their time with you. Having them organize their thoughts on paper will save you at least 15 minutes in every session.

Second, the prep form builds in deeper accountability, for you and for your salespeople. The prep form tracks the progress of your salespeople and outlines their specific and measurable goals and objectives. It builds further accountability, because it enables your salespeople to document clearly their expectations of every coaching session, their weekly wins and challenges, as well as what they are willing to commit to doing from one week to the next.

Conversely, if you did not have a prep form to refer to during a coaching call and no expectations are set, how will you and the person you are coaching know they are being met? Now, the salesperson can blame you for not meeting their objectives or getting the value they expect, avoiding the accountability piece that the prep form establishes.

Here's an example of a prep form that I use with my clients. Keep in mind, this is only a template, so take the time to fine-tune this form so that it fits best for you and for your situation.

The prep form provides a way for your salespeople to organize their thoughts, focusing on what they want to accomplish during their time with you. This way, they are sure to leave each meeting feeling they have made significant and measurable progress around what matters most to them.

Planning for your coaching sessions is critical, and it is important to make sure you and your salespeople have a clear understanding of how to make the most out of this form as well as each coaching session. Rather than simply telling them to fill it out, take a few moments to review the form together, going over each question and the reasons why it's important that they answer them all.

---

## THE EXECUTIVE SALES COACH

### Precall Plan, Objectives, and Expectations
### of a Coaching Call

Prep Form

Instructions: For each coaching session, please respond to each of the following questions and send to me pasted in the body of an e-mail. This form takes approximately 10 minutes to complete. Concentrate and be precise when completing this form. Please try to complete and e-mail this form the day before the scheduled call. Save the original e-mail as a master and work from copies of this form each week. It will expedite our work, maximize the value of our time, and keep us focused on the goals and results that matter most to you.

1. ACHIEVEMENTS:
    a. What I have accomplished since our last call. (Wins; insights; improved attitude; personal/professional successes, even the little ones.) What change in behavior, attitude, an added system, a process upgrade, an eliminated toleration, greater time/self-management, upgraded boundaries, standards, beliefs, etc., contributed to success in other areas of your life or career? Everything is connected, even if you didn't intend it to be.
    b. What upgrades/changes have you made in your thinking, attitude, or perception or are continuing to manage? (About yourself, others, your career/business, etc.) Have you eliminated or reduced the impact of a toxic/negative belief that's been holding you back from living up to your potential?
2. FOCUSED INTENTION AND EXPECTATION: I want to use my time with the coach to: (List specific and measurable outcomes, a strategy or skill to develop/improve, insights, guidance, or results you're seeking.)
3. ACCOUNTABILITY: On a scale of 1–10, where 10 represents full accountability, how would you rate yourself this week? (This doesn't mean that you're getting everything done, but that you're taking ownership of your life, career, and situations that are showing up in your life. We can discuss more.)
    a. #_____
    b. Commitment most proud of honoring. Where were you most responsible this week?

*(continued)*

    c. What I said I would have completed/worked on but didn't. Where were you most irresponsible this week? (Diversionary tactics/avoidance behavior, excuses, procrastination?)

4. FEARLESS: On a scale of 1–10, where 10 represents being fearless, not stressed/anxious, toleration free and not overwhelmed, how would you rate yourself this week? (Not that these feelings won't ever be present in your life; they will be. I'm referring more to how you are responding to them in a healthier, more productive way so that you manage the fear or experience, make it your ally, and grow from it rather than being consumed by it or having fear paralyze your efforts or rob you of your peace of mind. In other words, if you "Feel the fear and do it anyway," give yourself a 10!)

    a. # _____

    b. The consistent fear that gets in my way the most is _____.

    c. A fear that I've conquered or I'm working on conquering or keeping at bay:

5. CHALLENGE: The challenge(s)/problem(s) I am facing now. (What are you still currently putting up with that's dragging you down? What new or existing tolerations are surfacing that are getting in your way?)

6. GOALS AND OPPORTUNITIES: The opportunities and new possibilities that are available to me right now.

7. COMMITMENTS: What I commit to accomplishing by the next call: (This can also be cocreated during our call.)

8. OUTLOOK:

    a. Do you feel that the actions/tasks, activities that you had engaged in this week are moving you closer to your goals? Are you engaging in the right activities consistently?

    b. If not, where do you feel that you got sidetracked/diverted? What's getting in the way?

> c. What would you like your coach to do more of/less of during and after each call?
>
> 9. ACTIVITY/TACTICAL: Are you honoring your routine, your processes, your vision, your values?
>
> 10. SHADOW COACHING: Here's an opportunity for you to list specific clients, prospects, coworkers, or situations you've experienced that you would like to receive some specific coaching around. How did you handle a particular situation and what, if anything, could you have done to achieve an even better, more productive outcome?
>
> *Anything else?

## STRATEGIC COACHING QUESTIONS

The questions listed in the prep form have served my clients well throughout the years. However, in some instances, you may find that you need to ask more questions or different types of questions to gather additional information in order to make each coaching session count. Here are some additional questions I've used in other prep forms, depending on the goals and objectives that different clients have hired me to work on with them. The following questions can be used when there's a need to gather more tactical and specific information regarding a person's selling efforts.

1. Are you working off a template when cold calling and following up, do you typically wing it, or does your approach depend on who you're calling?
2. How many unique voice mails do you use? How effective have they been for you?
3. How many calls per day do you need to make to reach your sales goals?
4. How many are you averaging per day?
5. Do you call at different times throughout the day? Are you tracking this?

6. What are your closing percentages? (If you present to/ meet with 10 prospects, how many become clients?)

7. When cold-calling, how many questions do you typically ask on each cold call? Are these written out in front of you so when you ask them, the questions are precise each time?

8. My biggest challenge as it relates to cold calling is:

9. My biggest challenge as it relates to delivering a presentation and closing the sale is:

10. My biggest challenge as it relates to best managing my day and my time is:

11. The top three initial objections I hear when cold calling are:

12. The top three objections I hear when closing the sale are:

13. My biggest challenge as it relates to developing and maintaining a positive attitude and high level of self-confidence is:

14. My biggest fears/doubts I have when selling, cold-calling, or presenting to a prospect are:

15. The biggest hurdle that distracts me or prevents me from achieving my goals and the next level of success is:

## THE L.E.A.D.S. COACHING MODEL

If you refer back to the earlier section in this chapter entitled "The Anatomy of a Coaching Session," step 4 references the L.E.A.D.S. Coaching Model. Essentially, this five-step process encapsulates all of the coaching skills, strategies, tools, and principles that we have discussed throughout this book thus far.

L.—Listen

E.—Evoke

A.—Answer/Respond

D.—Discuss

S.—Support

Fast forward to the actual coaching session. There you are, in your office, face to face with the salesperson you are about to coach. Other than the questions you can use to open up a coaching conversation (see Appendix), how do you drive the conversation forward? The L.E.A.D.S. coaching model will guide you through a conversation in a natural way, allowing for a high degree of flexibility to dance within this conversation without feeling so structured or regimented in your coaching efforts.

## A FIVE-STEP PROCESS TO FACILITATING A COACHING CONVERSATION

**Step 1. Listen**   Listen for what the person is saying and not saying instead of filling in the gaps with faulty assumptions. Be silent, even if there is something you could say. Where ineffective listening can cause many breakdowns, effective listening enhances relationships, increases the level of trust between you and your employees, improves your credibility, gives you more confidence in dealing with certain situations, and makes the person you are communicating with more willing to listen to you.

**Step 2. Evoke**   Ask questions to gain more information or to clarify something. The art of coaching is the art of asking the right questions. Therefore, focus more on the question than on the answer. The question *is* the answer. This will prevent you from responding without substance, facts, or specific steps to back up a solution.

**Step 3. Answer/Respond**   Gain further clarity of a situation and what people are saying and feeling. Make them feel that you not only heard but also understood them by using *clarifiers* (Chapter 7). Acknowledge them for sharing what they said. Maintain the focus of the discussion. Even though you may have uncovered several symptoms of their condition or situation, you still want to reconfirm the actual source of the problem or the specific result they are seeking.

**Step 4. Discuss**   When you have clarified the intended message, the natural segue is to then talk about what was said. Discuss the situation. Ask more questions. Listen. This step enables you to go deeper into what your salespeople most need and want. Ask more questions to gather the relevant information you need to best serve them. What have you heard? Where are they stuck? What role did they play in creating this situation? What do they want most? Is it a blind spot, a story, a S.C.A.M.M., a coaching issue, or more of a training issue? In order for your salespeople to learn how to resolve their own issues, they usually need to hear it in their own words, rather than being told what their problem is or what they should be doing. Although there is a place for the coach to provide a solution, more information still needs to be gathered before doing so.

**Step 5. Support**   When you have uncovered what it is your salespeople truly need or want, here's the opportunity to provide support. Supporting is often the *how* in the conversation. What is the strategy needed to achieve the desired outcome? How have they handled this issue before? What's their take on the changes that they need to make in order to produce the results they seek? Provide the resources and structure they need to succeed or make changes. This can come in the form of sharing your observations; making a direct request of them; presenting them with a challenge, a task, or an action step; sharing the truths you see which they may not; offering further insight into their situation; providing the additional training around a certain area or skill that requires further development; collaborating with them on a step-by-step solution or strategy; even presenting an alternative way that they could look at their situation (adjusting their assumptions, beliefs, attitude, or suggesting they make a mental shift in their thinking).

When supporting your salespeople, give the issue, challenge, or request for a solution back to them in the form of a question in order for them to generate the solution on their own.

- How do you envision accomplishing this?
- What ideas do you have to resolve this situation completely?
- What do you feel you need?
- Why is that so important to you?
- What skill, if you possessed it or mastered it, would solve this ongoing problem?

- What are three steps you can take this week toward achieving this goal?
- Is there another way you can look at this?
- How can I best assist you around this?
- How do you want it to be?
- What can you do to make a positive change?
- What do you need to give up or let go of? (In your thinking or your behavior/habits.)
- Who do you need to be to achieve what you most want?
- What would be possible if . . .
- What is it going to cost you if you continue doing it that way?
- If you did know/have a solution, what would it look like?

At this point, you have all the tools you need to start developing your coaching skills and facilitating powerful coaching sessions with the intention of becoming a masterful coach. To provide you with some context and examples of how to use the strategies I've outlined in this chapter and what the conversation would actually sound like during a coaching session, what follows are three distinct conversations between a manager and a salesperson.

## THE MANAGEMENT CONVERSATION

The rest of this chapter details a situation that many managers experience with their salespeople: getting someone to be more efficient, organized, and prepared as it relates to managing their day as well as their sales activity. In other words, this manager is dealing with a salesperson who has a major issue with time management.

You will notice there are three distinct conversations. The first conversation outlines the dialogue that the majority of managers seem to have with their salespeople. The second and third conversations are coaching conversations, illustrating how you can coach your salespeople by applying what you have learned from this book in a way that creates a new possibility and solution.

Here is some background regarding this scenario. Jerry has been selling for LBI International for about seven years now. Jerry sells IT and telecommunications solutions for companies looking to either establish or build out their data centers, either as a fully outsourced solution or as the vendor who would handle only certain parts of a project with the rest of it kept in house.

Before working for LBI, Jerry had a history of being the top producer. Jerry's overall performance was not in question. However, Joe, his manager and Vice President of Sales, had noticed several key issues that relate to how Jerry manages himself and his time that have caused some problems. More specifically, Jerry was known for being late to meetings. Moreover, Jerry has been falling short on delivering the level of customer service and support that LBI strives to maintain and has built its reputation on. Not only has Joe noticed this himself but his customers have started to make comments. Joe received several voice mails from irritated customers who are not receiving the level of attention they expect, such as a simple returned phone call.

In addition to frequent tardiness, Jerry is constantly complaining about his ever-growing workload and tight schedule. Subsequently, Jerry fails to honor the majority of his commitments. The longevity of the sales cycle, the overall dollar amount of each sale, and the need for a formal written proposal compounds Jerry's time management dilemma even further, as he struggles to meet the agreed-upon deadlines for delivering proposals. In the spirit of finding a solution, Jerry has even inquired about getting a personal assistant that he could share with some of the other top salespeople.

What follows is a conversation between Joe and Jerry, before Joe developed his own coaching approach. This resembles a typical conversation between a salesperson and a manager. To set the scene, Jerry was working at his desk in the corporate office, the same office where Joe also works. Joe walked up to Jerry's desk and proceeded to initiate the following conversation.

### SCENARIO 1: A CONVERSATION WITH A MANAGER

> **Joe:** Hey, Jerry, I want to talk to you about something. Do you have a minute?
>
> **Jerry:** Sure, what's up?
>
> **Joe:** Well, I've been reviewing some of your statistics and activity for the last month. As it relates to hitting your

numbers, it looks like things are going well for you. So, congratulations on that.

Jerry: Thanks.

Joe: But here's the thing. Some clients are telling me that you're not even returning their calls.

Jerry: Listen, I'm doing the best I can, given the resources I have available to me. Which clients called and complained?

Joe: Let's take a look at my messages. Well, I see here just in the last two days I've gotten calls from Megatech as well as from Guardian Financial and one more here from Kane Investments. Why are you having such a problem getting back to these clients?

Jerry: I don't know why they are calling you. I've spoken to all of them over the last few weeks.

Joe: Jerry, I'm here to help you. It looks like you're struggling a bit with managing your day and honoring your commitments. What's getting in the way?

Jerry: Joe, you've been working for this company a long time. You even had my position so you know better than anyone the pressure and demands of this sales position. Between client service and managing their expectations, writing proposals, the training and orientation I have to provide for new clients to help set up their data center, initial meetings and presentations that I'm scheduling with new prospects, and the hours of cold calling I still try to fit in each week in order to keep my sales funnel full with new prospects, it's just tough to find a way to balance it all. At least I'm still hitting my numbers though.

Joe: Well, based on what I'm hearing you say, it sounds like you need to be more diligent in how you structure your day. Do you think there are some improvements that you can make around this?

Jerry: I'm sure there are, Joe, but that's not going to change my workload, and it's not giving me any more room to delegate some of these things that are taking up so much of my time and causing a lot of these problems. I'm not even referring to the tasks and responsibilities that only I can do effectively. The fact is, some of the client service issues and calls I get on a daily basis can be handled by an assistant. This would save me a ton of time that I could then use to focus on more sales activity and client retention.

Joe: I know you mentioned wanting to see if there's an opportunity to hire someone in an assistant role to support you. At this point, Jerry, let's not bank on this as an option. As you know, it's all about whether there's room in the budget to make this happen. Instead, I want you to focus on the things that you can control, which is how you're managing your day. Is that fair enough? Are you willing to do that for now?

Jerry: Sure.

This concludes the first dialogue between Joe and Jerry. So, what have you just heard? You may even read through this dialogue and think, "Hey, that's exactly how the majority of my conversations sound with my staff!" Maybe you read this and thought there's nothing wrong with Joe's approach. Joe was positive and was focused on finding some type of solution for Jerry. Finally, Jerry did acknowledge time management was an issue and did commit to making some changes based on his conversation with Joe.

Through the eyes of many managers, Joe facilitated a very normal and seemingly productive conversation with Jerry. Did Joe make any glaring management mistakes? Not exactly. And that's the point. Joe didn't make any serious mistakes. However, this typical approach does nothing to create a new outcome or possibility. What it does is enable the manager to continually manage mediocrity which generates mediocre results.

Making the shift from manager to coach is more about subtleties in dialogue, language, and approach that makes the difference between creating a breakthrough or conducting just another superficial conversation with your salespeople. The majority of conversations between managers and salespeople elicit no new outcome, whereas an effective coaching conversation creates accountability; a tactical, actionable solution; and fuels continued momentum, which leads to positive change.

## THE COACHING CONVERSATION

Now, we're going to explore this conversation using more of the sales coaching model rather than the traditional management model. Here's the same situation, yet an entirely different dialogue between Joe and Jerry. The difference is that in this scenario, Joe has already worked with his executive sales coach on developing his own coaching skills, language, coaching questions, and approach.

As you read through this, take the time to identify the steps I've outlined earlier in this chapter when facilitating a coaching conversation as well as the steps listed in the L.E.A.D.S. coaching model.

### SCENARIO 2: A CONVERSATION WITH A COACH

Joe: Hi Jerry. I know you're busy, but I was hoping we could talk for a few minutes. I've noticed how hard you're working, and I have a couple of ideas I want to run by you about making your workload more manageable and less overwhelming. Do you have some time now to discuss this?

Jerry: Sure, Joe. What were you thinking?

Joe: As you know, much of my tenure here has been spent in your position as senior consultant, doing what you are doing today. I remember the intense workload: all of the daily tasks and responsibilities I needed to manage.

Jerry: (Jokingly) And you'd be happy to know that the workload has not changed since you left the position.

Joe: I'm confident it hasn't. If anything, it's become more intense especially with the rise in the number of competitors we have now knocking on the same doors that we are.

Jerry: I agree with you there.

Joe: When I was selling, I didn't have any one specific manager I reported to who supported me. At that time, the company was fairly young, and we were going through some rapid and often turbulent growth. I learned most of my lessons through the painful on-the-job approach and through my experiences—both the successes and failures. And at times I'd be the first to admit, it got pretty stressful.

Jerry: Stress is an understatement. If I could bottle and sell my stress, I'd make millions because of the extra pounds I've taken off since taking on this job. Do you know that I'm putting in a 13-hour workday? It's now taking a toll on my personal life as well. And I still feel like I'm behind at times. Otherwise, I guess we wouldn't be talking now.

Joe: Well, it is one of the reasons why I wanted to talk to you today. Things are much different now, and what I want for you is to be able to leverage all of your great talents, continue your commendable levels of production, and I want you to be able to do so without the additional stress or pressure that seems to be taking a toll on your life and on your health, both mentally and physically.

Jerry: Okay, Joe, bring it on. What were you thinking?

Joe: Actually, I didn't have a specific agenda in mind. Instead, I was hoping we could explore how you're currently managing your workload and see if there's anything you're doing that we could identify as areas to improve upon. Is that fair?

Jerry: That's fair.

Joe: So tell me, Joe, how are you currently going about managing your week and all the responsibilities you have?

Jerry: I'm using the CRM software that you trained us in so that all of my appointments, my client and prospect meetings, as well as all of my contacts reside in there.

Joe: Okay, that's good. If you were to share with me three of your biggest challenges as it relates to managing your time and all of the tasks you're responsible for, what would they be?

Jerry: Well, first, there just isn't enough time in the day, period. And, as much as I continually run out of time at the end of each day, I still feel that things should be happening faster. I mean, some of these deals I've been working on really should be closing sooner than they are.

Joe: Thanks, Jerry. That really helps me understand your situation so I can best assist you. If I'm hearing you correctly, even though you're scheduling all of your client meetings and other appointments in your calendar, it's not leaving you with as much time as you feel you need in order to get to your other tasks. Is that accurate so far?

Jerry: Yes. And that doesn't include the other stuff that comes up unexpectedly and throws my entire day off. You know, things like clients calling with questions, dealing with certain emergencies, our own internal weekly meetings, and other issues that I have to take care of immediately that can't be put off.

Joe: Okay, Jerry, let me ask you this. How do you currently manage the other responsibilities you shared with me that you know still have to get done? You know, the things like prospecting and cold calling, returning client calls, making follow-up calls to prospects, working on proposals, doing your weekly sales reports, and any other administrative duties you have?

Jerry: How do I manage those things? As best I can, I guess. If I'm not on the road or at a meeting, that's the stuff I work on. Whenever I get a free minute.

Joe: Okay. I'm hearing that you are handling these additional tasks during the unscheduled times when you're not in a meeting or traveling. I'm curious, have you ever considered actually scheduling those tasks as a hard-line item into your schedule?

Jerry: Hmm. That's interesting. No, I have not.

Joe: It's a concept that I adopted myself years back. That is, to treat everything like an appointment. After all, if it takes up time, then consider it an appointment and schedule it. For example, what if you carved out certain time blocks throughout your day to handle each one of these additional tasks? Designate a time block for cold calling, for follow-up calls, for client service, for proposal writing, for administrative duties, and so on. Your routine can include not only the activities you're responsible for at the office but at home, which also take up time in your day. These activities can include getting ready in the morning, having breakfast, even your commute to work. Treating every activity as an appointment will allow you to plan better. It will also keep you honest about how much time you realistically have in your day and what you feel you can get done so that you can perform each task with a conscious intention. This way, instead of being interrupted by incoming calls or e-mails throughout the day, you now have specific portions of your day blocked out to make and return calls or respond to e-mails.

Jerry: I like the idea and would be willing to give this a shot. And being someone who is easily distracted, this would also help me focus on a specific task rather than look at my calendar when I have free time and ask myself, "What should I be doing now?"

Joe: It's great to hear how receptive you are to this. Let's take a quick inventory and see what your schedule would look like if we wove each of these activities into your day. Make a quick list of every task you feel you need to be engaging in on a daily basis. Then assign a time frame next to each activity that signifies how long you feel each activity would take or how long you would need to engage in that activity on a daily basis. For example, if it's something that you would be doing daily, such as cold calling, returning voice mails, or responding to e-mails, how much time do you need to put aside for each activity? We can do this together right now, okay?

Jerry: (After writing out the list with Joe.) Wow, that's a pretty long list, longer than I thought it would be.

Joe: That's good, now you're being more realistic with how much you actually have to do and how much time you realistically need to get it all done. To further drive this point home, tally up the total amount of hours of daily activity that you just outlined and tell me what you come up with.

Jerry: Whoa! Based on these calculations, it would take me 17 hours every day to complete all of these tasks! No wonder I haven't been able to get through my daily to-do list. I've been trying to fit a 17-hour day into 13 hours.

Joe: Well then, congratulations! You've uncovered the first challenge that can be easily remedied by more accurate and realistic planning, now that you're aware of how long each activity takes and the time you have available each day to get through them.

Jerry: Now that I think about it, I've tried something similar to this before. Not exactly like this but similar, and I still wasn't able to get through everything in my schedule for the day. Any thoughts as to where the breakdown is here?

Joe: Can you say more about what you experienced before?

Jerry: Sure. Basically, I time blocked my day with the specific tasks, just like you've mentioned. However, even with all the planning I did, there were always other things popping up throughout the day that I didn't plan for that still needed to be handled. These additional distractions, responsibilities, challenges, or emergencies ate up a lot of my time—time that I had initially designated for the other activities I wanted to get through.

Joe: And how did you handle it?

Jerry: I got frustrated and decided this strategy didn't work for me. So I dropped it and went back to how I'm doing it today, even though I know it's not the best way to manage my time.

Joe: I can certainly appreciate that, Jerry. When I first tried time blocking, I ran into a few challenges myself until I uncovered another trap that I'll now share with you. That is, I wasn't planning for the unplanned. There are essentially three reasons why it's so challenging to adhere to a schedule. Number one, as we've discussed, not being realistic with the number of hours we have in a workday compared to the number of tasks and, as a result, having too many activities scheduled. Number two, not engaging in the right activities that support our goals. And, Number three, not planning for the unplanned. These unplanned activities, which I call *externalities*, often go unnoticed and fly under our radar screen when we attempt to map out our week. They have a tendency to eat up our days.

These externalities can also take on the form of errands, time on the phone, a new project or proposal that has a rapidly approaching deadline, a conversation with a coworker you didn't anticipate, unplanned meetings, client emergencies, delays caused by other people's inefficiencies; the list goes on. These things come along and blindside us. Then we wonder why we're not able to finish everything for the day. Since we don't know about the things that will unknowingly consume our time, imagine if you were actually able to plan for these things, these same tasks that often go unplanned. Jerry, if you were to take your best guess, how many hours out of each day would you say are consumed with these externalities?

Jerry: Hmmm. If I had to guess, being conservative, I'd have to say probably three hours every day.

Joe: Okay, now tell me again how many hours you put into your workday?

Jerry: Thirteen.

Joe: And how many hours of tasks and appointments are you currently planning for? That is, how many productive hours are you banking on each day?

Jerry: Thirteen.

Joe: Now that I've shared with you the idea of planning for these externalities that you say eat up about three hours out of your day practically every day, tell me, how many hours do you realistically have that you can plan for?

Jerry: (Pausing for a moment, then responding reluctantly.) So, you're telling me I only have ten hours that I can realistically plan for?

Joe: That's right.

Jerry: (A bit resistant.) But, Joe, if I start planning for only a ten-hour day, then think of all the other tasks that are not going to get done or tasks that I could plan for if I had a full 13-hour day.

Joe: Well, let's recap. How is the current process you are using working out for you?

Jerry: That is true. No, it's not working.

Joe: Then you have a choice. You can still plan for 13 hours of tasks but think about the position you're going to continually put yourself in.

Jerry: You mean the situation I've continually been in?

Joe: Exactly. That is, feeling overburdened and not getting everything done that's scheduled. And, knowing you, it seems you're pretty hard on yourself when you don't get everything done that you said you were going to. Is that a fair observation?

Jerry: It sure is.

Joe: Then, let's say you continue to manage your time the way you are currently doing it. May I ask what your current approach is costing you?

Jerry: Well, continuing to beat myself up and make myself wrong every day certainly isn't the greatest way to end a day. It affects my sanity and peace of mind. Then I also begin to question my ability and my skills, which, in turn, starts affecting my confidence. That's something I definitely can't afford especially when selling. And the kicker is, I still don't get through my entire list of daily tasks!

Joe: So, what's another way that you can look at this?

Jerry: I guess as much as I may hate to admit it, I can start being honest with myself and with how much time I realistically have each day to plan my activities. At least I know that wishing for more time isn't going to get me through all of my responsibilities.

Joe: And if you're being honest with how much time you have by building in the time for unplanned activities, what's the upside that you can start enjoying and benefits you'll experience from doing so?

Jerry: If I'm truly being realistic with my time and how much I can fit into my daily schedule, I think the advantage will be that, at the end of every day, I can actually see myself getting everything done on my list! Wow, what a refreshing feeling that would be and a new experience as well.

Joe: Great work, Jerry. At this point, do you have any questions or anything that I need to further clarify as it relates to what we've discussed so far?

Jerry: No, this has been very helpful and insightful. I'm looking forward to putting these new strategies in place starting today.

Joe: It's good to hear that you're motivated enough to make a change. I applaud your efforts and admire your desire to want to make these changes, but I know that change can be a little uncomfortable. Let's start wrapping up this conversation and reconfirm action steps. First, you're going to begin the process of building in realistic time blocks throughout each day in order to find a home for all of the activities you need to engage in each week. Second, you are also going to build in the appropriate amount of buffer time so that you are effectively planning for the unplanned activities. Are you willing to commit to doing this and getting the first draft of your new routine done by our next meeting?

Jerry: Yes, Joe, I am.

Joe: Is there anything else you're willing to commit to doing before our next meeting?

Jerry: Given my workload, let me begin by completing this task first. That works for me.

Joe: (After scheduling their next coaching session.) Okay, Jerry, we are all set. Now keep in mind, if you get stuck on any of the things we've discussed today, that's perfectly normal. So, keep me in the loop about your progress, and we'll continue this discussion next Friday at 11 A.M.

Jerry: Thanks, Joe. I'm looking forward to meeting with you then.

This concludes the first coaching session that Joe facilitated with Jerry. Notice how different it sounded compared to the traditional management conversation I initially transcribed. Joe asked many more questions and probed deeper so that Jerry can find the solution on his own, rather than being told what it should be or what he needs to do.

This coaching process will continue during the next meeting that Joe will have with Jerry, one week later after the initial coaching conversation you just read. Become more sensitive to the subtleties or opportunities for coaching that Joe picked up on throughout this dialogue and how he responded to what he heard. In addition, notice how Joe supported Jerry through his reluctance by giving him the time, the space, and the additional questions that Jerry needed to continue his transformational process.

## GOING DEEPER—BREAKTHROUGH COACHING

The following dialogue took place during the second coaching session between Joe and Jerry. Here's what transpired.

### SCENARIO 3: A CONVERSATION WITH ACTION

Joe: Hi, Jerry. Thanks for sending over the prep form for our meeting today. It looks as though you hit a couple of challenges during the process of implementing your new schedule and would like to use our time today to work through them. Am I reading this correctly?

Jerry: You sure are, Joe.

Joe: Tell me what happened this week.

Jerry: Well, as you know, we met last Friday. So, I spent the weekend putting my weekly routine together, time blocks and all. And on paper, it looks really good! I was excited to take it out for a test drive on Monday. Well, by Monday afternoon, my new schedule came to a screeching halt. It totally fell apart. Tuesday, I tried to get back on schedule and honor all of the time blocks I entered into my calendar. But the same thing happened again. And then again on Wednesday and Thursday. So here I am, thinking this process may not work for me.

Joe: Okay, first, I want to acknowledge your efforts. That's number one. Second, can you explain in more detail exactly what happened?

Jerry: Oh, I know exactly what happened, Joe. Basically, it was all client-related. That is, whenever a client called with a request, it took me away from whatever I was in the middle of doing. I just dropped what I was doing to respond to their requests.

Joe: So, were you able to honor the requests that your clients made?

Jerry: That's the irony. Some of the requests that my clients made required a strong demand of my time. And even with dropping some of the other items that were on my to-do list, I still had a hard time honoring every request. One client I had to call back and tell them that I wouldn't be able to get the paperwork they wanted until the next day due to some backlog in the accounting and legal department. Needless to say, they weren't happy to hear that, especially since I had already told them I'd have it ready sooner.

Joe: Hmm. Maybe there's something else going on. What type of requests were you getting from your prospects and clients that caused such a rift in your schedule?

Jerry: Let me think about that for a second. Well, there were two prospects that I had to get proposals to. Then there were two clients who requested a training schedule for their managers who are operating the new data center that we just set up for them. Oh, and then there was one client who just sucks all the life out of me, as well as my time. They wanted me to put together another proposal for some additional work that they weren't going to get around to doing until next year anyway. And they also had some technical questions for me.

Joe: Thanks for bringing me up to date. One quick comment regarding the client you just mentioned who had some technical questions. I thought you typically delegate those to your technical support team.

Jerry: Yes, I know, but I'm pretty good with the technical stuff so I figured I might as well just answer their questions. I just didn't realize that it was going to take me two hours on the phone to do so.

Joe: Jerry, I'm curious about something. When people, especially your customers, make a request of you, on a scale of 1 to 10, where a 10 means that you are very comfortable using the word "No" and a 1 means that you are very uncomfortable saying "No" so instead wind up saying "Yes," where would you score yourself?

Jerry: Oh, without a doubt I'm probably at about a 2.

Joe: Thanks. Now Jerry, in the spirit of alleviating this challenge, I'm going to share something with you that you may have a reaction to. You might even resist it at first but as your coach, it's my job to take a stand for you and share with you the truth as it relates to what I'm seeing. Is that okay?

Jerry: Hit me.

Joe: Well, Jerry. Given how quickly and how frequently your schedule becomes overbooked, it sounds as if you may be what I call a "Yesaholic." It sounds like you often say "Yes" when you're better off saying "No." As a result, you wind up making promises you can't keep or struggle to honor. To compound this problem, I'm also hearing that you have a hard time telling your customers the truth about how long a project may actually take or cost. And you've mentioned to me on several occasions that you withhold information that you know your customers need to hear for fear of a confrontation or losing a sale.

Jerry: That wasn't so bad. I'd probably have to agree with you on that.

Joe: Well, that's good news. Would you also agree to use the word "No" more often?

Jerry: Other than using it right now? I'd have to say "No," Joe. As you can probably guess, given my score and considering the week I've had, I'm not very comfortable using that word, especially when it comes to saying "No" to my clients and prospects.

Joe: What makes it so difficult for you? Let me ask this question in a different way. What is the story or meaning that you're assigning to the word "No"? What do you make it mean if someone says "No" or if you say "No" to your clients and prospects?

Jerry: What does it mean? It means I'm not serving them. It means I'm not taking care of them or making their needs a priority. It means that if I say "No," they then go! That is, my clients leave us and start going to our competitors. Besides, if you want people to work with you and like you, you have to continually please them and honor their requests, right? Otherwise, they will not want to have any type of relationship with you.

Joe: Really? Has this ever happened to you before?

**Jerry:** (Thinking for a moment, searching for an example.) Well, not exactly. (Remember the S.C.A.M.M.s in Chapter 3.)

**Joe:** So, this has never happened to you before but you operate as if it has and will again. I'm curious, Jerry. This belief you're harboring as it relates to saying "No." What do you think it's going to keep costing you if you continue in this manner?

**Jerry:** I'd have to say the cost is pretty significant, once I stop and think about it. Every time I say "Yes" when I really need to say "No," I get put further behind a pile of commitments I need to get through. I'm stressing myself out trying to fulfill all of the obligations I have.

**Joe:** (After a long pause, ensuring that he gave Jerry as much space as he needed to share his thoughts and feelings.) What else is true, Jerry?

**Jerry:** Maybe I've overcommitted myself a little too much. My quality of life is dwindling the more I try to make up for stretching myself too thin. And I still manage to upset some customers when I can't honor the commitments I've made to them. This, in turn, throws me into a heightened state of stress and worry.

**Joe:** Okay. So, are you open to a new way of thinking around this? A way in which you can say "No" so that it still serves your customers and actually enhances your quality of life as well as your efforts, rather than continually saying "Yes," which consumes and depletes you?

**Jerry:** You now have a willing participant.

**Joe:** Then, what if we looked at this through a different set of lenses and assign a different meaning to the word "No"? That is, can saying "No" imply something else? Something that may be more empowering for you, something that would make you much more comfortable saying "No," especially when you really need to?

**Jerry:** I'm not sure. What did you have in mind?

Joe: Well, you mentioned that the concerns you have around using the word "No" actually never materialize. The fear you have has never come to fruition with any clients thus far. If that is the case, then let's begin the process of upgrading your relationship with using the word "No."

Saying "No" is often perceived as a bad thing. After all, you don't want to say "No" and worry about letting someone down, looking bad, or losing a sale. The irony is, if you say "Yes" all the time to keep everyone happy and don't follow through with your commitments, you wind up creating what you wanted to avoid from the start. That is, letting others down and creating stressful situations that cost time, money, and problems by continually overcommitting and not delivering.

Jerry, I want you to think about the people in your life who you respect and admire. Do you have an image of that person or those people in your head?

Jerry: Yes, I do.

Joe: Great. Now, what in your opinion makes them so attractive? What about them do you respect and admire?

Jerry: I'm not exactly sure. Let me think on that for a second. Well, they have a very strong presence, they're incredible communicators, they are passionate, fun to be around, they are clear about their goals and what they want. . . .

Joe: And what about when it comes to how they manage their time and the boundaries they enforce to protect their time?

Jerry: Oh, they're great at that. Now that I think about it, they're actually very good at saying "No" because if they weren't, everyone would be taking advantage of their time. Plus, they do it in a way that does not come across as self-righteous or condescending, and it does not drive people away. If everyone was taking advantage of their time, then they wouldn't be able to maintain that delicate balance they have in their life, which I also find appealing. These people have a great work-life balance, which I guess wouldn't be possible if they allowed others to violate their time boundaries.

Joe: You are right about that. The people who we admire and hold in high regard are people who have strong boundaries which protect them from the damaging behavior of others. These people are great at saying "No." That's why you have an opportunity to upgrade your perception of saying "No." Based on what you've just shared with me, saying "No" is actually an attractive trait. It's an admirable characteristic that people respect because it portrays you as someone with strong boundaries and, most of all, someone who has a very deep respect for time: both your time and other people's time. Isn't that how you want to be known?

Jerry: Most definitely. And, for the most part, Joe, I don't even think about it when I say "Yes" all the time! It's just more of a habit, I guess. I just automatically say "Yes!" without thinking it through. How do I break this cycle?

Joe: That's a great question, Jerry, and a perfect transition for us to begin discussing the tactical component to this solution. The next time someone asks you to do something and that also includes the promises you make to yourself, first, we need to break your habit of reacting with the word "Yes." We need to build in a safeguard, a buffer of space before you respond to give you time to process the request, determine if you want to take it on, whether you can even deliver on it, and, finally, develop a realistic time line to do so. Rather than responding with an outright "No" to people's requests, there is a softer, more appealing way to say "No" that still protects your time and allows you to make more realistic commitments without continually overcommitting yourself. You can build in this buffer by using one of the following statements the next time someone asks you to do something or makes a request of you. "Let me check my schedule, and I will get back to you" or "Thanks for the opportunity. I will consider it."

Once you've given yourself the time to review what you can realistically deliver on, what questions can you ask yourself before you respond with your commitment?

Jerry: Hmm. Well, I guess I'd want to get clear on a few different things. The first thing that pops in my head is, do I actually have time to deliver on what this person wants from me? If so, when would that be, given a realistic scenario? Next, will I be able to even meet their requirements? And, finally, is this something that I really want to be doing or is it something I have to do because it's part of my job and my responsibility?

Joe: Perfect. Great questions! Let's take what you just created and fine-tune those questions into a more linear process you can refer to each time someone makes a request.

After practicing this a few times you'll quickly see the benefits, since your life will become easier and more simplified once you eliminate the problems that result from overcommitting. Remember, either you run your life or other people and circumstances will run it for you. How is all of this sitting with you so far, Jerry?

Jerry: Joe, this sounds awesome! I just need to practice this, as you said. I'm going to want to get these questions on paper and have them in front of me all day long until it becomes a habit for me.

Joe: That makes a lot of sense. Great thinking! So, are you ready to go out and start using these new tools?

Jerry: I am. I just . . . Never mind.

Joe: (Recognizing an opportunity to explore something else that Jerry was hesitant to share.) What is it, Jerry? Please, I really want to hear what you have to say. I'm sure it's important.

Jerry: I just want to make sure that even if I'm saying "No" more often and I'm being realistic in determining when I can deliver on some of these requests, I guess I still worry that I'm going to cut my timelines too thin.

Joe: Say more about that.

Jerry: It's just that when I set a time frame to accomplish a task or carve time out for certain meetings and activities, they always seem to go longer than expected. I guess I have a hard time determining how long things actually take, let alone the challenge of handling the interruptions and other distractions that take me away from doing what I initially set out to do.

Joe: So, what options do you see that might resolve this issue permanently and prevent you from cutting your timelines short and overcommitting yourself?

Jerry: I don't know.

Joe: (With the intention of empowering and challenging Jerry, Joe initially puts the question, as well as the solution to develop, back in Jerry's court rather than simply giving him the solution immediately.) I understand. However, if you did know, Jerry, what do you think the solution could be?

Jerry: Let's see. Well, if my issue is that I'm not getting through everything because I'm not giving each task the appropriate timeline it deserves, I guess I would have to extend the estimated timelines that I'm assigning to each task.

Joe: Now that is a great idea. How do you currently go about assigning timelines to your tasks and activities?

Jerry: Do you mean what kind of system do I have? There is none. It's more my best guess in terms of how long I think each task would take. For example, if I'm driving to an appointment, I would think to myself, "Okay, this appointment is in the next town over, which is 30 minutes away." So, what I would then do is leave 30 minutes before my appointment to arrive there on time. Or, if I have a client issue to resolve, I would think to myself, "Best-case scenario, this should only take about 20 minutes."

Joe: And how is this system of establishing timelines working for you?

Jerry: If the goal is to arrive fashionably late to practically every appointment and go beyond my estimated timelines, then it's working fabulous! And the bonus is, I get to stress out even more because I'm already under the gun feeling that I'm going to be late to a meeting or not deliver value to a client. No, it's not working and it's also not healthy to show up at an appointment in this frenzied state of mind. This certainly isn't helping my selling efforts.

Joe: You know, Jerry, it sounds as if you're planning for the best-case scenario when scheduling tasks and appointments into your calendar. Is that true?

Jerry: I would say that is true, yes.

Joe: (After uncovering the limiting belief Jerry has about planning and managing his time.) Then, since we have established that planning for the best case is not an effective strategy, I want you to try this on for a moment. This is going to challenge how you currently plan. Instead of planning for the best, what if you planned for the worst? Just think about what is preventing you from realistically honoring your timelines or getting in your way, even with all of your best intentions.

Jerry: (Thinking for a moment.) I got it! It's those externalities you mentioned at our last meeting, right?

Joe: Yes. If you start planning for the worst, what new possibility have you created for yourself?

Jerry: For one, I'm going to be much more sensitive to the roadblocks or as you call them, the externalities, that can potentially get in my way. If I can identify these with greater accuracy, I can then better plan for them and plan around them. Regardless, it seems to me that if I plan for the worst and if the worst case actually happens, I'm covered. And if it doesn't, I have succeeded in overdelivering on my commitments or have some additional time to focus on another task or activity that needs to get done.

Joe: Exactly. By building in the worst-case scenarios, you'll wind up budgeting for the unforeseen events that are going to happen anyway at one point or another, which would otherwise prevent you from meeting other people's expectations, achieving your daily goals, and completing your tasks.

Jerry: I just need to get my head out of the sand and start being more realistic and responsible in terms of how I plan my day.

Joe: Notice what we just did. First, we uncovered and identified a way of thinking, a belief you had that wasn't working for you. Next, we upgraded how you think by replacing the limiting belief that was at the core of all of your scheduling challenges with one that would best serve you. Now that you're open to this way of thinking, based on this concept of underpromising and planning for the worst, what would a tactical solution around this new way of thinking look like? (Referring back to an earlier point in the conversation.) You mentioned earlier that you really don't have a system that helps you accurately develop timelines for each task or estimates in terms of how long each task or appointment would take. What would your strategy or approach be for underpromising and planning for the worst? What would that look like for you? (Joe purposely asked this question three different ways to ensure he was giving Jerry more clarity behind the questions.)

Jerry: If I understand the concept, then tactically speaking, I would need to build in some sort of safeguard, should something throw off my best laid plans. Similar to what we did during our last meeting when we talked about planning for the unplanned. Am I on the right track, coach?

**Joe:** You most certainly are. It's exactly what you want to do: build buffer time into each activity. The lesson here is to create your schedule so it reflects a healthier and more respectful relationship with time that you have developed as a result of underpromising on personal and professional deadlines so that you can avoid overpromising and overcommitting yourself. To plan your day around the worst-case scenario, let's develop a gauge, a formula, that would help you more accurately plan a realistic workday, starting with a more accurate estimate of how long each task or activity actually takes. Planning for the worst and using this formula will provide you with the additional cushion you need, just in case your best laid plans get derailed by life simply getting in the way. So let's do a quick debriefing of our meeting today. How are you feeling at this point?

**Jerry:** I feel really positive. Like there's actually hope for me. That I can really change for the better regarding how I manage my time.

**Joe:** I am very excited for you and admire your willingness to take this on, even with the feeling of discomfort you're experiencing. Finally, if we were to reflect back on our session today, what are some of the key points and insights that you are taking away with you?

**Jerry:** There are definitely a few. First, overcoming my fear of saying "No" was a huge breakthrough. And so were the questions I can use to help determine if and when I could honor the requests that I take on as well as the ones that I am better off declining. What else? Oh, underpromising and planning for the worst was a huge mind shift for me. Finally, having a tactical approach to planning for the worst is something I'm going to start doing as soon as we're done with our meeting. You know, theory is good but tactical causes the change. Really great stuff, Joe. Thanks.

**Joe:** You are very welcome, Jerry. I look forward to hearing about your new wins as a result of implementing some of these things. Just keep in mind, this is all new to you so it will take a little time for it to come naturally. With anything new, you've got to give yourself some time to adjust. After all, if this was easy, we would all be able to figure this stuff out on our own. If you run into any snags or upsets along the way, please reach out and let me know, since my commitment is to support you throughout this entire process, okay?

Jerry: That sounds fine with me. I really appreciate the additional help on this. Thanks again, Joe.

Joe: It's my pleasure. Jerry. Have a great rest of the day!

Joe successfully used all five steps of the L.E.A.D.S. coaching model throughout both of his coaching conversations with Jerry. First, Joe *listened for* the real issues and challenges Jerry was facing rather than making speculative statements such as, "Here's what your problem is" or "I've seen this before and here's what you need to do." To get a strong handle on Jerry's thinking and how he felt about the challenges he was up against, Joe *evoked* more information through better questioning, rather than make blanket assumptions of what he perceived was the core issue. Next, Joe *answered/responded* to what Jerry had shared with him, while gaining confirmation through the use of clarifiers that he received the message Jerry intended, leaving no room for misunderstandings or communication breakdowns. Once this step was achieved, it provided Joe with an opportunity to *discuss* the core issues with Jerry, asking more questions and exploring in greater detail exactly where the breakdowns were occurring in Jerry's current approach to managing his day. Finally, Joe was able to offer a resolution for Jerry's challenges and provide the *support* he needed to generate better results, specifically around Jerry's relationship with time and the way he managed it. Notice that the final solution consisted of both training and coaching. This included a change in Jerry's actions and behavior as well as in his thinking.

## HOW MUCH COACHING IS ENOUGH?

How much personal attention is enough? How often should you meet with each salesperson on your team regarding ongoing coaching?

A client of mine was telling me about a problem he was having with one of his salespeople. At a yearly review meeting, it came out that there were some things that management had done early on in the year that truly upset this person. Even though it was discussed during the review, it was practically a year later when this problem was finally put on the table and addressed. This same problem could have been defused immediately if management was connecting with their team on a more consistent basis.

Unfortunately, by this time it was too late and the person wound up leaving the company. The real cost is that this person could have been a star producer if only his issues had been handled and responded to on a timely basis. If only management had demonstrated their commitment to support him through ongoing coaching.

You may be thinking that you don't always have time to meet with your team. But think about the things that are taking you away from coaching and meeting with your team in the first place. I guarantee many of the issues and problems you're dealing with are actually a result of *not* coaching and connecting with your team or an individual more frequently.

Think about what this problem cost my client: having a salesperson who was unhappy for an entire year? How do you think this affected his performance as well as his level of commitment to the company and to servicing his clients? How many selling opportunities do you think this cost the company? And what kind of gossip, which spreads like poison throughout any organization, was communicated by this salesperson to the other members of the team? What damage was done there?

There are several factors that could determine the frequency of your meetings and one-to-one sales coaching sessions with each person on your sales team. First, how many salespeople do you have? If you have a team of five or ten salespeople, it's much easier to manage your time and your schedule to accommodate weekly one-to-one meetings. A larger team is more of a challenge due to time constraints. While group or team coaching is also an option to fill in some gaps, there is still no substitute for providing individualized attention. I suggest a minimum of two individualized coaching sessions per month for each member of your team, even though weekly one-to-one coaching sessions would be ideal.

Frequency and consistency are key, just like when going to the gym. The more time you spend at the gym and the better you eat, the healthier you become. The same rule applies to building and maintaining the health of your career and your team.

Ultimately, you'll find part of the solution to uncovering how much coaching each salesperson needs or wants by asking your staff how much additional support they need to reach their goals faster and how frequently they would like to meet with you. Other than a turnaround situation or an issue that needs immediate resolution, it's up to you and each salesperson on your team to find the balance and determine the frequency of ongoing coaching.

CHAPTER

# The Art of
# Enrollment

## IT'S ALL ABOUT CONNECTION

I was sitting in a hotel restaurant having breakfast and preparing myself for a day of back-to-back meetings. While I was working on my iPhone, a waitress came over and introduced herself. "Hi, I'm Maya and I will be your server this morning. May I get you something to drink?" she inquired. We've all heard this question a thousand times when dining at a restaurant. But for some reason, the way she asked me was different. "Let's start out with some coffee and orange juice," I said. "Great!" she replied enthusiastically. "I'll get that for you right away and will be back to take your order."

"That's what it was!" I thought to myself. She was smiling. "Big deal, a smiling waitress," you may be thinking. "Waitresses are supposed to smile. This doesn't sound like something that's so incredibly noteworthy."

Normally it wouldn't be, but this smile was different. You see, it wasn't like one of those smiles you're forced to put on when talking with customers, but a truly authentic smile. I could tell because it was coming from the inside. This woman was genuinely happy. "Okay, duly noted and dismissed." I acknowledged the observation, yet felt compelled to get back to my e-mails as quickly as possible, before the coffee and food came.

Maya returned a few minutes later with my beverages and took my order. "Another one out and 20 more to go," I thought. I had just hit the Send button on the fourth e-mail I managed to respond to before someone else came over to my table and began talking to me. "Good morning!" a friendly voice said. This time, it wasn't the waitress, but someone else who worked at the restaurant. A middle-aged woman had intentionally stopped at my table rather than continuing to walk by. I returned her smile and wished her a hearty good morning as well. I wanted to get back to my e-mails. Apparently, this was not part of her agenda. She didn't let me.

"I love your glasses," she said.

"Thank you," I answered quickly, doing my best to be polite while trying to let her know I was a bit busy, knee-deep in my daily dose of morning e-mails. "Couldn't she see I was working?" I thought to myself. I sensed myself getting a little annoyed that my daily regimen was being disrupted, then challenged that feeling for a moment. In a world where we need to question people's motives, was this person being truly sincere? I gave her the benefit of the doubt and began to further engage her in conversation. She had made herself more comfortable, leaning next to the booth beside me, obviously eager for an interpersonal conversation with me.

"So, are you here on business?"

"Yes," still convinced I could cut this conversation short, until she formally introduced herself and proceeded to talk about her children. When that happens, I can't help but be interested.

"By the way, I'm Tracy. I manage this restaurant. Where are you from?"

I put my iPhone down, surrendering to Tracy's persistence in wanting to have a dialogue. "New York."

"Oh, what a fun place to visit. I have two girls. It's my youngest one who goes to college out east. She's in her second year at Cornell. We had a chance to go into Manhattan when we were visiting her at school."

"My oldest daughter is about to graduate from UCLA and has already started the job interview process." Tracy continued, but with a different tone in her voice. "It is so tough out there to find a job that you not only love to do but can make a good living doing it." I could not only hear concern in her voice but I could see it in her eyes: the concern and protective instincts only a mother could project when worrying about her children.

At this point, my iPhone was back in my coat pocket, and I was practically ready for my second cup of coffee as Tracy continued telling me about her kids. Tracy had enrolled me in a conversation with her, but it was more than just a friendly exchange of words and pleasantries. Tracy and I were *connecting*.

"I just don't get it," Tracy shared, allowing her frustrations to surface. "These companies want to hire someone with a great education and experience. But other than holding some entry-level positions or finding a great internship, where are you going to get the experience if you can't get an opportunity to learn on the job and prove what you're capable of doing? They all say she has what it takes, except the experience."

I looked Tracy in the eye and said, "Tracy, I completely understand how you feel. However, I want you to know, your daughters will do just fine. They're not only going to make it, they are going to thrive. I know it."

My comment must have reinforced or reminded Tracy about the peace of mind and confidence she always had about her kids. "Thank you, Keith, but how do you know they'll be just fine? How can you say that with such certainty?"

I smiled at Tracy and asked her a question I already knew the answer to. "Tracy, are your children anything like you?"

She thought for a moment and smiled, "Why, yes, they are very much like me. My husband says they get their drive and bubbly enthusiasm from my side of the family."

"Tracy, your daughters are very lucky to have a mom like you. And if they sell themselves, that is, come across the way you do and share who they are naturally, people will notice the gifts, value, and talents they can bring to any position they apply for."

"Oh, you are so sweet for saying that. Thank you." Tracy's response was heartfelt. I could tell that she really listened to what I said and took it in rather than hearing my observation on a superficial level and dismissing it.

Tracy and I continued our discussion for another few minutes until she got called away by the hostess to handle an issue with another customer. I turned back to finish my breakfast. It had cooled off since the waitress came by and served it during the time I was talking with Tracy. But it was worth it. Yes, I made a difference that morning in someone's life.

As Tracy walked away, I glanced around the restaurant. Now that I was out of my head, or should I say, out of my iPhone, I started noticing more of what was happening around me than I had when I first walked into the restaurant that morning. I took a visual inventory of each person working in that restaurant. It was not just Tracy and Maya who were smiling. *Everyone* who worked there was smiling. The two hostesses at the front entrance were smiling, even if there were no guests for them to greet at the moment. Every busboy, waiter, and waitress was smiling, whether they were taking an order, serving a meal, or walking back to the kitchen where nobody could see them (unless you were like me and were purposely looking).

---

### ❧ FROM THE SIDELINES ❧

Every conversation you have is of vital importance. Even though some may seem trivial to you, each is deeply influential when compounded over time.

---

## MAKING AN IMPACT

How does this apply to your ability to become a great sales coach and master the art of enrollment which is what this chapter is about? Think about the restaurant experience with Tracy at the helm. She was the manager. She set the tone. Tracy was the one responsible for developing the atmosphere within the restaurant, which was a by-product of the culture she promoted within her team. This, in turn, created the positive experience every customer would leave with after dining at Tracy's restaurant.

❀ **FROM THE SIDELINES** ❀

The atmosphere, tone, and culture created within a company lead back to the efforts, actions, and behavior of one person—the manager.

Before you determine that you can't make a difference, before you conclude that you don't have enough power, think about Tracy. She is a manager who makes a difference every day with the people she meets. Not because of her experience or her training. Tracy makes an impact on people because she does something that other people, more specifically, other managers, are not willing to do or care to do: establish an honest, authentic connection with people. This is why I knew Tracy's kids would be fine.

## LEAVING YOUR LEGACY AS A MANAGER

The experience I had with Tracy, a restaurant manager, made me think about the other managers I know. Interestingly, the one thing I rarely, if ever, hear from salespeople is how much they've loved their prior managers. Think about your career and the path you've traveled, which brought you to where you are today. Reflect on managers you have had in the different positions you've held. Now, ask yourself the following questions.

- How many managers have you had that inspired you to live your greatness?
- How many managers throughout your career have you connected with on a deeper level outside of what needs to be done to maintain your sales numbers? A level where loyalty, trust, friendship, and a mutual respect are developed and cherished?
- How many of your prior managers have truly changed your life and career for the better?
- Do you still maintain a relationship with any managers you had in your prior positions?

If you want to make a difference, a positive impact that can be felt and measured by your team, first start by making a strong connection with your salespeople. Establishing a common ground and sharing personal experiences foster a deeper connection, leaving your salespeople with the feeling, "We are the same. He really understands me."

This connection you develop with your salespeople then leads to trust, loyalty, respect, and the authentic desire to want to succeed for themselves, for their team, and for you as their manager.

### ❀ FROM THE SIDELINES ❀

Before you can make a difference, you have to make a connection. The most effective way to make a connection is by sharing yourself, your humanity, even your vulnerability with others.

To build off this universal principle, we are going to discuss a powerful and compelling communication strategy that, without connection, would be very difficult to employ and benefit from.

## THE ART OF ENROLLMENT

Let's begin this section with a comprehensive definition of the word *enrollment*.

*Enrollment:* An authentic, powerful way of communicating that grabs people's attention, stimulates interest, and empowers others to embrace, support, and believe in your position, idea, or philosophy. This motivates people to want to become part of your cause (a cause that may be bigger than you and them), take ownership of it, and then act in their best interest to create the possibility that you have introduced to them and/or have taken a stand for. (For example: Creating a certain corporate culture, selling or making a purchasing decision, trying something new that hasn't been done before, or advocating for a positive, yet difficult change, etc.)

## ❧ FROM THE SIDELINES ❧

What do you do to be different, to be unique, to be eternal in the mind of a salesperson? True sales coaches leave not only a lasting impression but they also create one.

Like traditional management, traditional selling is dead. Unfortunately, many salespeople today are still using antiquated selling strategies. They no longer offer a competitive edge that separates them from every other company and promotes a healthy, winning relationship with their customers. Rather than change their approach, salespeople work harder and longer as they continually react to the changes in the marketplace, only to produce the same results as before.

Motivating employees is often exhausting and time-consuming work. Trying to get people to change or do things differently is even more of a challenge. Managers struggle to get their staff to become internally driven, self-motivated, and perform at their potential. Businesses are closing their doors not due to a lack of effort but because they are still attempting to sell, manage, or run their businesses the old way, not the way it needs to be done today.

The next evolution in communication and in the way we coach our salespeople is using the art and discipline of enrollment. Think about some of the great leaders of our time: Dr. Martin Luther King, Golda Meir, Gandhi, Nelson Mandela, Andy Grove (Chairman of Intel), and Oprah (actress, talk show host, philanthropist). What do these leaders have in common? Each had a *cause* that ignited them to act from a global perspective. It was their innate ability that enabled them to enroll millions of people to follow, not them, but what was bigger than them—their cause. They used the art of enrollment to achieve historical, unprecedented results.

What has been initially perceived as an inherent, genetic ability is now a documented process that allows each of us to tap into this hidden power we all possess. The dormant desire to want to express more of who we are, what we want, how we feel, and what could be possible can now be achieved through enrollment. Each of us can do so in a natural, conversational way that honors our personal strengths, talents, goals, values, passion, and style of communicating while remaining open to cocreating greater possibilities.

Enrollment is a way to unleash each person's purest form of open, honest, and authentic communication, using thought-provoking, curiosity-based questions that generate worthwhile results in any setting. When you uncover what you are passionate about, what you believe in, and then take a strong, unwavering stand for whatever it may be, while respecting the mutual differences of one another, only then can you start to communicate and achieve more through the enrollment process: the highest form of communicating and self-expression.

## ENROLLMENT IS A UNIVERSAL PHENOMENON

When top salespeople want to be better at their jobs while maintaining their focus and desire to deliver rich value and serve their clients' best interests, they stop selling and start *enrolling*. When an accountant, a coach, a doctor, contractor, financial planner, attorney, mortgage broker, or salesperson wants to build their practice or their sales, they *enroll*. When universities want to attract more students, they *enroll*. When parents want their kids to change or do something, they *enroll* them. When managers hire someone, they *enroll* that person in the position.

To make this more relevant, think about it in terms of your position. When handling internal conflicts or sharing a policy change that affects every salesperson's commission, managers must *enroll* people toward a positive, mutual mindshare. If you need your team to make radical changes in their behavior or in their thinking, you *enroll* them in that change. Here are some situations that would warrant an opportunity to use the art of enrollment.

1. Needing to get salespeople to relocate.
2. Developing an incentive program.
3. Defusing hostility and finding a common ground.
4. Making changes in company policy or procedure, such as a price increase, a change in commission or compensation, or a change in a person's job function.

5. Changing how salespeople will be developed and trained, such as taking part in a coaching program.

6. Recruiting and hiring a new salesperson.

7. Firing a team member and reducing collateral damage as well as toxic gossip.

8. Requesting a change in people's behavior or activity.

9. Getting people to own a certain problem which they have been avoiding.

10. Holding people more accountable around their performance goals as well as any administrative responsibilities.

11. Requesting that someone take on a task or do something they may normally be reluctant to do.

In practically any scenario where it requires opening up someone's thinking, modifying behavior, or taking action around something, the art of enrollment will become your primary communication strategy to bring about the changes you want without pushback, prodding, or resistance.

## CREATING THE POSSIBILITY FOR CHANGE

You may recall from an earlier chapter that coaching is the art of creating new possibilities. Enrollment allows you to communicate those possibilities in a way that people will be receptive to and motivates them to change. At its core, enrollment is all about facilitating positive, long-term change.

Whether you're selling a product, service, idea, or philosophy, no one likes to be sold. Everyone loves to feel as if they are making the decision themselves. If your salespeople perceive you as someone who is focused solely on helping them make their own decisions, they are going to want to be enrolled by you and will enjoy the process.

Take any situation or conversation in which there is a group of people who have conflicting interests, a conflict that needs resolution, an idea that needs to be communicated and embraced, a change initiative that needs to be launched, or a mutual goal that needs to be attained. Whether each person possesses a separate agenda or information that needs to be communicated, has a mis-understanding of each other's goals or has no business talking to each other in the first place, mastering the Art of Enrollment will unlock the door to full self-expression for all. It will enable you to communicate more powerfully, more authentically, and more confidently with everyone.

### ❊ FROM THE SIDELINES ❊

People don't want to be sold. They want to be enrolled.

## THE SIX STEPS OF AN ENROLLMENT CONVERSATION

Even though there is a systematic process of enrollment that you can follow, keep in mind that this is a guide and does have some flexibility. Therefore, depending on the flow of each conversation, you may tailor these steps so they fit each situation.

**Step 1.** *Get connected.* Share a story, either about yourself or someone else who might have been in a similar situation. This cultivates the relationship, creates a safe atmosphere to share more, and makes the other person more comfortable opening up to you.

**Step 2.** *State the possibility.* Here's where you share a general possibility the other person can realize. Typically, this is a broad, compelling statement of a desired outcome. Start off with a word or phrase that encourages the other person to suspend any doubts or limiting thinking when introducing what it is you want for this person or for the company as a whole. Here are some examples of words and phrases you can use: "Imagine," "Think about," "Picture," "Envision," "Consider," "What would it mean to you if," "What would be possible if," "Wouldn't it be great if," or "What if." One way of stating a possibility could sound like this. "Wouldn't it be great if we all came to work every day feeling motivated, fulfilled, and satisfied in our jobs. That's what I want to create for you."

**Step 3.** *Ask permission to have a conversation.* Follow up step 2 with a question that will give you permission to have this conversation. This question confirms that it is a good time for this discussion: what it is you want as well as whether the person is open to hearing it. Here's what that question could sound like. "Are you open to discussing how we can achieve/create this for you?" or "Is this a good time for you to discuss this now?"

Step 4. *Take a stand.* Whereas step 2 is a broad, compelling statement of a desired outcome, here's where you identify the specific proposition of the possibility that you want to create for that person. State your purpose clearly and concisely by using a *wanting for* statement. Here is one way to say it. "What I want for you is to come to work with a smile on your face, knowing that every day you're making a difference, delivering value, and enjoying the financial reward of your efforts."

Step 5. *Have the conversation.* Here's where you deliver the idea or request you want them to hear. The conversation may include a new concept or philosophy that you want them to buy into, a request to do or change something, or an invitation that may be more optional than mandatory.

Step 6. *Get complete.* This final step of the enrollment process is to establish the next course of action, gauging the person's feelings or response and determining a completion time. What are the next steps? How did this person respond to your ideas? How open was he? Here are some questions you could ask. "How do you see handling this?" "How are you going to handle this?" "In order to complete this, what steps are you going to take that make sense to you?" "How have you handled something like this before?" "What's your strategy going to be/look like?" "When do you think you can have this back to me?" "Is there anything that would get in the way of completing this by next Wednesday?" "How is this sitting with you?" "What concerns do you have?" "What are you most excited about?" "What can I do specifically to support you around this?" "How should we determine evidence of positive change?" "What criteria do you suggest we use?" This is the time to confirm the person's level of buy in or the clarity of your conversation. This is also the opportunity for you and the person or people you are enrolling to develop a strategy and deadline or finalize any steps to produce the result you seek to achieve.

To ensure that your enrollment efforts lead to the positive, worthwhile changes you seek, here are some final tips to keep in mind when using these six steps of enrollment. We have already discussed these observations and principles in preceding chapters, but it's a good idea to review them before attempting to enroll someone.

1. Surrender your agenda. When enrolling someone, there is no attachment to the outcome.
2. It's never about you but about a greater goal or good. The benefit that results from what it is you want to enroll them in will either be specific to that person, your team, your company as a whole, or for the greater good of society.
3. Sharing and being vulnerable (without putting yourself in harm's way) is the purest form of self-expression.
4. Focus more on the pleasure, vision, and dreams you want to create rather than the consequence of not doing so.
5. Whether you are enrolling and engaging a group or just one person, you have the power to continually create new and greater possibilities by harnessing your creativity.
6. Be sensitive to people's attitude and state of mind when you are attempting to enroll them. That is, are they receptive and open to hearing your message in that moment or did they just find out that they might be losing one of their largest clients? Their mood and mindset will affect the results of your efforts.

It's time to put enrollment into action. What follows are examples of situations and opportunities where the art of enrollment became the coach's greatest edge when managing people and promoting positive change.

## CASE STUDY: ENROLLING SOMEONE TO IMPROVE THEIR QUALITY OF WORK

Bill was a cosmetic surgeon who owned a successful practice in Washington, D.C. He had eight physicians in his practice who he personally hired and was also responsible for managing, as well as one manager responsible for marketing and new business development. He noticed that Jon, one of his physicians, was not being as diligent as he needed to be during and after patient exams. Although Jon's patient visits were high in terms of the number of patients he saw weekly, Bill felt that this issue needed to be addressed.

However, like most people, Bill did not like confrontation and avoided it at all costs. He was concerned about how to approach Jon in a way that wouldn't put him on the defensive and, instead, make him feel comfortable and open to discussing this matter. He wanted to discuss the diligence issue while honoring and acknowledging Jon's positive contributions to the practice.

Below is the dialogue between the two when Bill attempted to enroll Jon to change his approach.

**Bill:** Hi, Jon. I would like to talk to you about the work you are doing, which has been great, by the way. The way you're treating your patients has been wonderful and exactly what I expect. Do you have a few minutes to talk?

**Jon:** Sure.

**Bill:** I've been looking over the number of patients that all the physicians are seeing each week. You clearly rise above the rest when it comes to the sheer number of weekly patient visits. Listen, I'm always looking for ways to make all of our jobs here easier, so would you be open to having a conversation about how you can still maintain and even exceed those numbers and do so with fewer administrative problems?

**Jon:** Okay. What were you thinking?

**Bill:** Well, given the work that we do, I'm sure you're aware of the difference between being efficient compared to being effective. There's a subtle difference between the two. It's one thing to be efficient at each task as it relates to the sheer measurement of time and how long you take to complete a task or patient visit. However, you must balance being effective at everything you do as well.

Jon, you're highly efficient, seeing 90 patients a week; no one can argue with that. However, I'm thinking there may be a way for us to be more effective at the other tasks that we're also responsible for which would reduce our liability and the things that could be missed during a patient visit. You know, things like documentation, patient review, tests that have been done, and reviewing best solutions for our patients. And by doing so, you'll actually wind up with more time to see additional patients and less time feeling inundated with unfinished paperwork.

When you are working as hard as you are, sometimes it's easy to lose sight that it's not always about the numbers, especially when you put in the hours you do. Then, when you're diagnosing and treating the same or similar problems or performing surgeries over and over again, we even have a tendency to start looking at our patients as numbers, appointments, or visits rather than individual human beings. We have to always keep in mind that it's not about the number of patients seen but the number of patients we've helped today.

With the sheer number of patients you see, it's very easy to miss something. Anyone could. After all, you're only human. So, I'm really interested in hearing your thoughts about this, Jim. Do you have any ideas about some new processes or resources you could use that would help you improve on the other administrative areas that you are responsible for during a patient visit?

Jon: Actually, Bill, there are a few things I could use that may help. . . .

At this point, Bill and Jon identified some tactical strategies and solutions that would help Jon better manage his administrative responsibilities. Bill did a great job enrolling Jon in exploring some alternative ways to balance out his already heavy workload, especially when it came to the administrative tasks for which he was responsible. Jon, who is typically defensive when approached about his work, was not only open to having a discussion about this but was actually ready to share specific ideas that he'd be willing to try out in order to make this problem a thing of the past.

Given Jon's temperament, Jon may ask Bill to cite specific examples, such as a particular patient's paperwork that he did not complete or that was not done correctly. Jon may do this to gather some evidence that supports Bill's claims, which would put both Jon and Bill on the defensive and escalate this conversation into an argument. As a manager, you need to be prepared. Don't take the bait. Otherwise, you'll find yourself traveling down a rough road that focuses your attention on what isn't working or what Jon is doing wrong rather than on finding a resolution. Instead, collaborate on a solution rather than focusing on the problem.

## THE PRICE OF MAINTAINING MEDIOCRITY

Even though Jon may have recognized the advantages to making some changes, Bill sensed some resistance and felt that Jon was still not entirely on board and fully committed to improving this process. At that point, Bill thought that identifying the greater cost of not making these changes may be a more compelling case that would motivate Jon to make the necessary changes.

Below are some questions that Bill used to evoke the cost or pain associated with not changing the way Jon was currently operating and handling postpatient visits. These questions will enable Jon to recognize the costs on his own.

1. What do you think it's costing you by not being as effective as you are efficient? (Tell a story. Paint a picture.) For example, take the situation with patients who are on Medicaid. How will it affect our ability to get reimbursed as well as serve more of these patients if we are not abiding by their strict reimbursement guidelines, especially their requirements regarding how they want patient visits documented?

2. What is the cost to you and to the practice if you rush through the paperwork?

3. What would it cost you and the patient if you were to misdiagnose or miss something as a result of not giving the documentation process the attention it requires? What could happen if you misdocument a patient chart?

4. What would it cost the practice if you misdiagnosed a patient's condition?

5. What if you mistakenly, in your haste, prescribed the wrong treatment?

Bill now wanted to see this conversation through to its conclusion. After listening to Jon's responses to his questions, he interjected additional possible costs that Jon may not have mentioned or were outside of his line of vision.

Next, Bill wanted to ensure that he uncovered any additional concerns that might get in the way of Jon changing his ways by asking him the following questions.

- What concerns do you have at this point that might prevent you from following through with the solutions we've developed today?
- What do you see that may get in your way of making this part of your daily routine?

Finally, Bill confirmed that Jon agreed with his assessment and articulated the additional benefits that were strong enough to motivate him into action and make these positive changes. Jon finally understood how it would make his job even easier and less overwhelming by building in nonnegotiable time at the conclusion of every patient visit for his additional responsibilities. Jon realized that by making these adjustments, he would be able to see more clients, generate more referrals, maximize his income, experience greater peace of mind, and have fewer headaches.

## CASE STUDY: ENROLLING SOMEONE TO BECOME MORE ACCOUNTABLE

Silvia has owned her own retail clothing store for 20 years. Because she is innovative and creative, she listened to her coach when he suggested enrolling each of her employees in creating their own job description. Even though the majority of her staff of eight salespeople turned in this assignment by the imposed deadline, there was one person who did not.

It didn't come as a shock to Silvia that Jackie, her floor sales manager, missed the deadline. It seems there has been a history of disorganization, negligence, poor time management, and excuses that Jackie relies on to justify her attitude and performance. "If it wasn't for how great she is with customers on the floor. . . . " thought Silvia. But Silvia knew that continuing to put up with Jackie's behind-the-scenes blowups and highly reactionary style would cost the company more money, more arguments, and more headaches down the road.

Silvia needed to confront Jackie rather than continue to avoid the issue or fool herself into thinking, "I'll get around to this next week." Silvia thought about what precedent she would be setting and what message she would be sending to the rest of her team if she continued to tolerate Jackie's behavior.

The following dialogue took place after Jackie failed to honor the commitment she made to write her job description. Notice that the language Silvia used empowered Jackie to become more accountable, move away from her usual excuses, and instead focus on the solution.

After Silvia got confirmation from Jackie that it was a good time to talk and permission to proceed with this topic of conversation, here is how the remainder of the conversation unfolded.

**Silvia:** Jackie, we're trying to develop uniformity in our company culture and together, grow this business. We all share in the same goal of wanting to be the leading design center in the area. I noticed that I did not receive your job description, and, quite frankly, I was looking forward to seeing yours and getting your input. Were you aware that there was a deadline imposed on this exercise?

**Jackie:** Yes.

**Silvia:** Did you know that everyone on our team was responsible for turning one in?

**Jackie:** Yes.

**Silvia:** Listen, Jackie. I know how hard you work and the hours you put in. I certainly appreciate the time and effort you put forth in your work on a daily basis, but we're all still responsible for honoring deadlines, especially as a manager who would then request the same from her team. I'm the first to realize how much you have on your plate. We are each responsible for a huge workload, which makes it even more critical that we manage our time as effectively as possible. The thing is, great time management doesn't happen naturally. It's a strategy that first needs to be outlined, then put into practice.

Let me ask you this. Now I know this may sound like a stretch, but what would it mean to you if you were able to meet each deadline without becoming stressed or overwhelmed?

Jackie: Quite frankly, I don't think it could be done.

Silvia: Well, Jackie, look at it this way. Is the process you're using now getting you the results you want without having to stress over it?

Jackie: Not exactly.

Silvia: Well then, if it could be done, would you at least be open to trying it?

Jackie: Sure.

Silvia: Besides, if you don't honor a deadline, what is the message you're sending to the other people in the company, including your team? What type of culture do you think will then be created?

Jackie: Hmm. I didn't think of it that way. Actually, now it makes more sense as to why I get some pushback from my people when it comes to meeting their deadlines.

Silvia: In order to reduce or even eliminate the stress you experience from how you're currently handling your workload, what do you need to change in how you manage your schedule and your day? What has to happen so that you can meet every deadline you have?

## INSTILLING CONSEQUENCE AND ACCOUNTABILITY—A COLLABORATIVE EFFORT

Jackie and Silvia continued their conversation, focusing on what Jackie needed in order to become more organized and efficient.

Silvia asked more questions in her effort to uncover what Jackie needed most and how she could best support her, such as, "How would you like me to support you around making these changes?" Some of the needs that Silvia uncovered included individual, one-to-one coaching, and an accountability partner to keep her on task as well as several additional resources such as a laptop, software to manage her schedule, a portable PDA, and a better filing system, just to name a few.

If there's a deadline imposed on your employees, then it is their responsibility to come to you or their supervisor to discuss their concerns of potentially not being able to honor the deadline rather than waiting until the due date and not being prepared. Of course, this all begins with the manager. After all, if employees are not following through on deadlines or procedures and the manager is not holding them accountable for doing so, then it's ultimately the manager's fault. Since a person's behavior speaks volumes over their spoken word, the manager would be sending a message to his staff that sounds like, "Following protocol and honoring deadlines is not all that important."

But the manager does not need to take on the full burden. Rather than including or defining a measurable consequence if Jackie did not honor her commitment, Silvia enrolled Jackie in developing the consequence and asked Jackie to report back to her within two days. If Jackie fails to honor her commitments from now on, she has only herself to blame. Silvia is no longer the scapegoat or tyrant, because Jackie came up with a self-imposed consequence that she is now responsible for as well as how she wants her manager to hold her accountable. Here's what that conversation sounded like.

> **Silvia:** Now that we've flushed out some solid strategies, there's one other thing that is important for us to establish mindshare on. Would you agree that it's your responsibility to come to me if you feel you can't meet a deadline?
>
> **Jackie:** Yes.
>
> **Silvia:** Great. Then to reconfirm, in the off chance of this happening again, will you approach me beforehand so that we have the opportunity to discuss it?

Jackie: Of course.

Silvia: Thanks, Jackie. I'm glad to hear that. If you really want me to coach you on reaching this goal faster, then I need to know that you will be okay with being challenged and stretched more than you're used to and held accountable for the commitments you make. Remember, it's all in the spirit of having you reach your goal. Is that fair?

Jackie: I guess so. I mean, yes. I'm going to have to do the same thing for my staff so the same guidelines need to apply to me as well.

Silvia: I appreciate you saying that. Let's go a little deeper on this for a moment. Part of my role is to hold you accountable for honoring your commitments in a way that will sound supportive and won't come across as negative or micromanaging. That said, how do you want me to approach you if you don't follow through with the commitments you make? How do you want me to handle it? (Here's another way of asking the question: "What would be a good way to bring this up to you so that you will be open to hearing it?")

## THE WRITTEN WORD: CRAFTING A COMPELLING MESSAGE

### ASKING TO COMPLETE A COMPANY APPRAISAL

E-mails are probably one of the leading causes of communication breakdowns, problems, conflicts, lost sales, and damaged relationships within the workplace. And it's no wonder. With nothing more than the written word in front of you, the rest of the message—the tone, pace, volume, attitude of the message, tonality, and inflection—is then left up to the reader to decipher. Even though the writer of the e-mail may try to reduce or eliminate any possibility of misinterpretation, the writer cannot control or be aware of the reader's state of mind when the e-mail lands in the inbox and is read.

Here is an e-mail that I helped design for a client who was about to do appraisals on every employee in the company. The first appraisal was going to be focused more on the company as a whole before individual appraisals were to be completed. This e-mail was used to enroll the client's team in the benefits of completing an appraisal of the company.

---

MEMO: To All Team Members
RE: Company Appraisal
From: Larry Anderson
Greetings,

As you may have noticed, we are making some changes within the company that will impact each of us in a positive way. My commitment to you is to create a work environment that you can thrive in as well as enjoy.

That's why we're asking for your help so that as we advance in our careers, you feel that you are getting the support, training, and guidance you need to excel in your career in a culture that also supports your personal and family goals. In order to create the atmosphere needed for each person to excel, we would like for you to share your thoughts and take part in creating a company that we all can aspire to bring to fruition.

As such, please complete this online company appraisal no later than 9:00 a.m. on Friday, February 20. To get the most value out of this exercise, please be as honest as possible. Your replies will be kept anonymous. We value your open and candid input, so please don't hold back your thoughts and suggestions. Your response is deeply appreciated and will enable us to make long lasting changes.

With your help, we are confident that we will all have the ability to impact the company and bring about healthy change that everyone can be a part of. These positive changes will enable you to make a profound impact within the culture of this company, in your career, as well as with every customer we work with.

*(continued)*

Thanks again for your time and input. If you have any questions regarding this appraisal, please don't hesitate to contact me anytime.

I wish you continued success.

With sincere regards,

Larry Anderson

President, Best Health, Inc.

## ASKING TO COMPLETE A PERFORMANCE APPRAISAL

Now that you have enrolled your team in completing a company appraisal, it's time for them to complete their own performance appraisal. The example below could be used as a memo to enroll your team in the benefits of completing a performance appraisal.

MEMO: To All Team Members

RE: Personal Appraisal

From: Larry Anderson

Greetings,

As you may have noticed, we are making some positive changes within the company that will impact each of us in a positive way. I can certainly tell you since starting this company 25 years ago with my dad, we've truly transformed into something even greater since our inception. My commitment to you is to create a work environment that you can thrive in and enjoy. The more we know about you, the easier it will be for us to make long lasting changes we can all benefit from.

That's why I'm asking for your help. Please complete this personal appraisal. This personal appraisal is designed to gather more information about your skills, competencies, as well as your experience within the company and industry so that together, we can uncover the areas of opportunity that we can work on improving, additional resources needed, and the skills that require further development in order for you to reach your goals. This way, as you move ahead in your career, you can rest assured that you will receive the support, coaching, and resources you need to excel and live your potential.

In addition, if each of us takes the time to uncover the areas we can further develop and refine, we now have the opportunity to impact our coworkers as well as every customer we serve.

Please complete and return this appraisal no later than 9:00 a.m., March 1, attention Larry Anderson. To get the most value out of this exercise, please be as honest as possible. Your response is deeply appreciated. Please note that your appraisal will be held in the strictest of confidence and will not be shared with anyone other than your manager(s).

Finally, it is important that you know the results of this appraisal are for professional development only. This is not an employee evaluation. As such, the results of your appraisal will not be tied into any compensation, bonus, year-end raise, or performance evaluation.

Thanks again for your assistance. If you have any questions about this appraisal, please don't hesitate to contact me anytime.

Sincere regards,
Larry Anderson
President, Best Health, Inc.

## ASKING TO CONTRIBUTE TOWARD CREATING A SHARED COMPANY VISION

Here is a memo you can tweak when introducing another exercise I would also suggest doing with your team—crafting a company vision.

MEMO: To All Team Members
RE: Bringing About Positive Change in Your Career
From: Larry Anderson
Greetings,

*(continued)*

As you may have noticed, we are making some changes within the company that will impact each of us in a positive way. Along with any change comes a degree of discomfort, as we stretch outside our comfort zone to do something new, unknown or something that hasn't been proven yet.

We are truly excited about the new standards we are setting in our company. Standards of excellence, teamwork, honesty, professionalism, accountability, consideration, cooperation, overdelivering on value and integrity. As our company grows, it is critical that each member of our team makes a conscious choice to want to grow with us. After observing other companies going through a similar transition period, those people who are uncomfortable with rapid growth become challenged within the workplace and begin to struggle if they resist adapting to the changes. Considering that our company's location is in the heart of Silicon Valley, you can imagine how critical it is to become a change master.

That's why we're asking for your help designing a corporate vision. This way, as we move forward, you will feel that you are working toward a shared goal that you personally took part in crafting, as well as bringing to fruition.

Without a clear vision and goal, a compass to guide us, something that would empower each of us and pull us forward on the same path to achieve the same goals, we cannot successfully build what we all want to be a part of. Therefore, your help is needed to chart this exciting path and build a blueprint of what Best Health could evolve into. Your suggestions are needed to create and define that vision, that shining North Star, which will guide all of us throughout the years to come.

We are asking each and every employee to take about 10 minutes out of your extremely busy schedules to write down what is important to you in your workplace. We're looking for some quick gut reactions. In order to best provide continued support for each person during our time of rapid growth, we would like you to share your thoughts and suggestions and take part in creating a company vision that we all can aspire to achieve.

As such, please jot down some quick responses to the following questions and return them no later than 9:00 a.m., Tuesday, March 20, attention to Larry Anderson. (Feel free to send them anonymously if you would prefer or you can also fax them to 123-456-7890.) To get the most value out of this exercise, please be as candid and honest as possible. Your input is deeply appreciated.

1. List three characteristics or qualities that you would want to use to describe this company. (Remember, these characteristics don't have to be present now but how you would like it to be at some point in the future.)

2. What would you like your customers to say about the company you work for? (What level of value do you want to deliver to them?)

3. What are three or more factors or qualities that you consider to be most important in your job and in your company? (If you cannot think of three or more, give just one.)

4. If you were to describe your ideal client, what would that sound like? (Characteristics, qualities, traits, etc.)

5. In an ideal setting, how would you like to describe the atmosphere within our company? What would you like to see different from how it is today?

6. What would you want to be said about you? (From your coworkers, supervisor, clients, etc.)

With your help, we are confident that over the next few months we will all have the ability to impact the company and bring about healthy change that everyone can be a part of. These changes will enable you to make an impact on the direction this company travels, on your career, as well as on every one of our customers.

Positive changes are coming and, remember, we can't do this without you and our unified, collaborative efforts.

*(continued)*

Thanks again for your support and assistance. If you have any questions on this, please don't hesitate to contact me anytime.
Sincere regards,
Larry Anderson
President, Best Health, Inc.

The art of enrollment is a practical application that can be used in virtually every conversation we have, especially as it relates to motivating a team of salespeople to bring about long-term, worthwhile change. Enrollment is a way of communicating that requires a shift in your thinking around what it means to be a powerful, inspiring communicator, your communication goals and objectives, as well as your language and strategy when delivering your message. Once embraced and put into practice, you will soon see what a robust and influential tool it can be in your daily communication, in your leadership, and with every person you interact with.

CHAPTER

# The Seduction of Potential

## POTENTIAL IS THE HOLY GRAIL

There are three areas in which managers constantly struggle. One area is deciding who to hire and where to find good talent. The second is deciding who to invest the time in turning around, and the third is determining who to let go and when to do it. These are the tasks that managers complain about the most.

When it comes to making these decisions about their employees, the questions I hear most often, the ones that keep managers up at night, sound like this:

- "I'm not getting the production I need from my team, even when I continually push them. How do you turn an under-performer into a top producer or at least into an average, acceptable producer?"
- "When does it make sense to invest your time, money, and resources into someone who you feel you can turn around?"
- "How can I determine (with great certainty), based on a defined set of criteria, benchmarks, and measurable steps, when to cut the proverbial cord and let someone go?"

233

During a coaching workshop, on the first day of a weeklong conference, someone asked a question about how to handle an underperformer. While this manager was sharing in great detail the challenges she was having with a salesperson she hired several months ago, I noticed an interesting reaction from the audience. I glanced out at a sea of people, their heads nodding up and down in agreement, as if she was sharing not just her story but everyone's story.

She talked of an experience that practically every manager and business owner in the room was able to relate to: an all too familiar tale of a new, promising hire with incredible potential who wasn't working out.

Everyone has a story about an underperformer. This manager's story continued about a candidate with a wonderful resume, great background, stellar references, and a seemingly positive attitude and disposition. A candidate who was given the opportunity to work with her. A candidate whom she felt had the potential to live up to her expectations. A candidate whose experience seemed to be a perfect complement to this new sales position.

I listened intently as she described this experience. Her once positive level of exuberance, her hopes and dreams, evaporated before our eyes, as she painfully explained how this promising young superstar became one of her biggest disappointments, frustrations, and expenses. And it wasn't as if she just called it quits after a few weeks and fired this person. Like most managers, she invested precious time trying to turn the person around. The more she invested in supporting and training this person, the more her expectations were shattered.

### ❧ FROM THE SIDELINES ❧

Are you tripping over your own potential? Or worse, are you relying on other people's potential to ensure your success?

This manager was stuck. She didn't know what to do. At this point, this new hire was costing her money, time, selling opportunities, and resources every day. This manager completed her story, sounding as drained as if she and the rest of the audience were reliving their personal staffing nightmares, touching what seemed to be an open wound that simply would not heal. With what sounded like a desperate cry for help, she concluded with something I hear quite regularly, "Keith, what should I *do*?"

The room was silent. All the managers and business owners were gripping the edges of their seats, waiting, anticipating a magnificent piece of brilliance, a solution to this common and painfully eternal dilemma.

My response was, "Do not be seduced by the ether of potential."

## THE SEDUCTION BEGINS: THE ETHER OF POTENTIAL

Yes, we are often seduced by the potential that we believe we see in others. We see potential in the people, as well as in the opportunities, all around us. We recognize the untapped potential in people who we have a vested interest in: our children, spouse, coworkers, partner, supervisor, and, of course, in our staff. We see potential in our new hires as well as the untapped potential in the veterans on our team.

We believe that sometimes, if we wait, if we're patient, if we give them just a little more time, more resources, better training, more attention, they can finally live up to their potential. We believe our employees when they tell us, "Just give me a few more weeks. I'm about to close in on two big sales. Yes, I know my performance has slipped, but as I told you, those personal problems that have been distracting me are no longer there."

### ❈ FROM THE SIDELINES ❈

Quite often, managers are seduced by and get hung up on potential opportunities and past defining moments.

We think, "Okay, if they really could turn it around that would make my life so much easier. After all, it sure beats the painful and time-consuming process of having to recruit someone new, let alone having to figure out how to cover a territory with no salesperson!"

This belief is counterintuitive. Ironically, it costs you more to keep someone like this on your team. More time, more lost sales, more money and resources, more lost selling opportunities, more conflict, more internal problems. Then you have less time to focus on growing your business and on the people who *are* performing: the people who make you look great, who are coachable, and who want to truly live their potential today.

And that's when it happens. The seduction begins. Now, you begin making decisions based on your emotions, feelings, hopes, and unrealistic scenarios, rather than on the facts and what is best for you, the company, as well as the person in question.

The seduction of potential clouds your better judgment. If you're looking for evidence of this conundrum, then just glance over at the people on your team today. Think about the people you have hired in the past who did not work out. How many people can you think of who you hired, when, in your heart, there was a warning sign, something telling you that this person was not the right fit? Call it your gut reaction, your instincts, or intuition. Your internal barometer was desperately trying to tell you something, and you chose not to listen.

## THE HARD COST OF COMPLACENCY

How many times have you been in a situation with an underperforming employee when every week you convinced yourself and others, "Just one more week. He'll turn it around. I know he can do it. If he just follows the program. Just let him get through this next project. I hope he brings in some new business soon." I refer to this type of behavior as Mother Teresa Syndrome. Signs that you might be suffering from this condition would also show up in your internal dialogue. "I can save him. Just a little more time. And I will sacrifice more and more in order to do so!"

> ❈ **FROM THE SIDELINES** ❈
>
> "Wait and see" is not a contingency plan. Hope is not a strategy.

We often hire people based on their potential rather than on what they have truly and measurably achieved. As such, we try to develop the potential we see in them. After all, the goal of management is to make your people more valuable. The key here is investing your time in making the right people more valuable. Otherwise, it's a time-consuming and exhausting exercise in futility.

You continue this internal battle, as you struggle to come up with the right decision. "If he stays, maybe he will turn it around. If I fire him, then what do I do? I have to start the recruiting and training process all over again. What if I fire him and he goes to work for the competition and becomes a superstar? Let's just wait and see what happens tomorrow."

Creating extreme scenarios, relying on costly assumptions, and making decisions that are fueled by hope, fear, and consequence still keeps you from recognizing the truth. The truth is, as human beings we have a tendency to lie to ourselves and then believe our own lies.

## YOU CAN'T BUILD A BUSINESS ON POTENTIAL

There is no *potential* in terms of how you currently define it or embrace it in your life. The way managers rely on potential is more of a smokescreen, a diversionary tactic, an attachment to a certain outcome, a rationalization for their salespeople's performance, a justification for their own behavior or for doing something they want to do, or an excuse not to take certain actions.

### FROM THE SIDELINES

Potential lives in the future; possibilities are created in the present moment.

You don't hire people based on their potential. Here's a more vivid and beneficial definition of *potential*. Potential is based on something that you have not seen yet nor have evidence to support. Potential resides in the future, fueled by your own personal expectations. Besides, if you are attempting to make hiring decisions based on people's potential, and the candidates haven't been living their potential by the time you meet them, then what makes you think they are going to start living it when you hire them?

Either people strive to live their potential each day or they don't. It's that simple. It's management's responsibility to ensure each person on their team has the systems, tools, resources, training, and coaching that allows them to live their potential every day.

Besides, if you don't know whether you have made the right hiring decision within the first 30 to 60 days, then you are in deep trouble. If you think giving the new hire one more chance, more time, or more training is the answer, it is not. This is a lie, a justification, and a story that you're telling yourself (S.C.A.M.M.). Eventually the pain of keeping that person around will become so evident that the person either quits or gets fired. Consequently, you as the manager have surrendered all of your power to act by choice and, instead, are now in a state of reaction and in dire need of a new candidate. Inadvertently, you have put yourself in the dangerous position of having to hire a new person out of desperation; a person who you know in your heart is not the right fit.

If neither you nor your staff are currently using and leveraging your talents every day, then none of you are living your potential. It's not that you cannot improve. The difference between working off potential and lifelong improvement or building a high performance, collaborative team of self-motivated people is this. With potential, you're looking for something that you have not seen yet nor have evidence for. With lifelong improvement, you're working with a known quantity and have the empirical evidence (possibly from past experiences) that supports your belief that turning this person around is truly possible. You have the verification and evidence that the situation can be made better.

The real problem is, managers wind up collapsing potential with possibility. So, what truly seduces you is the *potential of possibility*.

What's missing for managers is *certainty*. It's the uncertainty, the unknown, the fear that paralyzes managers who have to make the decision whether to terminate someone or invest the time in turning them around. Managers rely more on their fear-based gut reactions than on the facts.

Having certainty and confidence in their people supported by evidence is a healthier, more productive model when creating new possibilities. This is what I refer to as authentic human potential. The certainty comes from having an executive sales coaching program. Once you have a structured coaching program that holds people accountable on a daily and weekly basis, you no longer have to make the decision to keep them or terminate them. Now, underperformers will make that decision for you, based on the defined set of criteria and measurable action steps they need to take to demonstrate their commitment to their position and to dramatically improve their performance. A step-by-step turnaround strategy that you can employ is covered in detail in Chapter 12.

If you are responsible for hiring, developing, and managing a team, what process do you have in place to leverage their strengths from the time of hire through their first 30, 60, 90, even 120 days in their new positions? Would having a Thirty-Day New Hire Orientation Program for every new hire based on measurable productivity steps and objectives help you and your team? Wouldn't this simplify your life dramatically? Now that you have a proven process documented, either the new hire is sticking by the program and achieving the expected results, or not. At this point, there's no room for you to be seduced by the potential of possibility. There's no probation or waiting for the year-end performance appraisals.

You can now run your business or manage your team with greater efficiency. Once these processes are in place, you'll be able to get back to doing what every manager is destined to do in the first place: make your talented people more valuable.

## WHEN TO GIVE UP AND LET GO

"The most rain we've had in about 80 years!" That's what the news reported as a result of the constant rain that had been falling for days, fully expediting my lesson about the downside of having a fully finished basement.

In home after home in the New York area, people began the arduous task of pumping hundreds, sometimes thousands, of gallons of water out of their basements. Streets were like rivers, running with water from all the basements that were being drained.

And then there was the damage, not only the structural and cosmetic damage to the houses, but to all the possessions: miles of carpeting, furniture, appliances, and everything else that once made a house a home.

At this point, I had been living in my new home for only about five months, following a 15-month construction project. When we first moved in and the movers arrived with our lifelong possessions that had been in storage for over a year, I couldn't believe how much stuff we had accumulated! Stuff that I've lived without for 15 months. At one point, I asked Eddie, my mover, to take it all back. He said, "You'll probably wind up throwing most of this out."

Well, dozens of unpacked boxes later, we found a place for everything that Eddie was kind enough to bring back to me: in the garage, the attic, and the basement.

Now ironically, not five months after moving in, this flood forced me to throw out at least 80 percent of the boxes stored in my basement. These were the same boxes that I paid to have in storage for 15 months, the same boxes I paid to have moved out of my old house, into storage, and then into my new house, the same boxes that were taking up precious real estate in my new home. The kicker is, for the most part I had no idea what was even in the majority of these boxes!

I needed to give up. That's right, I needed to quit. Without the flood, these boxes would probably have remained undisturbed for years, simply taking up space and adding to household clutter. Yet, because of this natural disaster, I was forced to clear out this clutter, the things that I did not use or that no longer served me anymore.

## MASTER THE ART OF ABANDONMENT

Doesn't the same philosophy apply to our business, our career, and our life? The fact is, there are things you are doing right now that are creating the very results you want to avoid. And you may already know this! Yet we still hold on to things that are not working: the toxic people or relationships that we're better off without, the strategies we keep thinking will eventually work, the limiting beliefs we have about ourselves ("Well, that's just how I am"), the philosophies about selling, serving our customers, as well as developing and retaining our staff.

The most productive people on the planet have mastered the art of abandonment, that is, the ability to let go of the stuff that no longer works. This is not only limited to what you do but also to how you think: the limiting beliefs that keep you prisoner and stall your progress, preventing you from moving ahead.

## THE TOP TRIGGER POINTS OF SEDUCTION

The seductive ether of potential can show up in many areas, not just when determining whether to turn around or terminate a salesperson. Potential can cloud your judgment and overshadow what would be considered more prudent and productive choices.

Here are 10 additional areas that have been known to seduce managers who become tainted and corrupted by the ether of potential. Even though it is critical that salespeople possess many of the following characteristics, they do not replace the salespeople's inability to reach their performance goals and maintain a certain level of acceptable production.

1. *Loyalty.* Loyalty is essential, but is it paying the bills?
2. *Skills.* They may be talented, but are they using their talents to produce the results you expect?
3. *Efforts and commitment.* Sure, they can put forth the effort and possess an unwavering commitment to you and the company, but do they have the innate ability to perform at an acceptable level?
4. *Passion.* Their enthusiasm can be contagious but ineffective in posting higher sales numbers.
5. *Product knowledge.* No one may know more about your product and service. However, since this person has trouble even closing a door, your competition thanks you for keeping this salesperson employed.
6. *Overcompensating qualities.* A gregarious, outgoing, and warm personality certainly makes for a pleasant atmosphere,

in spite of the low numbers this salesperson continues to post each month.

7. *Perceived additional value.* They told you they know *who* and can bring in more business from *which* company, association, or organization? Are their people connections, networks, and what they say they can do for you (which has yet to materialize) keeping them around a bit too long?

8. *Fear.* Nothing is more seductive and paralyzing than allowing your decisions to be governed by fear as you ask yourself questions like, "What's worse, not having a salesperson or having an underperforming salesperson who might be able to turn his sales numbers around? Hmm, let me chew on this one for about seven months."

9. *Ego.* Allowing yourself to be driven by your ego prevents you from learning some valuable lessons, especially as you continue to sell yourself on the idea that it's not your fault.

10. *Mother Teresa syndrome.* The hard reality is, it is not your job to try and save every salesperson nor does it mean that if you can't, you're a failure. If you can't let this one go, then you might be better off working for a charitable organization.

Here's something I would encourage you to do. List 10 things that you can abandon either in your behavior, actions, or in your thinking. List the things that you are holding onto that are either no longer working or not generating the results you really want. Learn to let go. Who or what can you give up on today?

CHAPTER

# Develop an Internal Coaching Program

W ith the work you've done up to this point and a new coaching approach to unleash, you must realize how powerful a manager you can become. And with any great power comes a greater responsibility to use your power for the good of your team. But beware of the kryptonite that robs managers of their strength, influence, and confidence. The seduction by potential can very quickly render you the hostage of your career and of your team: a helpless victim of your own thinking. While the persuasive ether of potential can become your worst nemesis, it will be the defined, focused intervention of a turnaround strategy that will break the shackles of seduction that bind you.

This final chapter incorporates many of the skills, upgraded thinking, and techniques that we have discussed throughout this book, which are all necessary to contend with an underperformer. Using an actual coaching scenario, I will give you a ground-level view of how one well-intentioned manager guided one problematic salesperson on their transformational journey and the conversations that transpired throughout this intense, demanding, yet ultimately rewarding process.

At the conclusion of this chapter, you will be able to rely, with great confidence, on a four-week program that will provide you with the blueprint to turn around underperformers in less than 30 days or quickly determine whether you and your company are better off without them.

## IDENTIFYING A TURNAROUND OPPORTUNITY

"Someone couldn't sleep last night," I thought to myself. It was 5:30 in the morning, but the e-mail I was reading from Steven Hamilton had been sitting in my inbox since 3:30 A.M. when he had sent it.

"Need Your Advice" read the subject line. What I read in the body of the e-mail didn't surprise me. Here's what it said.

"Having some trouble with Brian Grazier, the salesperson I mentioned that I hired about a year ago. I thought he was turning his performance around for the better but he's still struggling; and so am I. Out of our entire sales team of 27 salespeople here in the U.S., he has become my greatest challenge. What makes it so challenging is that this guy has the heart of a lion and is truly committed to the company. However, I'm not sure if his commitment alone is going to be enough. So, I just wanted to give you a heads up so you know what I want to focus on during our next coaching session scheduled for 10 A.M. today."

Steve was the Vice President of Sales and Business Development for Genesis Industrial Solutions, one of the largest manufacturers of industrial parts and equipment for a variety of industries. Given the nature of their business and an average sale in the range of $500,000 to $800,000, Genesis was overly sensitive to the length and depth of their sales cycle. Given the complexity of each sale and the number of decision makers who are involved in the process (from engineers to C-level executives), it can take a year if not longer before a sale is made.

The company had experienced tremendous growth over the last few years with a new signature product line. And as happens quite often, strong growth is accompanied by a need for more new talent. To sustain such growth, the company recently launched a major hiring initiative for new salespeople, as well as a new sales manager who would be reporting directly to Steve. This new sales manager would be hired to take over Steve's current responsibility of managing the sales team, adding a new layer of reporting between Steve and the sales team. However, until that position gets filled, Steve will continue to be the person on the front line, managing and building the sales team.

At 10:00 A.M., Steve called for our scheduled coaching call. Even though Steve and I have worked together for two months now, we had never met face to face.

"Did you get my prep form?" Steve asked, anxious to dive into the heart of the staffing challenge he had e-mailed me about earlier this morning.

"I did, and thanks for sending an update. It sounds like you want to focus on resolving this issue with Brian," I confirmed.

"Yes. Do you remember me telling you about this guy?"

"Yes, you told me that you hired him about a year ago. You initially felt he would be a great addition to your team and early indicators suggested that he was. Yet, for reasons that are still unknown at this point, the person you thought you hired has now become a trigger point of contention for you, and you are unsure why this happened and what you can do about it. So now you're faced with a tough decision, which is, Do you invest your time in turning around an underperformer or are you better off letting him go? Did I get it right?" I asked.

Steve took a deep breath and let out a long sigh, "You got it, Keith. That about sums it up."

I followed up with a series of questions that I could have predicted the answers to based on his current dilemma. (As a coach, you never make assumptions regardless of how accurate you may feel you are.)

"Have you made Brian aware of the sensitive nature of this situation?"

Steve shared with me that Brian is well aware of the fact that he's not performing up to expectations. According to Steve, Brian sounded as if he was truly committed to wanting to turn his performance around. They discussed the measurables that Brian needed to achieve regarding his sales and how far off he was from making quota. Typically, most managers don't struggle with pointing out a problem, until I ask the next few questions.

"And did you establish weekly benchmarks of activity that you could manage which would build the momentum needed for him to start performing at an acceptable level?"

"No."

"Steve, how do you typically hold Brian, as well as your other salespeople, accountable for doing the things they need to do?"

It was evident that these questions made Steve a bit uncomfortable. Not because he didn't want to answer but because he never really stopped to think about a defined process that would hold people accountable. After all, most people don't like confrontation and do what they can to avoid it.

"In the last conversation I had with Brian, he told me about an opportunity he had on Monday to meet with one of the senior production managers for a top U.S. automaker, as well as a couple of other opportunities he was trying to move through his pipeline. He sounded very excited about these. I told him to keep me in the loop regarding these meetings, especially if he needed me to go along with him. Not only did Monday come and go and I never heard a peep from him regarding the meeting, but I'm not even getting the weekly sales reports from him that I asked for months ago. So, I did what I felt needed to be done and called him into my office for a face-to-face meeting. I asked him why I never heard from him about Monday's meeting. Brian told me it got pushed back because of some scheduling conflict. I then asked him about his sales reports. He apologized and told me he'd have them done for me this week."

I listened carefully to Steve as he shared what he considered to be his way of holding his salespeople accountable for their performance and results. Steve continued sharing how the rest of the conversation flowed.

"I asked Brian about his business development activity and how much time he was carving out to make these calls. He admitted he wasn't being as consistent as he needed to. We reviewed his production goals and even used your prospecting calculator to come up with exactly the number of calls he needs to make each week and each day to attain his goals. Brian told me that he struggled balancing new business development activity with the customer service issues that he is also responsible for."

After a brief pause, I jumped in with a question. "And that's how you hold Brian accountable?" I wanted to reconfirm and make sure I didn't miss anything.

"Pretty much," Steve replied. "I addressed the issue and explained to him, as I have many times in the past, how important it is for him to be organized so he can balance all of his responsibilities without any of them falling through the cracks. I told him that inconsistent results lead to inconsistent sales. I reinforced the importance of consistency and alluded to the fact that if he doesn't start posting some numbers, he may find himself looking for another job."

I followed up with Steve and probed further about what transpired next. "Did you schedule a follow-up meeting?"

"Of course I did, Keith," Steve said.

"And what did that follow-up meeting unearth for you?"

"It never happened. I got called away from the office and had to travel out of the country. So, we never had a chance to sit back down and assess his results."

"So, when did you get a chance to speak with Brian again?"

"I haven't had a chance yet. With the intensity of my own workload, I'm off to putting out the next fire. But I'll definitely shoot him an e-mail when we're done with our call today," Steve declared, as if this would continue the process of supporting Brian, without considering the collateral damage that Steve had already and unknowingly caused.

"Steve, what role do you think you're playing in this situation?" I asked gently.

It was evident I caught Steve off guard. From years of experience, I could tell that Steve was expecting a different response from me.

"The role I'm playing?" Steve restated, as if to confirm he heard me correctly. "I'm not too sure what you mean, Keith."

"Well, Steve, based on what you've shared with me over the last two months, this isn't the first time you've had to deal with an underperformer. And the one common thread in all of our problems, challenges, and successes is *us*. You've heard me use the expression, 'Avalanches roll downhill.' Teams take on the complexion of management, both the strengths and weaknesses of the manager. That's why we need to look at ourselves and the things in ourselves that we can truly control and change: our actions, our thoughts, and how we respond to the events in our life.

"Let me ask you a question to drive this point home.

"You shared with me that you've made certain requests to Brian which he failed to honor. And the requests he failed to honor were never acknowledged. You mentioned to me that, due to your schedule, you never had a chance to follow through and see if he honored your request and the deadline you imposed. So consider this for a moment. By not following up with Brian on the timeline you created, what was the unsaid message that you sent to him?"

Steve thought for a moment, pondering the weight of the question. "That it's okay not to follow up? That if I'm not following up on this, then it may not be that important to me. And if it's not that important to me, then how can it be important to him?"

That's why I tell managers that they are typically creating the very problems that they are desperately trying to avoid.

## HOLDING YOUR PEOPLE ACCOUNTABLE

Steve and I spent the next couple of coaching sessions putting a turnaround strategy together, one that he could easily implement. At the same time, he would be empowering Brian to become fully accountable for his success or failure in his position.

What follows is the course of action Steve took and the conversations that transpired over a four-week period between Steve and Brian. At the end of this chapter, I will provide you with the same program that you can use to coach your salespeople, hold them accountable, and, if necessary, what you can do to either turn around or terminate an underperformer.

## WEEK ONE: INTRODUCING THE TURNAROUND STRATEGY—AN ENROLLMENT CONVERSATION

Within 18 hours of our coaching session, Steve had gotten on the phone with Brian and, based on the model that Steve and I developed, was preparing to have his first conversation with Brian about developing a turnaround strategy.

Steve scheduled to meet with Brian the following day at 10:00 A.M. in his office. When Brian arrived at Steve's office, it was evident that Steve had not fully clarified the intention of today's meeting, leaving Brian with the burden of interpreting the agenda and forming his own negative conclusions as to why Steve called this meeting. Based on Brian's current performance, his mind wandered to the worst-case scenarios: probation or, worse, termination.

Steve began the conversation, starting out on as positive a note as he could. "Good morning, Brian. Thanks for coming in. First, I'm sorry if I kept you in the dark about this meeting. That was not my intention. So let me take a moment to clarify what the intention of this meeting is. I want to talk to you about what we can do to get you on a path to greater levels of performance. Brian, when I first hired you I had all the confidence in the world that you would become a star player here. After all, you wouldn't have been named Rookie of the Month if you didn't bring in appointments with key decision makers when you first started here. But your recent performance has not been nearly as strong. As your manager, I do take some responsibility for this. And what I want for you is to get back on the right path that will lead you to greater success."

Steve paused for a moment, giving Brian some time to take in what he was telling him, then continued. "As a team we're all responsible for hitting our sales numbers, myself included, and you are an integral part of that success equation. So, falling short of hitting your numbers over the last several months is affecting the team's ability to meet our collective goal, let alone the cost that you feel personally, not only financially but also a sense of enjoyment and satisfaction that I know you can have in this position."

Brian sat in front of Steve, nodding his head and acknowledging Steve's comments in silent agreement, as if waiting for the bomb to drop in his lap.

Steve continued. "I know this job can be challenging, especially given our long sales cycle. I remember how demoralizing it can be when you work an account for so long and wind up with nothing to show for it. And I know that you are tasked with more than just new business development. I remember when I was in your position, how easy it was to get distracted from focusing on the revenue-generating activities. But looking back when I was in a sales role with the company, I was fortunate that I had a manager who showed an interest in me and in my abilities and because he saw how driven and committed I was, he chose to support me and help turn my performance around, which is why we are talking today."

As Steve talked, you could see some of the tension lift from Brian's shoulders and face, the more he realized that his imagined worst-case scenario was not about to come to fruition, at least not today.

"Brian, I truly believe that while your heart is in the right place I'm not certain if all of your efforts and actions are in alignment with the job's goals. Based on early indicators I know you have the talent and the ability to turn your performance around. And I want you to know that I am here to support you 100 percent in doing so. You shared with me when I first hired you that you wanted a long-term career here. If you're willing and able to get on the right path, you will be rewarded financially and will achieve a greater sense of satisfaction in your career. The question then becomes, how badly do you want it?"

Brian paused for a moment, carefully and deliberately reflecting on Steve's question. After several more seconds of pondering the weight of the question and the repercussions of his response, Brian said, "Steve, I appreciate you sharing this with me. And I am certainly glad that I have you as a manager as well as the fact that you're willing to help me change the direction I'm traveling. To be completely candid, my first reaction to your question is a resounding 'Yes, absolutely, I want this badly! I know I can do this job and do it well, even better than most.' However, what follows right behind that reaction are thoughts of skepticism, doubt, and uncertainty. In other words, sure, I want to be successful here, but quite frankly, I'm at a loss of what to do at this point other than what I'm doing now."

Steve thought for a moment, digesting what Brian had shared and felt that it was an appropriate time to set up the expectations and the commitment he needed from Brian. "Brian, I want you to know that I'm fully committed to supporting you and giving you the additional attention and resources you need to start meeting the expectations and goals set for you. However, what's more important is your commitment to wanting to do this.

"So here's what we need to do. Together we will set measurable parameters and results. We'll create a step-by-step action plan that I expect will turn around your performance within the next four weeks. And at the end of four weeks, we will regroup and together determine what the best course of action would be for you. Whether that means building on the newfound success we've achieved or getting you into a different position, either with this company or another. So, if you are truly committed to this company and to your success here, is this turnaround process something you are willing to commit to?"

Steve stopped talking and waited for Brian's response. It was clear to Steve that Brian was seriously contemplating and deliberating, demonstrating the importance of his decision. "I'm in. Fully on board and committed to making this work, especially since you feel this is something I can do."

Even though Steve felt the sincerity and commitment behind Brian's decision, he still wanted to give him the out, just in case he didn't make it crystal clear to him earlier in the conversation. He took a stand for Brian, looked him in the eye, and said, "Brian, if you are not committed to turning your performance around, I want you to know that it is perfectly fine. I support your decision either way." Steve gave Brian the space for him to fully digest and internalize what Steve had just proposed, letting his message sink in completely.

This time, with more excitement and energy than Brian had displayed in a long time, Brian did not hesitate to reconfirm his commitment to doing whatever it takes to become a top producing sales champion.

For the next 45 minutes, Brian and Steve worked together, outlining a four-week plan and a turnaround strategy that would achieve the primary objective. They established measurable targeted activities which Brian would need to engage in on a daily basis, knowing that if he did so, the results would follow. Here are the eight areas that Brian and Steve outlined, establishing measurable targets for each activity.

### Sales Activities
1. Appointments
2. Follow-up contacts

3. Cold calls via phone
4. Networking
5. Asking for referrals
6. Collateral piece
7. Request for proposals
8. Development/refinement of the sales process. (This would include a cold-calling script, a follow-up strategy, e-mail templates, and a better routine to more effectively manage his time.)

In the spirit of creating deeper accountability and ownership, rather than giving all the answers to Brian, Steve had Brian come up with as much of the strategy as he could on his own.

When Brian and Steve finished outlining the measurable objectives and the strategy and action plans to achieve them, as well as the role that Steve would be playing in terms of how he could support Brian, they concluded their first of four meetings by scheduling their next turnaround coaching session.

## WEEK TWO: A MINOR SETBACK OR IMMINENT FAILURE

It was Thursday morning, a few minutes before 10:00, exactly one week after Brian and Steve had sat down and confirmed their turnaround strategy. It was the time they scheduled for their second meeting.

About 10:15 that morning, Brian walked into Steve's office. "Not a good sign," Steve thought to himself, interpreting Brian's tardiness as a testament to a waning commitment he made only seven days ago. But rather than jumping on him for being late, he let it slide temporarily, until he had all the facts about Brian's situation.

If pictures can speak a thousand words, then the expression on Brian's face, as well as his overall disposition, told the story of a struggling salesperson whose initial commitment to boosting his performance was being challenged by his lack of activity and focus. Brian looked as if any excitement or hope he had from the prior week had been squeezed out of him by the results he was about to share.

Brian opened up with an apology in an effort to defuse a potential rift and display some accountability on his end, as well as a respect for Steve's time. "I'm sorry for being a few minutes late. It won't happen again."

Steve seemed satisfied with Brian's sincere apology and jumped in to initiate the conversation "So, Brian, here we are one week after our first meeting where we both made some clear commitments. Let's begin by reviewing some of the things you said you'd commit to accomplishing by today's meeting."

Brian didn't have to say anything for Steve to know the answer to his question. Brian hesitated, let out a deep breath in preparation for delivering some less than positive news. "It's been an abnormally busy week," he began. Steve had heard this statement from salespeople many times over in the course of his career. He knew full well that in the wake of a comment like this would come the avalanche of excuses salespeople use to justify their failure, their mediocre performance, or their inability to honor their commitments.

The excuses started rolling off Brian's tongue. He then continued, "And the deal I was working on with the International Automotive Buying Consortium was in jeopardy of falling apart, which required doing some additional work and creative maneuvering to avoid any further potential collateral damage. I think we're now back on track with them, which is good." It was clear to Steve that Brian was doing a great job justifying his lack of performanc in his own mind, going as far as selling himself on the idea that his actions should be rewarded and acknowledged! He even seemed a bit proud of his achievement, as if he forgot about the core objective as to why they were meeting in the first place.

*He can't be this blind to the problem, can he?* Steve thought to himself, then said out loud, "Brian, that's great to hear that you saved that deal. I'm sure you feel pretty good about that. How about we get refocused on the real intention and reason why we're meeting here in the first place and talk about the action steps and tasks you had committed to completing this week. Can you share your results with me?"

Steve anticipated the next comment but didn't want to make any assumptions. "It didn't happen," Brian admitted quietly.

"What didn't happen?" Steve asked, looking for some clarity.

"The assignments we discussed, they didn't happen. I did make some follow-up calls to existing accounts but it wasn't consistent, and I wasn't able to bring myself to make any new business development calls." He struggled with being so frank and honest with his boss, but did so at Steve's request. Even with this additional reinforcement and encouragement, it was the vulnerability that he opened himself up to that made Brian so uncomfortable.

"I appreciate you being so up front with me. Now let's focus on the solution so this doesn't happen again, okay?" Steve said in a supportive tone. He continued. "Brian, regardless of your efforts over the last week, is your commitment still as strong as it was last week when we first met?"

"It is, Steve. I just. . . . " Brian hesitated, as if what he was about to say would upset Steve but then remembered the commitment that Steve made to him. "I can't believe I'm saying this, but I'm experiencing some heavy reluctance to picking up the phone and making the calls I need to. It's been so long since I've had any consistency in making outbound cold calls that I've lost all momentum and, with that, some confidence in my ability as well."

Instead of reacting with an empty, hollow statement devoid of value, Steve sat quietly, patiently, and attentively as he listened to Brian. Convinced that this was more of a coaching issue, rather than a tactical issue, Steve shifted to more of a question-based coaching approach.

Steve waited until Brian didn't have anything else he wanted to share at that point and then responded, "You know, Brian, what you said really does make a lot of sense. And I admire and respect your willingness and ability to admit to what your challenge really is, as uncomfortable as it may be for you to do."

Steve wished at that point he had a camera to capture the expression on Brian's face. It was clearly evident to Steve that Brian had been anticipating a different reaction. A typical, ineffective reaction would have sounded something like this: "You just need to be more disciplined." "C'mon, you're a big boy, get over it, and just get on the phone." "Well, let me get you a sample of some other scripts or templates that the other salespeople are using when making calls." "Listen, this is just part of your job. You just have to carve out the time and make it happen." Or some other variation of a disempowering comment that would shut down any future opportunity for Brian to continue sharing how he really feels openly, safely, and honestly.

But Brian didn't hear any of that. Instead, Brian heard his manager *agree* with him. And if that wasn't enough to take him by surprise, hearing his boss compliment and thank him for being so honest about his feelings was almost too much for Brian to digest.

Sensing now that Brian was beginning to feel more comfortable and trusting of him, Steve went on with an analogy. "After all, I remember when my fourth child was born with a medical condition. He had some special needs that caused me to cut back on work activities so I could devote more time to my family. And the two main activities I had to temporarily suspend were going to the gym and golfing. When my son started doing better and no longer needed the additional care and attention, I remember how challenging it was to get back into the gym on a consistent basis. What I found was my lack of consistency around these activities started to challenge my confidence and whether I'd be able to get back into shape. It was the complacency that bred doubt and uncertainty. However, once I started engaging in these activities on a consistent basis, it wasn't long before I was back to where I wanted to be. Brian, it sounds like this may also be true for you. What do you think?"

Feeling reassured by his analogy, Brian agreed with Steve that getting back in the habit after falling out of a routine was certainly a major contributor to his dilemma. Nevertheless, Brian still felt some resistance to reengaging in this activity and openly admitted this to Steve.

"That certainly helps," Brian declared. "But even so, the idea of picking up the phone and making about 50 calls a day to decision makers who really don't want to talk to you, let alone meet with you, feels so daunting." His call reluctance was glaringly obvious. Steve saw the need to probe deeper into this issue.

"What exactly is it about cold calling that's causing such resistance?" Steve inquired in a neutral tone, with no edge or opinion attached to it.

The more Steve probed into the mindset, beliefs, and fears that Brian had around cold calling, the more obvious the root of the issue was to him. Just as we discussed in Chapter 3, Brian was a victim of his own negative or misaligned thinking. Through careful questioning and gentle, supportive challenging of his current way of thinking, Steve was able to get Brian to see how it was his thinking that was getting in the way of his taking the necessary actions he needed to engage in. That is, Brian was fueling his call reluctance because he was making the selling process about him and what he stands to lose or gain with the prospects he speaks with, rather than making the selling process about the prospects and the value he can deliver to them. Brian was putting so much pressure on himself to look good and avoid looking bad, that he was focusing on himself rather than on his prospects.

Steve continued to coach Brian on his beliefs around cold calling by uncovering what Brian felt the initial goal of a cold call actually was. To compound his call reluctance, Brian felt the initial goal of a cold call was to get the appointment. The more Brian pushed for the appointment, the more resistance and pushback he got from his prospects.

Steve continued exploring this line of thinking by asking, "If the way you're currently thinking about cold calling isn't working, then what would be a different way to look at it?"

Through Steve's continued line of inquiry, Brian was able to see that the initial intention of a cold call was not to get the appointment but to determine if there's a fit with a prospect that is worth pursuing. This opened up a whole new way of thinking that made Brian much more comfortable and receptive to picking up the phone and making his daily calls.

This lit the proverbial lightbulb in Brian's head. "This is going to save me so much time, now that I won't be booking appointments with people who aren't qualified," Brian said with a renewed sense of excitement.

For the rest of their meeting, Brian and Steve shifted their efforts from coaching Brian's mindset to now focusing on a tactical solution he can execute. They brainstormed and created a solid list of the most effective qualifying questions to ask every prospect. Even Steve was strangely surprised how excited he was getting over the new strategy they put together and the possibilities that were opened up during this meeting.

With a few minutes left in the meeting, Steve made one final suggestion to Brian. "I know we're about to wrap up our meeting but before we do, I want to share another idea with you. As it is with anything new, our tendency is to slip back into our old ways, unless there's something there to prevent us from doing so. Since we're building in some new strategies around cold calling, it would probably serve you best if we could develop a few more check-in points throughout the next week leading up to our next scheduled meeting. This way, rather than waiting until our next meeting to report where you got stuck or what you weren't able to accomplish, I can support you throughout the week to ensure you don't fall into this trap and help keep you motivated and focused on the right activities.

It suddenly dawned on Brian that this was exactly what he needed. Brian was so used to operating on his own that an idea like this would never have crossed his mind. And even if it did, he would never have imagined any manager being willing and committed enough to do this for him, especially given the history of managers he'd had throughout his career. Brian and Steve scheduled a five-minute daily check-in point every morning over the course of the next week.

As Brian walked out of the office with his revised action plan and week-long commitments, Steve noticed something different in Brian that he couldn't put his finger on. The person who walked into his office about an hour ago wasn't the same person who left. Brian looked different, and Steve was correct in his assessment. After all, when someone leaves a meeting 100 pounds lighter than when they walked in, it's bound to affect their appearance, their attitude, and their overall disposition.

As Steve reflected on his meeting with Brian, he felt something he hadn't felt in a very long time. Steve smiled with great pleasure and satisfaction when it hit him. "I'm finally making a difference. I'm helping someone achieve a worthwhile goal."

## WEEK THREE: ON THE WINNER'S PATH

Thursday came around quickly the following week. Brian arrived 10 minutes early for their next weekly meeting and was putting some final touches on the outline he had created so he could efficiently report on the results from the last seven days. Based on his disposition and the coaching prep form (Chapter 9) he had sent Steve earlier that morning, it was clear that Brian's mood and attitude had changed from the previous week. He was looking forward to this meeting.

Steve started the meeting, looking for measurable evidence of activity and progress. "So, Brian, here we are at week three in our overall four-week turnaround strategy. How have things progressed for you this week?"

Brian didn't hesitate to jump in. "It's been a great week, Steve. Those five-minute daily reports to you made it more successful. Knowing that I had to report to you every morning helped me stay focused and accountable. They were a great suggestion."

Without hesitation, Brian forged ahead. "I am happy to report that I honored that commitment and made on average 50 calls from my targeted prospecting list every day. And, I actually scheduled four meetings with key decision makers over the next two weeks."

"Congratulations, Brian. Great efforts, especially given your full workload of maintaining existing accounts. That's got to feel really good, yes?"

"You have no idea, Steve. I've been living in fear and anxiety for so long, it's like a rebirth of my career and what I see I'm capable of doing. It's awesome! But I haven't told you the best part yet."

"You mean there's more?"

"Oh, yes, there is. What I didn't tell you was how I got these meetings and how I was able to save myself from wasting countless hours on the wrong prospects! As you can guess, the questions we created were responsible for these results. That's where I seemed to be dropping the ball. But now, I'm totally over my call reluctance with the new outlook I have around cold calling and know exactly what to say when calling on a prospect for the first time."

Steve smiled silently as he listened to Brian's report, energized by Brian's enthusiasm and success. Steve began to set the expectations of their third coaching session. "Well, then, let's keep building on your new successes. I reviewed the prep form you sent me this morning. Thanks for sending it. However, I see you left question 2 blank regarding what you wanted to focus our time on today. We can answer that right now. So, what would you like to work on today that will keep you moving toward achieving your goals?"

Brian jumped right in. "When I went to write in there, I drew a blank. I feel like I've made some great progress over the last couple of weeks. I know I still have a way to go, but wasn't completely sure what to focus on next. Actually, I was kind of hoping you'd have some thoughts on that."

Determined not to lose the momentum or the accountability and fire that had been rekindled within Brian, Steve asked Brian another question, "Looking at your activity over the last week, where do you see the biggest opportunity for improvement?"

Brian paused. "I'm not exactly sure. The cold calling is going much better now, so I feel I have a good handle on that. And I'm honoring the time I need to put aside and make these types of calls. But I haven't really focused on the follow-up calls I need to make. Actually, to be completely honest, I'm probably getting stuck making the follow-up calls. You know how it is. With such a long sales cycle, it's hard enough to engage prospects the first time you call, but keeping them engaged up until the point where they may be able to make a purchase, and do so without being overly annoying or aggressive, I'm struggling there. I mean, how many times over the course of a year can you call to 'check in' or 'touch base' with someone without them eventually telling you to stop calling?"

For the next 15 minutes, Brian and Steve explored both the mindset and the strategy of following up and staying in touch with the qualified prospects that Brian had identified. Rather than dump a process onto Brian's lap and send him on his way without knowing exactly where he stood on this, Steve asked some strong coaching questions: "Tell me the process and strategy you're using when making follow-up calls." "What results are you experiencing?" "What results do you expect?" Brian's replies gave Steve the insight he needed to uncover the gap (Chapter 4) in Brian's thinking as well as in his approach that provided the coaching opportunity for today's coaching session.

Here's what Steve learned through his process of inquiry.

- Brian didn't have a process for follow-up, which created inconsistencies and redundancies in his messaging, specifically in the mundane voice mails he left customers.

- Brian called prospects without having a primary objective when he got them on the phone. Nor did Brian set up the expectation in the prospect's mind. He needed to develop his skills so that at the beginning through to the end of each call there was a plan of action that both he and his prospects followed.
- Brian was harboring a limiting belief that sounded like, "If I keep calling, then I'm going to be annoying to them." Brian wasn't giving value to the customer in his follow-up calls. As such, he came across just like every other salesperson who calls on the same prospects.
- Brian didn't have a process to further qualify his prospects, whether or not they are still a fit and when they might be able to make a purchase.

Once Steve recognized the gaps in Brian's overall strategy he asked, "Based on what you've just shared with me, and what we've uncovered so far, what changes do you feel need to be made to make your follow-up strategy more effective?"

"I really don't know, Steve."

Steve recognized his salesperson's cry for the answer. Being more sensitive to this than ever before, Steve noticed there were still traces of some old programming going on, as Brian turned to his boss for the solution.

"Well," said Steve, "if you really did know the solution to this, what do you think it would look like?"

Steve was certain that the look on Brian's face said, "What happened to the guy who would just fire back the solutions when I presented him with a problem?" Brian hesitated for a few moments, then offered his opinion. "Similar to the solution we came up with that got me cold calling again. I really need to document my process," admitted Brian.

Steve could see that Brian was getting it. However, he still sensed there was something else he needed to challenge him on. "Brian, I want you to put yourself in your prospect's shoes for a moment. Now let me paint the picture for you. You're at your desk, handling the barrage of tasks that you are inundated with on a daily basis. Your phone rings. It's a salesperson. Ironically, this salesperson uses the same exact approach that you are currently using on your prospects. Now that you are a prospect who is the recipient of your own cold calling strategy, how might you react when hearing it?"

"Ouch!" Brian reacted. "That really puts a whole new spin on analyzing my approach. What would I do? Probably what most of my prospects do, which is tell me they're not interested, to call them back, or simply hang up the phone."

"I admire your willingness to look at yourself and share your honest insight," Steve acknowledged. "Why would you feel that way?"

"Probably because my approach isn't very compelling, let alone as professional as it should be," Brian fired back. He was slightly frustrated about how obvious the solution was to this ongoing problem, yet he still knew he wasn't able to uncover it on his own. "I'm probably coming across sounding like every other salesperson who calls on them. And if that's the case, then how could I expect better results?"

"Let's keep going with this," Steve persisted. "What else is true?"

"I'm probably getting tons of calls like this every day. And many of my prospects comment about the 20 or so calls they get like mine every day. So now I am just another interruption. I definitely could make the calls more exciting, maybe focus more on delivering value rather than asking if they're ready to buy, which is more about me and my need to push the sale through."

Steve probed further. "And if you're finding your prospects resistant to your calls, what could that tell you?"

After a brief silence, Steve saw the lightbulb over Brian's head as he gasped and exclaimed, "I am not getting permission to follow up with them!" Brian sat on this for a moment, and then continued. "I'm reluctant to call on them because I have little to no idea when they actually want me to reconnect with them, if at all. I'm making that assumption, which is fueling the hesitancy on my end to reach back out to them, since I have no idea whether or not my timeline to call them back is aligned with the prospect's timeline and their needs. I'm calling them based on my agenda, rather than theirs."

Steve sat silently, listening to the realization that Brian arrived at on his own.

Brian then continued. "Even if I come up with a more effective follow-up strategy, I really don't know *how* they want me to follow up with them, let alone when. I'm actually guessing around this as well."

Steve listened intently. "These are some very powerful observations," Steve said. Sensing that it was time to transform these insights into something tactical, he asked, "What adjustments can you make in your system that would prevent these problems from ever happening again?"

Steve and Brian spent the remainder of their meeting examining Brian's current follow-up strategy. Step by step, they dissected Brian's approach; building a new follow-up system that included compelling language Brian could use that would neutralize initial obstacles and objections, as well as the call reluctance he reported experiencing.

Brian's new documented follow-up strategy will now include the following components:

- The frequency pattern, how many times to call on each prospect and at what interval, a template that provides language to use when connecting with a prospect that focuses on delivering value to them and the questions to determine if they are even a fit.
- Nine powerful voice mail messages which grab the attention of prospects and stimulate more return calls. These scripted voice mails deliver a substantial message and make the salesperson feel confident that he's developed a unique edge which sets him apart from his competition.
- Distinct time blocks for making both cold calls and follow-up calls. This provides a way to balance each salesperson's weekly sales efforts and maintains the level of consistency needed to drive sales over a longer period of time.

Brian now does a remarkable job setting and then managing every prospect's expectation starting with the first contact. Not only is he getting permission from his prospects to continue calling on them but he also now uncovers each prospect's preferred method of contact and timeline for him to follow up.

When the two of them agreed the new strategy was complete and ready to be tested, Steve felt that it was important to gather some feedback from Brian that would help gauge how effective this coaching session was. In addition, he would have Brian come up with the commitments he would see through over the course of the next week.

"I think we got it!" declared Brian, who was seemingly happy with what he and Steve had put in place.

Steve agreed. "Before we wrap up our meeting and you start implementing your new approach, I'm curious about what you're taking away with you from our time today. What new opening or possibility did this meeting create for you?"

Brian reflected on their meeting. "If anything, this meeting, and even going back to the first one we had, has driven home for me the importance of having a written and documented process. It's funny, I was an athlete in high school and college, so you would think that having a consistent process would be something I would have engrained in my thinking. I just never brought this philosophy into my career, until now. I can't believe what a difference it's already made and will continue to make, once I start implementing this new program we've put together."

"That sounds fantastic." Steve continued with another question to ensure continued momentum over the upcoming week. "What would you want your specific action steps to be this week that would give you a sense of accomplishment that you can experience by our next meeting?"

Brian thought a minute and then responded, "Based on my schedule I can commit to making a minimum of 25 follow-up calls over the next week. I think that's realistic."

Given the depth and length of Brian's list of prospects to follow up with, as well as the sensitivity to keeping the process moving along, Steve sensed this was a perfect time to challenge and stretch Brian a bit more. "That sounds like a fair commitment. I'm wondering though, given the aggressive nature of your goals and your desire to want to turn in some new orders fast, is there anything else that you are willing to commit to accomplishing this week that would stretch you a bit farther while at the same time move you closer to reaching your goals?"

Brian pledged to set an additional two appointments with new prospects through his cold calling and new business development efforts.

When the meeting was over, Steve reflected on the work they had done, and smiled. This was the type of smile you see on a coach: a smile that sends a clear message that says, "I am genuinely smiling for you, not for what your efforts are going to produce for me. I am so very happy for you, for the path on which you are traveling, and for what you are creating for yourself."

Steve was already anticipating their fourth and last meeting. He is now recognizing things in Brian that he hasn't seen in a long time: a reignited flame of focus, excitement, confidence, and a desire to live up to his potential.

## WEEK FOUR: A SUCCESSFUL TURNAROUND

Steve wanted to have their final meeting at the Elk Room, one of the top three restaurants in the area, and Brian's favorite.

"Thanks again for inviting me out to lunch, Steve, especially here. And it's not even my birthday!" announced Brian with an upbeat lightness in his tone that Steve had not heard in a while.

"It is my pleasure," Steve replied sincerely. "Now just keep in mind, this is a working lunch so we do have an agenda to stick to," he continued lightheartedly. "After all, this being our fourth meeting and based on our initial agreement three weeks ago, this was the meeting that we were going to use to determine whether or not it made sense for you to continue along your career path with Genesis Industrial Solutions or if you would be better off moving onto a different career path or possibly working for a different company.

Brian looked at Steve and smiled. He knew that even though Steve was serious, his cheerful disposition indicated that a celebration of some sort seemed imminent. Over the last seven days, it seemed that Brian had become an unstoppable force whose efforts and results have now captured the attention of the other salespeople, as well as several senior executives within the company. And for good reason, as it's not too often that a salesperson can turn in a half million dollars worth of new business in 14 days. Brian also succeeded in completing the commitment he declared to Steve regarding his follow-up calls and new business development activity. As a result, Brian's schedule is now booked for the next four weeks with meetings that would position him in front of the key decision makers of the top five companies in the automotive industry.

Their initial conversation over lunch revolved around the new successes Brian has experienced and the continued efforts and steps that need to be taken as a by-product of all his new activity.

When Brian had brought Steve up to date on all of the things he was working toward, Steve asked, "So, Brian, have you taken a moment to pat yourself on the back for a job well done?"

Brian thought for a second, then responded, "Actually, I've been too busy to do so. It's certainly been a whirlwind of a week."

"Well, then, now would be an appropriate time to do so, don't you think? Besides, this is why we are here today, to celebrate you. You did it, Brian, and I wanted to not only congratulate you but also do something special to show my admiration and appreciation for all of your hard work, effort, and the diligence you put forth over the last four weeks."

And with that, Steve reached into his briefcase and pulled out a plaque for Brian. It read "Most Valuable Player for Q-1, 2007." As Steve handed it to Brian, he said, "Maybe it should read *Turnaround Champion of the Year*! But since your numbers put you ahead of the rest of the team for the quarter, I thought this would be more appropriate."

Steve gave Brian a few moments to appreciate and enjoy this acknowledgment before continuing. "I would like to invite you to continue our coaching and the work we've been doing. After all, why stop here? I'm proud of you, Brian, for who you have become and I am truly honored to have you on my team. And since every great athlete has a coach, it only makes sense to keep supporting you to stay on top of your game. So, what would you say if we kept the momentum going and meet one to one starting off on a bi-weekly schedule?"

"I'd say sign me up! That is awesome news, and I'm thrilled to hear that you are willing to continue doing this."

"Brian, I've learned a tremendous amount about myself and about what it takes to truly manage and support my sales team. The most important thing I learned through this process is that there is nothing I can do throughout my week that is more valuable and essential than investing my time with my team, and, specifically, making the time each week for those who really want to make profound changes. For that, I thank you, Brian, for allowing me the opportunity to be your coach and a part of your future success."

It was the last turnaround meeting that Brian and Steve would ever have to schedule again. From then on, their meetings centered around what Brian could do to continually raise the bar on his performance and what Steve could do to continue supporting Brian as he progressed in his career.

To this day, when Brian reflects on his successful career, he always remembers having Steve as his guide and model for what a manager's role truly is as a coach, and how powerful a manager can be, especially when it comes to making a measurable impact. And regardless of company culture, resources, products, or philosophies, managers can make a difference. Every manager can feel empowered rather than play the victim. It all starts with managers making the choice and then standing behind their commitment to transform themselves first. Then and only then, can managers make a profound difference that leads to positive, long-term change—one salesperson at a time.

## DESIGNING AN EXECUTIVE SALES COACHING PROGRAM

As challenging as it may be to turn an underperformer around, it is not a complicated process. If I were to offer a simplistic model of what encapsulates this process, it would be broken down into seven concise components:

1. Consistency in weekly or biweekly one-to-one meetings and making these meetings a priority rather than something that can easily become optional or pushed aside to engage in a perceived more important task.
2. Clear commitment to the turnaround (or coaching) process from both the sales coach/manager as well as the salesperson.
3. Focus on accountability and specific and measurable objectives.
4. Authentic and unconditional support. (Being unconditionally supportive is key to this process.)

5. Strategic, timely, and creative use of the right questions asked at the right time (as well as offering the tactical steps, processes, or even the verbiage needed when it's more of a training issue), which moves people to uncover the real truth of what's getting in the way or the solution which they, in turn, would execute.

6. The outline and completion of weekly measurable action steps, tasks, or specific results that fuel constant movement and momentum from one meeting to another.

7. A realistic timeline that would give both the salesperson and the sales coach enough time to demonstrate a successful turnaround.

In the course of my career working with business owners, managers, and executives, I have realized that there are many truths relating to uncovering and overcoming the core issues that need to be addressed. There are a myriad of reasons why salespeople fail and why a turnaround strategy is a vital component needed to ensure their long-term success. Managers need to understand that, despite all their efforts, some turnaround situations will result in termination or the salesperson's own decision to leave. Sometimes, the ability to implement the right solution to defuse the problem will be out of your control. For example:

- Sometimes the salesperson does not fit into the overall culture of your company.
- Sometimes it's the salesperson's attitude or a lack of willingness and desire to do what it takes to be successful.
- Sometimes it's the salesperson's language or inability, for various reasons, to upgrade the quality of communication.
- Sometimes the person simply doesn't have the ability. After all, even with all the effort and commitment you're willing to put forth, everyone can't become a professional athlete.
- Sometimes it's the wrong person who should never have been hired in the first place.
- Sometimes a person has to leave a position for personal reasons.

These reasons aside, for those salespeople who may be failing, a turnaround strategy effectively executed will result in a positive transformation. While the more obvious solutions to turning someone's performance around may focus primarily on the tactical side of the selling equation, that is, the strategy or approach they use to sell; their organization and time management stills; or the language or dialogue they use when cold calling, presenting, or closing the sale; you are bound to run into situations where the primary reason for their subpar performance is more elusive. For example:

- Sometimes they feel alone and unsupported.
- Sometimes they want to know there is someone who really cares about them—their well-being and career path—who will offer encouragement and positive reinforcement to back this up.
- Sometimes (and it's more often than you think) it's their attitude and mindset that's causing havoc and getting in their own way.

Steve, the Vice President of Sales in our story, was able to turn a potentially costly and toxic situation into a winning opportunity. He could just as easily have made the choice not to do anything because he felt he didn't have the power or ability to foster a transformation due to a lack of skill, a lack of talent, or a lack of time. And rather than doing something about it, Steve could have watched Brian silently and with great predictability drown in his own self-defeating behavior. If this had been the choice Steve made, he never would have realized that he possessed the ability to turn Brian around to become the star producer that he is today.

When managers do not have the awareness and discipline to develop and execute a turnaround strategy when needed, the costs to every company are great. Companies that lack a clearly defined strategy to handle underperformers tend to overcompensate in other areas for the weakness this void creates. They are more apt to accept turnover and a certain level of attrition as a natural course of doing business and building a team.

What's worse, these companies often reinforce the wrong lesson through these experiences and adopt inaccurate and limiting philosophies when it comes to hiring, retaining, and developing their salespeople, such as, "Either they have it or they don't." "You either make it through the first few months in this position and demonstrate your ability and commitment to learn through hands-on training or you're not going to make it in this business." "Hey, it's entirely up to them whether they're successful here. After all, I have people making really good money here because we have a great product and service that we sell to an audience who really needs it." I have often overheard sales managers tell their salespeople, "Listen, all you need to do is just follow the system we've laid out for you. If you do, you'll make it here. But don't count on any additional support or training because we're all stretched pretty thin and just don't have the time to devote to that. It's really all up to you."

Companies that fall victim to this type of disempowering philosophy and culture avoid the question: "I wonder what role we are playing in this ongoing problem?" As a result, these organizations suffer, often unknowingly, as this philosophy continues to cost them more than they realize. They squander more time, waste more money, and expend more energy hiring someone new rather than investing their energy in the right strategy to turn someone around. They are simply unwilling to change their approach or own the role they need to be playing, thus they are destined to continually repeat this insanity and their futile efforts indefinitely.

Brian was clearly an employee worth saving, and Steve did so with great success. And while this story illustrates what a successful turnaround would look like, keep in mind that everyone is not salvageable and sometimes the wrong hiring decisions are made. Everyone makes a hiring mistake sometime. Every manager I've ever known or worked with would admit that over their career they've certainly made more than one hiring mistake.

Regardless of the initial underlying or perceived reasons why a salesperson isn't performing to desired expectations, a four-week program like this will help you accurately identify what's really going on. It will provide you with the framework to quickly determine how you can turn around an underperformer or whether you and your company would be better off without him.

The story about Steve and Brian is packed with powerful and practical examples of better ways you can manage your own force of sales champions. It is essential that every manager develop and master this new approach to building and maintaining a world-class team. I encourage you to review this story several times and use it as a reference guide.

Finally, I want to bring to your attention what Steve did toward the end of the fourth scheduled meeting he had with Brian. He invited Brian to continue the one-to-one coaching they had been doing on a more consistent and permanent basis. Steve took this four-week model and now uses it as part of what he does on a weekly basis with all the salespeople on his team, even the ones who are his top producers. In essence, this turnaround strategy became the springboard that evolved into a comprehensive internal coaching program for all the salespeople within the entire organization, especially all new hires, further protecting what is every company's greatest investment—their people.

In order to help you apply this turnaround strategy and ongoing coaching process in your own organization, the following section outlines the steps you can follow to turn around underperformers, keep your people on top of their game or make the educated decision that they are better off somewhere else. This section also includes some questions you can use to help coach your salespeople through each step of this process and is identical to the process that Steve took Brian through.

Steve also developed interim check-in points throughout the week, when he had Brian check in with him between their regularly scheduled weekly meetings. Depending on the situation and the attention that each salesperson requires, you may want to implement these additional sessions to ensure continuous momentum, maintain focus on the objective, and build in more accountability, further demonstrating the salesperson's commitment to make the necessary changes. These interim meetings can be held in person or on the telephone.

## HOW TO TURN AROUND OR TERMINATE AN UNDERPERFORMER IN LESS THAN 30 DAYS

### EMPOWERING PEOPLE TO BECOME MORE ACCOUNTABLE

Keep in mind that, as with all templates, you may need to fine-tune this so it fits best for you and your organization.

### STEP ONE: INITIATE AND SCHEDULE THE FIRST CONVERSATION ABOUT A TURNAROUND STRATEGY

### STEP TWO: SET UP THE EXPECTATION AND COMMITMENT FROM YOU (THE MANAGER) AND THE SALESPERSON

This is the enrollment conversation. Here's where you would explain the need for a turnaround in performance, why it's important, and the benefits the salesperson will experience by going through this transformational process, rather than the consequences of not doing so. (Motivate through goals and pleasure rather than fear.) The conversation Steve had with Brian is a great example of what it would sound like when enrolling a person in this process. Below is an edited version you can use as a template.

"I want you to know that I'm fully committed to supporting you and giving you the additional attention and resources you need to start performing like the top producer I know you can be. However, what's more important is your commitment to your own success. Here's what I'm proposing. Let's look at what you are committed to doing, set some measurable parameters and results to achieve, and work on a plan to turn your performance around. At the end of a four-week period, we will regroup and determine what's the best course of action for you. Whether that means building on the newfound success we've achieved or getting you into a different position. So, if you are truly committed to this company and to your success here, is this turnaround process something you are willing to commit to?"

If you want to give the salesperson an out, you can continue with this statement:

"Just so you know, if you are not committed to this process, I want you to know that it is perfectly fine. I support your decision either way. This is optional, not mandatory."

Then, proceed to schedule the first of four coaching sessions.

**Optional:** Draft a memo detailing the commitment and stipulations that you both have agreed on, both sign it, and keep it on file.

### WEEK ONE: THE FIRST COACHING SESSION

**Step One: Establish measurable targets for both of you to commit to**
- Create specific sales and marketing activities
- Determine a specific number of appointments

- Generate a specific number of qualified prospects
- Determine a specific number of follow-up calls and contacts
- Determine a set number of cold calls via phone
- Define specific networking activities, meetings, lead groups, etc.
- Develop certain sales and marketing tools and collateral materials
- Determine set number of requests for proposals and number of proposals delivered
- Create components of the sales process such as scripts, templates, an overall sales methodology and approach, a defined strategy to achieve sales goals, a schedule to best manage time, and so on

### Step Two: Coaching questions to ask during the first meeting

- What is your action plan and strategy to meet these goals?
- What steps do you need to take to move forward?
- What are the concerns you have that may get in the way of achieving these results?
- What are the potential challenges and roadblocks that you may run up against that would prevent you from generating these results?
- How can I best help support you to achieve these objectives?
- Would you like to schedule check-in calls in between our regularly scheduled meetings to ensure you have all the resources you need and are staying focused and on task?

### Step Three: Coaching questions to ask at the end of the meeting to establish accountability and expectations of what will be accomplished

- What can you do this week that would give you a sense of accomplishment you can experience by our next meeting?
- What would be easy for you to do this week?
- What would be a stretch for you to have completed by next week?
- What would you like to have done by this time next week?
- What is the one thing you can have completed by our next meeting that would give you the evidence that you're on the right path?

## WEEK TWO: THE SECOND COACHING SESSION

### Step One: Review progress and the prep form

- Discuss the efforts, activity, and tasks that were accomplished.
- Provide encouragement and acknowledgment if targeted goals were met or exceeded for the week.

### Step Two: Coaching questions to ask during the second meeting

- What would you like to learn today that would raise the quality of your performance this week?
- What is going remarkably well for you? What are you most proud of accomplishing this week?
- What skill, if you could develop and master it, would propel you forward?
- What would make our time today incredibly valuable for you?
- What can we work on today that would move you closer to achieving your goals?
- What is the biggest challenge you're still running into that if eliminated would dramatically accelerate your success?
- How can I best support you today?
- What would you like for me to do most during our time today?

### Step Three: Coaching questions to ask if commitments that were made were not honored

- What prevented you from honoring the commitments you made during our last meeting?
- What would be another way to look at this situation?
- What additional support do you need?
- Who do you need to be in order to achieve your goals?
- How can I help you stay on track to meet your goals by our next meeting?
- Do you feel you focused more heavily on revenue-generating activities or do you feel you got sidetracked and distracted by engaging in revenue-draining activities? If so, what where they?
- Are you honoring your daily routine, which details the specific and measurable activities you are to engage in throughout the day?

- Are you honoring the prospecting system we put in place?
- Where is the breakdown that prevented you from following through with the commitments we outlined?
- What is the fear or concern that's getting in your way of doing what you need to do in order to turn your performance around?
- What would it mean to you if you were able to bring in three more sales over the next two weeks?
- What do you think it's going to cost you if you don't make the changes we've discussed?

**Step Four: Coaching questions to ask at the end of the meeting to establish accountability and expectations of what will be accomplished**
- Refer to Coaching Session 1, Step 3.

### WEEK THREE: THE THIRD COACHING SESSION

**Step One: Review progress and the prep form**
- Discuss the efforts, activity, and tasks that were accomplished.
- Provide encouragement and acknowledgment if targeted goals were met or exceeded for the week.

**Step Two: Coaching questions to ask during the third meeting**
- Refer to Coaching Session 2, Step 2.

**Step Three: Coaching questions to ask if commitments that were made were not honored**
- Refer to Coaching Session 2, Step 3 or continue with some of the following questions.
- What is really preventing you from meeting your goals?
- What do you want your W2/income statement to read at the end of the year?
- What is your commitment to making this work?
- What behavior or way of thinking do you need to abandon?
- Is this really the problem or is there something underneath?
- What question, if you knew the answer, would solve that problem?

- If you were listening to yourself right now on the other end of the phone, what would you say?
- Can you remember a time when you had a similar problem? How did you handle it then?
- Can you remember a time when you were achieving the results you want? Cite a time when this occurred. How did you handle it?
- What is the central problem that, if eliminated, would make the other problems disappear?

**Additional questions to uncover the cost of inaction, why they failured to honor commitments, or complacency**

- What keeps getting in your way of doing what needs to be done to reach your goals?
- What does it cost you and the company when it doesn't get done?
- Do you feel this is your responsibility?
- How is your thinking around this giving you what you see?
- What is a better solution that we can implement immediately?
- What are three things you can do starting today that will turn your performance around?
- Would you be open to having me coach you each day for the next week to help build in further accountability to your commitments while giving you the additional support or training you need?
- As human beings we don't do anything unless there is some type of payoff, even if the payoffs are not obvious. What payoff are you getting from not engaging in the activities that are going to help you achieve your goals? (Examples of payoffs: I don't have to be accountable; I want you to make the decision for me; I want to see what I can get away with; I'm testing you; I'm getting some type of adrenaline rush; I thrive on chaos; I get to stay busy so I don't have to look at the real problem; I get to justify my performance; and so on.)

**Step Four: Coaching questions to ask at the end of the meeting to establish accountability and expectations of what will be accomplished**

- Refer to Coaching Session 1, Step 3.

## WEEK FOUR: THE FOURTH COACHING SESSION

### Step One: Review progress and the prep form

- Discuss the efforts, activity, and tasks that were accomplished.
- Provide encouragement and acknowledgment if targeted goals were met or exceeded for the week.

### Step Two: Coaching questions to ask during the fourth meeting

- Refer to Coaching Session 2, Step 2.

### Step Three: The final coaching conversation

- If targeted objectives have been achieved, congratulate the person and suggest that you both continue the coaching sessions.

"I wanted to congratulate you and let you know how much I admire, respect, and appreciate you for all of the hard work and effort you put forth over the last several weeks. It was an impressive challenge to take on with an aggressive timetable to turn things around. But all in all, you persevered and you did it! You deserve the admiration and success that has come as a result of your successful transformation, and I hope you've taken a moment to pat yourself on the back for a job well done. I would like to invite you to continue our coaching and the work we've been doing. Since every great athlete has a coach, it only makes sense to keep supporting you to stay on top of your game. So, what would you say if we kept the momentum going and meet one to one, starting with a biweekly schedule?"

Here are several different ways to deliver the same tough message to people who don't make the cut, and you now have to inform them that their tenure with the company has ended.

1. "Based on our agreement and what we initially discussed, looking at the results over the last four weeks, it seems you've already made your decision. What do you think?"

2. "Based on the efforts we've put forth and the struggles we've had to meet our objectives over the last several weeks to further develop and coach you into the type of person who

succeeds here, it doesn't look like you are a fit for this team. Looking at the stark evidence, would you agree?"

3. "Reflecting back on the last several weeks, and looking at the efforts you've put forth, I'm sensing that you really don't want to be here. Is there any truth to what I'm saying?"

4. "I think it would be best for you to go and find a company that better fits your skills and style more. Is this roughly the same conclusion you've come to as well?"

5. "Do you remember the initial conversation we had before starting this process? We both committed to achieving certain results by the end of the four-week period, which would determine whether you should continue to work here. And based on those measurables, you were not able to achieve them (or honor your commitments). As such, it's best for you to find a company that's better suited for you. As hard as this may be to hear, would you at least agree with it?"

6. "We both committed to this turnaround process with some clear measurable goals that needed to be achieved. Your results are just not good enough to build a successful career here. Listen, I know this is a tough message to hear, but looking at the results, what do you really think?"

## FIRE THEM AND THEN HIRE THEM

In some instances even though salespeople may not have achieved the results needed to justify their position, it may be less about their commitment, integrity, work ethic, or intelligence and more about their ability, acumen, or personality to be a salesperson. Therefore, if you have someone who didn't meet the agreed-upon objectives, yet is still the type of person you would want working for you and feel you can find this person a different position within your company, below is an example of the dialogue you can use to deliver this message.

"If you remember, and based on this memo that we both signed, at the end of four weeks, we were going to regroup and determine what the best course of action would be for you, whether that meant continuing your career here or getting you into a different position, either with this company or another that is a better fit for your goals, abilities, and talents. Well, looking at this agreement and the results you've experienced, it looks like this position is just not a good fit for you. And that's okay. After all, everyone is not cut out to be a salesperson. However, you have a great work ethic, enjoyable personality, and really fit well within our culture. We think we can still use your skills and talents in another area within the company. So, if you are still committed to this company and to your success here, is this something you would be open to discussing in greater detail?"

## TIPS FROM THE COACHES PLAYBOOK

- Steps one through three can be used on a continual basis as an ongoing sales coaching model for your salespeople.
- Try to schedule one-to-one weekly meetings at the same designated time each week. If weekly one-to-one meetings are truly unrealistic based on the number of salespeople you manage and your current workload, then schedule meetings every other week.
- Have each person complete the precall prep form before your meeting to establish further accountability and map out objectives and expectations for every coaching session.

# Conclusion

## FINAL THOUGHTS ON BEING
## AN EXECUTIVE SALES COACH

At this point, I hope you are feeling much more confident about making the transition from manager to executive sales coach. You can now decode and eliminate the myths and misconceptions about managing and coaching that weigh you down, cause improvement paralysis, or make you vulnerable to being held hostage emotionally by your staff.

Please realize this process is not going to be easy nor is it going to happen overnight. If it were easy, then everyone, including your competition, would be doing it. (What a great way to develop an immediate edge over your competitors!) So, if you don't fully internalize these first lessons completely, that's perfectly natural. After all, you've been married to your current way of thinking and operating system for a while now (your whole life).

Training to become a master at coaching requires the same time, commitment, patience, practice, and diligence that would be required to become a professional athlete, entertainer, or musician. Give yourself some time to get comfortable with your new approach. Remember, it's the repetition of consistent, productive actions that will generate the consistent, productive results you want.

I hope this book has opened your eyes to the changes you need to make so that you can get your team to perform like champions. Awareness is the first step. Now that you're aware of what needs to be done, it is up to you to implement the strategies that you have learned.

While the coaching process and techniques outlined in this book are not complicated, the biggest challenge you're facing is putting these newly learned strategies and skills into everyday practice. That's why the process of making the transition into coaching can initially be frustrating and tedious. However, it will ultimately become one of the most enriching, fulfilling, and rewarding parts of your career.

If you are still feeling a bit overwhelmed or not sure what to do first, keep it simple. Start with implementing just one chapter at a time. You can even break it down to one strategy or mindset you want to work on adopting. Give yourself a break and don't feel that you have to do it all at the same time. Try the parts that feel comfortable for you while respecting your relearning process so that you can begin the momentum and start moving forward to achieve breakthrough results.

Use this book as a daily resource and your personal sales coaching playbook. Take the time to continually review the techniques you've learned until you feel that you've internalized them to the point that this new way of thinking and behavior is now an integral part of you.

For now, just being aware of the changes you need to make and bringing them to your conscious attention moves you toward the understanding that you can, in fact, upgrade your management style to improve upon the results you've been getting from your salespeople. Doing so creates awareness. And awareness creates choices.

Realize that when you are coaching people, one of your objectives is to open up their thinking to the new possibilities that you can cocreate with them in order to provide a better solution or eliminate a recurring problem. As such, if you are looking to change the perception, mindset, or actions of your salespeople, your mindset needs to be changed first.

Michele, the business owner introduced in Chapter 2, assimilated these lessons and the changes that followed with great success. Although she would admit having some doubt when her coach told her that "A year from now, you'll have an entirely different team," not one year had passed until Michele had effectively top graded her entire sales team (other than Jennifer, the one salesperson who turned her performance around and reinvented herself, thanks to Michele's coaching and turnaround strategy).

What makes Michele's success story so inspiring and relevant is this. Michele was a real person. Even though the company name was changed to protect confidentiality, what transpired with Michele was very real.

Today, out of the 250 companies operating under a licensing agreement with the founding company headquartered in New York City, Michele's company was rated Number One throughout the country.

How's that for a measurable win? Michele generated more sales volume with less than *half* the number of salespeople that she used to have on her team. Three of her rookies were doing better than *eight* of her veteran salespeople from a year ago. Her turn-around experiment with Jennifer was not only successful but Jennifer is now the *number one* producer out of all the company's offices in the country.

When asked how she achieved this, Michele responded:

1. Having the courage to let go of certain people, strategies, and thinking
2. Becoming fully accountable for my team and to my own development as a coach and leader
3. Working with my own coach

Michele continued to report the following results. "The words 'you can't build a team on potential' continue to echo in my head and have helped me make better hiring decisions. Looking back at the resumes I've reviewed, everyone looks good on paper. However, I now look at resumes through a different set of lenses. It's interesting how much more sensitive I am and I can now easily recognize holes and inconsistencies in resumes. These were the very same gaps and red flags that I was blind to before when I was seduced by the ether of potential."

Today, Michele is thriving, even admitting she's having more fun than she's had in a while, rekindling the excitement and passion she had when she first started her company. She's even working fewer hours and spending more time doing the things she really wants to do. This is exactly what I want for you. After all, Michele was only able to achieve these unprecedented results through the work she did with her coach!

Call me and I will be happy to help you find the right executive coach for you. And if you're interested in using the content in this book for your own personal use, whether for your sales team or for your own consulting or coaching practice, we have coach the coach programs and licensing opportunities available for you. For more information on executive sales coaching, corporate training, or my keynote presentations and workshops delivered in person or via teleconferencing, you can reach me at 1-888-262-2450, info@ profitbuilders.com, or visit my web site at www.ProfitBuilders.com, as well as www.coachingsalespeopleintosaleschampions.com. I'd also love to hear about the successes you've had as a result of using the materials in this book, so please shoot me an e-mail anytime.

Finally, thank you for the opportunity to do what I love most: contribute to your future success. I'm fortunate to live my passion and share my greatest gift with others. You have given me my greatest gift.

Now, it's your time, coach! It's time for you to start coaching your salespeople into sales champions. And as you continue to develop and leverage this ultimate power of coaching, may your coaching efforts become effortless.

# APPENDIX

## THE PLAYBOOK OF QUESTIONS FOR SALES COACHES

The salesperson you want to turn around. The problem you need to resolve. The tension among coworkers or teammates that desperately needs to be defused. The sale that must be closed. The passion and drive within each salesperson, especially your rookies, which are essential to uncover. The underperforming veterans who are in a slump and require additional support, gentle encouragement, and a deeper sense of accountability in order to bring out their very best. The candidate who you would love to hire but is considering a position elsewhere.

Whatever the situation, challenge, or solution, the one common denominator and the tool used consistently by the world's best coaches when approaching any scenario are questions. Not just any questions but powerful, creative, and well-crafted questions delivered at the right time, in the right way, to the right person.

Questions are at the very core of all coaching tools and strategies. Questions are the essence of coaching. Coaches draw their power from questions and questions are where the magic of coaching originates. Questions are where great opportunities are born, new ideas are ignited, self-imposed limitations are exposed, and vast possibilities are discovered.

Paradoxically, questions can very quickly become the prime source of devastation, damage, and disappointment for the manager who misuses or abuses them. Oddly enough, questions can put people on the defensive, make them wrong, come across as accusatory, and keep people drowning in the problem rather than maintaining their focus on the solution. Any of the many barriers to effective coaching or the coaching mistakes we've discussed in this book will prevent you from using these questions in a way that will achieve the positive impact you're hoping for. The flagrant abuse and misuse of questions can easily create the negative outcome you were trying to avoid.

## ❊ FROM THE SIDELINES ❊

Every time you give a solution rather than present a question, you rob your salespeople of their power, increasing your risk of becoming a victim of babysitter syndrome. That is, instead of making your salespeople more self-driven, you are making them more dependent on you to solve their problems.

The use of questions plays a critical role throughout the entire coaching process, during every coaching session, and also throughout daily conversations between you and your salespeople.

Rather than put the questions into a compelling and entertaining story, I decided to present the following section in a more academic and tactical format. This chapter is your Playbook of Coaching Questions and a tactical reference section, as I've listed some of the most powerful coaching questions, all of which are broken down by category. This way, you can easily search through and locate the right questions to use depending on the unique circumstances or situations you find yourself in throughout the course of your week.

This chapter is a practical guide for you to choose the most effective questions at the appropriate times. Whether it's during a coaching session, an enrollment conversation, or to defuse a potentially volatile issue, you will find questions that will enable you to create the breakthroughs you're looking for in any conversation and allow you to get to the real truth behind every issue.

With these hands-on tools, you're now ready and equipped to get out in the field and start coaching!

**The Playbook of Questions for Sales Coaches**
1. **Accountability: Attraction, Being Responsible, Self Management**

    These questions uncover the salespeople's level of ownership and accountability around their goals, their job, and their problems. These questions shift the responsibility back to the salespeople who are avoiding it and build in further accountability around their position.

    - Where are you most irresponsible?
    - What gift are you not being responsible for leveraging?
    - What are you committed to?
    - Who are you if you are not your word?
    - I hear your intentions behind reaching your goal, but can you share with me the evidence or activity that demonstrates your commitment to it?
    - What role are you playing in all of this? What part did you play in creating that in your life?
    - How have you demonstrated ownership of this?
    - Do you believe that you are responsible for everything that shows up in your life? (If not, what do you feel you are responsible for?)
    - What are some of the challenges that keep showing up?
    - What is currently on your plate that will get in the way of your meeting this deadline/expectation?
    - How long do you think it's going to take you to complete this task?
    - Looking at your schedule and your current commitments, when can you realistically devote the time you need to complete this?

2. **Acknowledgment: Evidence of Change Results, Growth**

    These questions reinforce positive behavior and the success that follows. Acknowledge your salespeople using these questions to have them affirm their wins and achievements. This reinforces a continued positive attitude.

- What's working for you now?
- What changes have you made this week?
- What are the three biggest wins you've experienced this week?
- Have you noticed that there are fewer problems you're dealing with? (How many fewer problems are coming at you?)
- How are you feeling as a result of the changes you've made?
- What are you most proud of accomplishing?
- If you were to look at where you were a month ago compared to where you are now, what difference do you see?
- You have done some remarkable things over the last few months. Have you taken the time to pat yourself on the back and recognize what you've accomplished?
- I want you to stop for a moment. Do you realize how much you've grown?

3. **Action: Getting Them Moving, Making Requests, Fieldwork, Assignments**

   These result-driven questions get people out of their heads and stories and into the activity. Shift the focus to the actionable, measurable tasks they can engage in to achieve the specific and measurable results you seek.

   - What do you want to be able to do quickly that you are unable to do now?
   - What's the right action for you to take in this situation?
   - What are you going to do to resolve this issue?
   - What are the three activities you can commit to doing this week that will move you closer to your goal?
   - Who do you need to be or become in order to generate these results?
   - What shift do you feel you need to make in your thinking to achieve this?

- What drastic changes can you make today that would support your goals?
- What would you like to have completed by our next coaching session? (What are you willing to commit to?)
- What's the biggest change you are willing to make this week, starting today?
- What are you going to begin doing immediately after our meeting today?
- What are you willing to commit to doing this week that would give you a sense of accomplishment you can experience by our next coaching session?
- What are you willing to do or change in order to achieve this?
- What do you need to give up or abandon in order to achieve this? (In thinking and in action, old habits, etc.)

4. **Appreciation: Recognizing Value in Their Life**

These questions shift the focus to what is present and magnificent in someone's life or career. It's easy to recognize the things we don't do or are not achieving and gloss over the things we are accomplishing. Sometimes it takes these questions to position the good stuff back under the spotlight. They're also useful for getting someone out of a funk or helping them replace their negative thinking with a more positive mindset and attitude.

- Why aren't you satisfied with what you have?
- What is wonderful in your life right now?
- What is working well for you?
- What do you love about yourself and your life?
- What in your career/life are you taking for granted that if you no longer had it, the quality of your life would be diminished?
- It sounds as if you are looking through your binoculars backwards. You're magnifying what you're not doing and

minimizing what you are accomplishing. If you were to turn your binoculars around, what might you start appreciating and acknowledging more of each day?

- What's stopping you from celebrating your achievements today?
- What are the three things you love and value most in your career/life?
- It sounds like you have a perfect life. Congratulations. You've worked hard at it. It's great to meet someone who is pleased with exactly how things are.

5. **Attachment: Control**

These questions break the pattern of thinking that's causing anguish or problems. Maybe the salespeople are being resistant to making the changes needed for them to succeed. Maybe there's a fear that's getting in their way. Give them the space to explore these questions when you pose them to open up their thinking to a different possibility they haven't considered before.

- What are you attached to?
- What are you holding on to that's preventing you from recognizing or creating a better outcome?
- What belief has you gripped that's causing you to feel stuck?
- How should it be?
- What are you trying to control?
- It sounds like you're suffering from either-or thinking. Do you know you can have it all/both?
- What can you change within yourself that you have full control over?

6. **Attitude: Paradigm, Come From, Mindset, Assumptions, Limiting Thinking, Beliefs**

These questions challenge someone's core beliefs, limiting thinking, and negative assumptions, creating the opening to explore healthier thinking, which leads to positive changes in behavior.

- What has to happen for you to feel (more successful, happier, more confident, more passionate, more organized, more motivated, less stressed, and so on)?
- How is that way of thinking working for you? What is it costing you?
- What does _____ mean/look like to you?
- How can you approach your situation in a way that would better serve you?
- Do you know that your attitude and way of thinking are choices you make rather than a condition of your experiences?
- How would your mindset change if you walked into each appointment as if it were already a sale for you to lose?
- What assumptions are you making that's giving you what you see?
- Is it possible there may be another way to look at this?
- What evidence do you have that supports how you feel?
- May we change the focus of our calls from goal setting and reporting to making some internal changes regarding your attitude and skill set?
- Could you reframe this? Is there another way to look at it that would better serve you?
- If there is another perspective, what would it be?

7. **Challenging Them**

   These questions are formulated to stretch a person to reach their fullest potential. They challenge someone directly, yet supportively and positively, to achieve more and do better than they have before.

   - (When the person says, "I can't.") Okay, but if you could, how would you do it?
   - (When the person says, "I don't know.") Okay, but if you did know, what would it look like?

- What would doubling your effectiveness look like?
- What could you do that would be uncomfortable for you but would cause a breakthrough and move you forward?
- What would be easy for you to do this week? What would be a stretch for you? (You can't stretch or challenge people until you know what would be fairly easy for them to accomplish during the course of a normal week.)
- What is one thing you could do this week that would clearly demonstrate your commitment to your goal? (Look for evidence.)

8. **Choice, Being at Choice**

   These questions reinforce the most powerful tool at our disposal: the power of choice. It broadens people's peripheral vision; giving them more options. It allows them to come from a place of abundance and empowerment rather than feeling confined or powerless to make the changes they want.

   - What can you do to remind yourself that you are at choice around how you feel?
   - Do you believe you are at choice? Is stress a choice or a condition?
   - What path are you on? Is this the same path you would continue to travel down by choice?
   - Is this a choice for you, an obligation, or a *should*?
   - What's getting in your way from making a better choice?
   - Do you know that you've made a choice to be in this situation?
   - What change is needed in your thinking to make the choice you want to make?
   - What choice can you make that would demonstrate how powerful you can be?
   - Sounds to me like you have to make a choice, and you have several. What options do you have?

9. **Communication**

These questions focus on how effectively people communicate and uncover the strengths as well as the deficiencies in their communication style. You will also be able to challenge them to become more accountable for their communication and the areas they need to further develop.

- How do you normally communicate?
- What does that sound like?
- How much of the responsibility are you owning up to regarding your communication with people and the outcomes of each conversation?
- How would you describe your communication style? How would your (friends, coworkers, family, etc.) describe your communication style?
- What needs to happen for you to boost the impact of your communication?
- What do you need to let go of (in your thinking or strategy) to boost the impact of your communication?
- Who do you use as a model for clear, powerful, and collaborative communication?
- Do you notice any communication tactics you are using that might be causing the problem you're describing?
- Do you think you're really listening or are you too caught up in your agenda (closing the sale, getting people to agree with you, etc.)?
- How often do you allow other people to contribute to you during a conversation?
- It sounds as though you've already made a determination before hearing the entire message. Is there any truth to this?

10. **Confirming Value of Coaching, Takeaways**

These questions are used at the very end of a coaching conversation. They confirm the value received by the people you're coaching based on their agendas and expectations, not yours. You can quickly uncover the coaching that's having an impact, the message they're receiving, and the follow-up you need to do to uncover the evidence of positive change.

- What part of what I said was useful? How so?
- What value did you receive from this meeting/conversation?
- What new opening did this conversation create for you?
- How did this coaching session meet your expectations?
- What is now possible that didn't seem possible for you before our meeting?
- What are you most excited to try out?
- Can you share with me the shift in your thinking that occurred during our coaching today?
- How are you feeling now?

11. **Consequence, Uncovering the Cost**

These questions hit on the cost of negative thinking or behavior. Unfortunately, pain is always a greater motivator than pleasure. Sometimes, when people uncover the cost on their own, it leads to the momentum needed to create something new.

- What is this costing you (to continue doing things the way you're doing them)?
- How is that strategy working for you?
- Do you feel that continuing this way is costing you something?
- When you keep engaging in that behavior, what are the repercussions you may experience? How does your behavior affect you and those around you?
- If you continue doing what you are currently doing, where do you think you will end up?
- How does that affect you?
- How much longer are you going to put up with that?

12. **Empower: Have Them Create the Answer, When They Are Looking for the Solution**

    These questions are perfect for coaching your salespeople to come up with the solutions to their own challenges and problems. No more do you have to foster a team that's reliant on you for all the answers. These questions challenge the salespeople to come up with the answers, while you guide and support them through the process.

    - If you were me, how would you coach yourself around this?
    - What is a gift you have that you would feel great about orienting your life around?
    - What do you suggest?
    - Listen to what you just said. What are you hearing?
    - How have you typically handled something like this in the past?
    - What question, if you had the answer, would give you the solution you're looking for? (What question, if you knew the answer, would solve that problem?)
    - How should I coach you on this one?
    - Why is that important to you?
    - Look in the mirror. What did you just hear?
    - If you had to (generate more qualified prospects, boost the effectiveness of your presentations, qualify your prospects better, get more organized, etc.), what would that process look like?
    - Imagine for a moment that you are the client. How might you respond to your approach?
    - If you want to generate that specific response from your customers, what approach do you think may be more effective?
    - If you were the coach in this situation, what changes would you like to see made?

13. **Enrollment**

These questions build out the space of possibility by having people use their imaginations to craft the positive visions and outcomes they seek or what would be possible if they were enrolled in what you are sharing with them.

- These problems seem to persist. What would it be worth if you could eliminate them?
- What would be possible if . . . ?
- What would it look like if you were enjoying your ideal career today?
- Imagine for a moment . . .
- If you were achieving all of your personal and professional goals, what would that look like? How would it be different than it is today? Who would you be, compared to who you are now?
- If you are able to make these changes, what new possibility can be created for you?

14. **Encouragement, Uncovering the Source, Quitting, Loss of Desire and Motivation**

These questions tap into the source that has caused people to lose their drive, spark, or motivation. Do you have salespeople who are moping around, unhappy? If they aren't moving or are hesitant to act, you'll soon learn why.

- What part of you is just waiting for the right person, the right opportunity, or the right time to act?
- What is the goal or dream that you've given up on?
- What motivates you to want to improve?
- What part of yourself have you given up on attempting to make better?
- What goal or part of your life have you put on the back burner?
- When do you think you will be ready to make yourself and your life/career a priority?

15. **Evidence of Change: Proof of Shifts, Leaps, Results, Activities**

    These questions get right to the evidence of change in either result or in action and activity. What have the people done specifically? What did they do differently? What results have they experienced? If you ever wonder whether someone's feeding you a line or are truly being sincere, at the end of the day these questions focus on what counts: the indisputable results.

    - What shifts have you made in your thinking this week? How has it affected you?
    - How would you handle this situation differently than you would have a year ago?
    - What area did you choose to strengthen this week?
    - Tell me about the progress you have made this week.
    - Can you share a specific example with me? (Cite a time when this occurred.) Then follow up with the next three questions.
        - What action did you take?
        - What result were you expecting?
        - What actually happened?
    - What actions do you take consistently to enhance the quality of your relationships with your coworkers and clients?
    - Finish this sentence. What I accomplished today was . . .
    - What would a full step forward look like around your prospecting efforts?

16. **Fear**

    These questions are very effective in coaching people around identifying the fears that are holding them back or paralyzing them, while upgrading their relationship with fear. Fear can be a toxic source that can rot the motivation and effectiveness of any salesperson or sales team. It is critical that any fear be contained and addressed; otherwise, it simply continues to grow. Remember, you can't coach what it is they fear because what they fear is never real (Chapter 2).

- What are you afraid of?
- Even though the feeling of fear is very real, is what you fear real?
- What (consequence) are you avoiding?
- Can you remember a time your worst fear came to fruition? What happened?
- If you follow your concern to its conclusion, what is the worst that could happen?
- What are your three biggest concerns or fears you have about yourself?
- What are your three biggest concerns or fears you have regarding your career?
- What are your three biggest concerns or fears you have about success?
- Is your fear real or the result of an overactive imagination?
- What's more real: your fears or your dreams? (They are both created using the same tool;—your imagination.)
- At what point does the fear live? (In the future. That's why that which you fear is never real.) And where do you live? (In the present.) So if you can stay in the moment, then the fear can't get to you.
- Instead of focusing on the fear or what you don't want to happen, can you share with me what you do want to happen?
- Although I can't coach you around what you fear, I can coach you around your relationship with fear. Are you someone who embraces or resists the feeling of fear? Is fear your ally or your adversary? What if I told you that fear can be one of your greatest teachers?

17. **Finding Their Gifts, Natural Strengths, Passions**

These questions make for a powerful and exciting conversation, since you're focused on uncovering the natural strengths, passions, and gifts that all people possess. This way, you can align their career, responsibilities, as well as their sales strategy and approach with their natural style of selling and communicating. Cookie cutter, one-size-fits-all sales tactics put limitations on people's abilities to fully express their full talents and potential.

- What is your special gift or natural talent?
- What is it you love to do?
- When was the last time you did it?
- What do you feel you do well with little effort?
- If you could rewrite your job description, how would it change?
- What would you like to be doing more of or differently?
- In what areas of your life do you feel naturally strong?
- What about you has contributed to the level of success and power you have experienced to date?
- What excites you and gets you out of bed each morning?
- What is the most exciting aspect of your work?
- What is the most fulfilling aspect of your work?

18. **Goals**

These questions encourage healthy collaboration and development of value-based goals. Salespeople will come up with goals they are passionate about that are sure to motivate and drive them internally, above and beyond any other external *should*-based goals.

- Where do you want to be in 10 years? What will make it happen?
- Let's select a goal for the next 60 days that you really, really want. Forget about the *shoulds*. What if there were no limits?
- What is motivating you?
- What would you want to change right now?
- What is the deadline to achieve this goal?
- What is your strategy to accomplish this goal?

- What don't you want?
- What is the one regret that you don't want to have in this lifetime?
- Is that your goal or someone else's?
- Is that what you really want or what you think you should do?
- What resources are missing that you feel are necessary for your success?
- Can you share with me three improvements that you would love to make as it relates to: (Pick any topics from the suggested list below.)

  - Relationships
  - Career
  - Motivation
  - Selling skills/professional skills
  - Communication
  - Time management/organization
  - Attitude
  - Quality of life
  - Finances
  - How you are seen by others

19. **Money, Finances**

    These questions create the space for a healthy and productive conversation about money. Discover just how much people are truly driven by money and what limiting thinking they may be harboring around it that will have a direct and negative impact on their sales numbers.

- How much profit should your business/department be making?
- How is your financial situation?
- How much money is enough for you?
- How stable is your income stream?
- What holds you back financially?
- On a scale from 1 to 10, 10 meaning it's of the highest priority, how important is it for you to make more money?

- What is your relationship with money?
- What actions could you take that would double your current income?
- What mistakes do you seem to make with money?
- Do you feel your personal worth and the value you bring is aligned with your income?
- Do you feel you are worthy of making a seven figure salary? If so, why? If not, why not?

20. **No: Saying No, Being Selfish**

These questions will help you unmask any Yesaholics on your team. The good news is, these questions will help them reframe their relationship with the word "No" in a way that will build their confidence, close more sales, boost their efficiency, and create more time.

- How else can you create more space and time in your days?
- What does it cost you when you continually say, "Yes" all the time without thinking whether or not you can deliver on your commitments?
- What does being selfish mean to you? Where did you learn that?
- When you give of yourself, does it always have to cost you something? Giving doesn't always have to come at a sacrifice.
- What would it mean to you if you started to say, "No" more often?
- Think about the people you admire. Do they have strong or weak boundaries? That is, is it easy or difficult for them to say, "No?"
- Do you realize that when people make requests of you, you don't have to respond to them immediately?
- If it's difficult for you to say, "No," then what if you responded to other people's requests with, "Thanks, let me take a look at my schedule and get back to you" or "Thank you for this opportunity. Let me consider it, and I will call you within the next couple of days" or "Before I commit to a delivery

time, let me check what is already on the schedule and call you back with a firm date."

21. **Opening Up a New Coaching Session**

If you're always in search of new and interesting ways to open up a coaching conversation in a way that would move it forward and get the salesperson to set the agenda and focus, these questions are perfect for you.

- What are your expectations of our coaching session today?
- What do you need most from me today?
- How would you like me to coach you today?
- Is there anything you would like me to do more of or less of during our meeting?
- So, let's start by hearing what is wonderful in your world.
- What do you want to leave with today?
- What do you want to learn today?
- What have you learned this week?
- What have you done this week to become more of who you want to be? (Or to achieve your goals.)
- How do you want to feel at the end of our coaching session?
- If there was one thing that would be worthwhile for you to achieve today, what would it be?
- What is one thing we could work on together that would be incredibly valuable for you?
- Before we jump in to what you want to discuss today, how about we begin by reviewing the fieldwork/activities we identified during our last meeting that you committed to completing by our meeting today.
- What's the single focus for our coaching that will help you reach multiple goals?

22. **Opening Up a New Possibility, New Opportunities, New Way of Thinking**

These questions break old patterns of thinking and encourage people to explore beyond the self-imposed boundaries they have created, which have prevented them from maximizing their talents and abilities.

- Why wait a decade or two to get what you want when you have what matters to you now?
- What would it mean to you if you could be happy and successful this year instead of feeling as if you have to wait for it at some point in the distant future?
- What are five business opportunities that you are currently not taking full advantage of?
- What could you do differently the next time you find yourself in a situation like that?
- How would your decision change if you made it from a place of abundance rather than fear and scarcity?
- What other choices do you have?
- What are you willing to give up that's preventing you from creating a new and better outcome?
- What would be possible if . . . ?
- If you were to go to sleep tonight and a miracle were to happen, what would the miracle be?
- What would your life look like after the miracle? How would you know it occurred?
- What new possibility can be created here?

23. **Payoffs: Uncovering the Benefits of Self-Sabotaging Behavior and Thinking**

These questions are meant to uncover a seemingly paradoxical behavior that stalls professional growth. That is, every action and inaction is a choice that comes with a payoff. Here's a chance to expose some negative and damaging behavior and thinking that ironically is working for people in some way. Otherwise, they simply wouldn't do it.

- What do you have invested in continuing to do it this way? What benefit/payoff is there for you?
- What are you getting out of living your life/managing your career the way you are now?

■ While this may sound strange, as human beings we don't do anything unless there's some type of payoff even if it causes suffering or difficulty. So, what do you think you might be getting from (tolerating this behavior, engaging in these activities, not making any changes, avoiding accountability, avoiding a regimented routine, complaining, blaming others, etc.)

24. **Prioritizing, Ownership**

These questions help people sift through the mounds of data, call backs, appointments, projects, and prospects quickly and prioritize what's most immediate and important now.

■ What is so important about that?
■ What is your most urgent or pressing problem?
■ What problems feel unsolvable for you right now?
■ What are the three biggest changes you need to make over the next 30 days?
■ What are the three biggest opportunities you need to focus on over the next 30 days?
■ What is the one core problem that, if handled, would eliminate the majority of challenges you're experiencing?
■ What is the most important activity or task you can complete this week that will move you closer to your goals and provide you with a sense of fulfillment?

25. **Resistant**

These questions are a great way to gently respond to a person's less than positive reaction to what you did or said. Whether overtly or using your intuition, you feel something is off and know the situation needs to be talked about. These questions will help you get complete and allow the person to safely share exactly what it was that caused the reaction or resistance to something you may have discussed. Another universal law: We resist what we need to learn the most.

- It sounds like you are a bit resistant to what I've just shared with you. May I ask why that is?
- I'm sensing that you're being a bit close-minded around this. Is that true?
- Are you truly being open to my point of view?
- Are you this resistant in other areas of your life?
- What could I say that would appeal to you in a better way?
- Are you receiving this or resisting this message?
- It sounds like you're having a reaction to what I just said. Is that true?
- I'm sensing that you are resisting this. Can you share with me what part of you is?
- What part of you needs to change in order to embrace this?
- We resist what we need to learn the most. If that's the case, would you agree there's an opportunity here worth exploring?

26. **Results**

These questions help people get a clear focus on the measurable results they are working toward. The more you can measure results, the better you can manage them and the process needed to get to the desired outcome.

- What sort of measurable results are you seeking?
- What do you hope to accomplish by having that conversation?
- What do you hope to accomplish by doing that?
- What do you expect to have happen?
- How do you plan to achieve that result?
- What's the ideal outcome?
- What would it look like? How would you like it to be?
- Can you be more specific regarding the measurable outcome you're hoping for?
- What's the measurable result you really want and the deadline to achieve it?

27. **Segue**

These questions are meant to create some flow and more natural transition throughout a coaching session. You can also use them to tie up some loose ends or conversations you started and then stopped throughout your meeting. They also work well when you succinctly and tactfully need to immediately redirect the conversation elsewhere.

- I'd like to press Pause on this part of our conversation for a moment and explore the comment you just made in greater detail.

- We will definitely spend more time discussing this, but for now it sounds like there's something more pressing we need to talk about.

- I know we're jumping around a bit during our meeting. However, you'll soon see how it all ties together.

- Do you feel complete around this conversation? Are you ready to move on to the next topic for today?

- I know that what we are discussing is very important to you, and as your coach I don't want to skip anything. That's why I want to shift our focus on to something else I'm hearing. We will certainly come back to this conversation later. Is that okay with you?

28. **Stress, Anxiety**

These questions assist you in getting to the trigger point with people (their angst, worry, sense of being overwhelmed, or stress), which is affecting their attitude and productivity. Once you identify the source, you can do something about it.

- How is the stress you are under right now affecting you and your work?

- Where is the stress coming from in your work?

- What conflicts are you having at work?

- What might happen that is causing all your worry? (What are you worried might happen?)

- How do you define stress?
- What is the most difficult or stressful part of your work?

29. **Surrender the Fight, Pushing too Hard**

These questions get to the core motivating factors behind the goal, battle, or attachment that people invest all their energy in that's producing nothing more than unhealthy and toxic results.

- What fight are you fighting that's not worth your time or energy? (For example, trying to fit 32 hours in a 24-hour day.)
- What different possibility can we create that would still make you feel accomplished?
- You're pushing real hard for this. Why is this so important to you?
- What are you avoiding that you're not ready or willing to look at?
- At what point are you going to have all the evidence needed that would let you know it can/can't be done?
- If you want to figure out what you need to embrace or let go of, just ask yourself, what am I complaining about the most?

30. **Setting the Expectations of the Coaching Relationship**

These questions are essential to establish clear and measurable expectations around the coaching relationship from the onset.

- What is your expectation of our coaching?
- How will you know the coaching was successful and that you're getting the value you expect (a feeling, who you become, or a measurable result)?
- What changes will you need to make in order to make the most of what we talk about?
- What's the most empowering and helpful thing I can do for you during our coaching sessions?
- Other than encouragement, support, and advice, what are four additional ways I can deliver value to you?

- What should I do/not do if you fall behind on your goals and commitments?
- What would you like to do or talk about toward the end of each coaching session?
- What should I do if you miss a coaching session?
- How would you like me to coach you?
- What type of coaching and support do you respond to best?
- How long will we be working together in this capacity?
- What's the most exciting part of working with a coach?
- What concerns do you have about working with a coach?
- How can I best support you to achieve your goals?
- How can I hold you accountable for the results you want to achieve in a way that will sound supportive and won't come across as negative or micromanaging?
- How do you want me to approach you if you don't follow through with the commitments you make so that you will be open to hearing it?

31. **Stuck, Blocks, Resistant, Reluctant, Can't Take Action, Problems**

    These questions help people chip away at the barriers they have created in their thinking that are preventing them from moving forward. These are perfect for a turnaround situation, dealing with a sales slump, or for handling an underperformer.

    - What is stopping you from doing what you know needs to be done?
    - What do you need to let go of or give up? (In thinking or in behavior?)
    - What is not working for you?
    - What is keeping you from doing that right now?
    - Where do you feel most off: in your head or in your heart?
    - How is what you are doing standing in the way of who you want to be right now?

- If I could give you the single most brilliant piece of coaching that would move you forward and add value, what would it be?
- How can I best coach you around that?
- What do you need to move forward?
- What are you getting out of (not taking action, your current way of doing things, your behavior, your current way of thinking, etc.)?
- What is the (fear, story, concern) you have around this?
- Has this happened before? How did you handle it then?
- Can you remember a time when you were (achieving your monthly goals, able to do that well, living your potential and were happy with the results, feeling positive and excited about your job, etc.)? What was different then compared to the situation you're in today?
- What's the biggest challenge you are facing right now?
- What motivates you?

32. **Tactical, Hands On**

    These questions help you identify the step-by-step solutions and tactical activities and tasks your salespeople need to engage in to achieve their sales goals. These questions are useful for uncovering the gaps in their processes and selling strategies so that you can continue to provide a coaching or training solution to fill them.

    - What system can you design that would prevent this from ever happening again?
    - What's the first step you need to take?
    - Since it's much safer to practice on me rather than on your customers and prospects, let's role-play. (For example, I'm the client who just cancelled and you're about to call me. What are you going to say?)
    - What steps do you need to take to move this project through to completion?

- What are the five things you spend most of your time doing during your workday?
- What steps are necessary to move the project forward?
- What is the simplest solution here?
- What steps will you or the team assume responsibility for?
- What is the best way to bridge the current gap?
- Who else needs to be involved to ensure the project's success?
- What do you need to put in place to accomplish this?
- What obstacles to success need to be eliminated?
- What tasks are you going to have completed by tomorrow?

33. **The Coaching Edge: Delivering a Strong Message, Making a Big Request**

These questions create space for the coach to deliver a strong message; typically one that would traditionally be tough to deliver and difficult for people to hear. Questions like these soften the blow by clearing any ambiguities other than your well-intended efforts. Finally, these questions give you permission to deliver the message in the first place, opening up their listening and the chance that they will hear what you have to say.

- Can I point something out to you that may be tough for you to look at right now?
- It sounds like there's something you're not willing to own up to. Can I share with you what I see and then we can work through this together?
- You are not going to like what I have to say. But if I don't tell you, I would be going against my integrity, my commitment to supporting you, and what I believe is in your best interest. I just ask that you hear it that way, okay?
- I have something I need to tell you that is going to sting a little bit, but I need you to know that I'm sharing this with you for your own good. I just need you to be open to hearing it, okay?

- This is going to be really difficult for you to hear and, quite frankly, I'm not certain if you're going to be able to hear it right now. Can you commit to at least being open to what I have to tell you, even if you don't agree?

- You may not be able to hear this, but my role is to speak the truth about what is going on. Can I share with you an observation that may be uncomfortable for you but is sure to cause a major breakthrough in your performance if you can embrace it?

- There's something that I see that may be a little uncomfortable for you to hear, and I just want to make sure that you are ready to hear it. Is it okay if I move forward in telling you?

- If you really want me to coach you on reaching this goal faster, then I need to know that you will be okay with my challenging and stretching you more than you're used to and holding you accountable for the commitments you make. Remember, it's all in the spirit of having you reach your goal. Is that fair?

- Do I have your permission to say something to you each time I notice you reverting back to your old destructive habits or behaviors?

- May I have permission to cut you off during the course of our conversations if I see an opportunity to coach you on something you could improve on? More specifically, if I see you communicating from a place of weakness, I'm going to jump in and coach you to speak from a place of power, which will double your effectiveness. Is this something you would be open to?

- Can I push you a little harder around the way you're currently managing your schedule that will more than double your productivity each day?

- You sacrifice yourself for everyone else's interests, put up with people's unacceptable behavior, and let your clients walk all over you. The good news is, it sounds like you are ready to stop tolerating this, and I can help you do so. Is this true?

- Your beliefs are killing you. Are you ready to make some changes in your thinking that would enhance you instead?
- The way you come across is keeping you from becoming extremely successful. Are you ready to abandon some self-defeating behaviors, which would set you free?

34. **Truth: Uncovering the Truth, Getting People to Look at the Truth**

These questions eliminate wasted time coaching people around symptoms, excuses, stories, and diversions and enable you to penetrate through to the truth of what's really going on.

- Is this really the problem or is there something underneath?
- What aren't you telling me that's keeping me from coaching/helping you?
- What's the real truth?
- What does your soul/heart/gut say?
- What is your intuition telling you?
- Go deeper. What are you not facing?
- And . . . ?
- What else is true?
- What is underneath that?
- What are you not saying?
- What is missing here?
- What else do you have to say about that?
- Do you feel that you are operating at your absolute potential?
- How can you change to increase your capacity and capabilities?

35. **Uncovering the S.C.A.M.M., Dealing with a Diversionary Tactic or Story, Interpretations, Excuses**

These questions help redirect the focus of the conversation to the facts, rather than the S.C.A.M.Ms that do nothing more than fuel avoidance behavior and justify performance.

- Okay, I'm having a little trouble understanding this. Can you please explain to me how this has a direct impact on your (performance, behavior, activity, mindset, attitude, etc.)?
- That's your story. Now, can you share with me the facts that support what you see?
- What else is really going on here?
- Sure, that's one way to look at this situation. Now, what would be another interpretation that would serve you better?
- If that is the truth, can you share with me the evidence that supports it?
- What did you make that mean when the customer said . . . ? What action did you take then?
- What did that mean to you?

36. **Uncovering Their Processes, Way of Thinking**

    These questions are essential for your coaching toolbox. Understanding what salespeople do in a selling situation, the language or dialogue they use, the specific steps they take, all help you accurately pinpoint the weak links in either their thinking, system, approach, or activities. It's the second best thing to observing them in an actual selling situation.

    - Explain to me how you (typically go about scheduling your day).
    - Share with me your process when (following up with prospects).
    - What approach do you typically take to handle any objections you hear? (If you hear a prospect say, "I'm not interested," how do you typically respond?)
    - When you make a cold call, what does it sound like? How do you open up the call? What do you say to grab a prospect's attention?
    - What questions do you use to qualify your prospects?

- During a meeting or presentation, what steps do you walk each prospect through before asking for their business?
- What's your take on our industry and competition? How do you combat that?
- How do you ask for the sale? What does that sound like?
- What is the intention of a (cold call, presentation, follow-up call, networking function, etc.)?
- How is your thinking getting in the way of taking the actions you need to succeed/complete this project?

37. **Vision**

These questions motivate people to think beyond today, next week, even next month. They provide you with an opportunity to coach people on creating their ideal careers and life visions toward which they are working. The vision then becomes their guiding light or North Star, as they can now begin to identify and navigate through those activities that will take them where they ultimately want to be.

- What is your lifelong dream that is worth living, starting now?
- What are you building toward?
- If you could describe your ideal life/career, what would it sound like/look like?
- What is the one personal quality you want to be known for/ skill you want to master that will affect everything you do?
- What does the next level of success look and feel like for you?
- If you took a Polaroid of your life 20 years from now, what would it look like?
- How would it be different from the way it is today?
- What do you want to be known for? Your legacy?

38. **Who**

These questions move the focus away from the tactical and the doing and on to *who* the person is, who they want to be, or the qualities the person wants to ultimately possess. You can learn so much by listening to someone's feelings.

- Who will you be if you do that/achieve that?
- Who do you need to be in order to achieve that objective?
- Who are you now? Who would you like to be?
- What confining beliefs about yourself do you need to abandon to become the person you want to be?
- How would you want to feel differently about yourself?
- What would you like to say about yourself that you can't say now?
- How do you perceive yourself? Finish this sentence. I am someone who is . . .
- How do you come across to others?
- When you look in the mirror, who do you see?
- What is the one standard you choose to live by that is non-negotiable?
- How is the belief in yourself getting in the way of achieving your goals?

## THE 80-20 RULE ON COACHING QUESTIONS

There is an important 80-20 rule in coaching. During any true coaching session (not training or advising), the person you are coaching should be doing approximately 80 percent of the talking, and you, the sales coach, should be doing about 20 percent.

It's essential to realize that one well-crafted question can cause a tremendous breakthrough when coaching someone. You might find yourself using only three questions in total during a 30-minute coaching session. Remember, if you emphasize everything, you wind up emphasizing nothing. Give each person you coach the space to process one issue at a time.

Asking questions is an art form. The questions listed here and the way they are arranged may seem simple to use, and they very well can be, as long as they are used properly.

After all, you may know the inner workings and mechanics of the proper golf swing, yet in order to master your swing, it still requires a level of discipline and consistency that few are willing to invest the time to master.

One final observation: Before attempting to infuse these questions into your coaching style, it may be more effective to first assess your team and identify the opportunities for coaching and improvement within each person and within your entire sales team. This way, you can focus on the areas you feel need immediate coaching.

Keep in mind these questions can be used at any point in time, whether you have a team of 1 or 100, regardless of what you are selling, your salespeople's responsibilities, or the size of your organization. So, treat these questions as you would a buffet: Take the questions you like and leave the ones you don't like or are unsure of. Even though I've organized these questions by category to make it easier for you, many of the questions can be used in a variety of settings and situations. Most important, take these questions out for a test drive and use them in your coaching sessions in order to uncover the ones that work best for you. You'll be amazed at what happens. When you give people the space to digest the right questions, you will open up new possibilities that neither you nor your salespeople have ever experienced before.

# INDEX